PRAISE FOR NICHOLAS LEZARD

'It all makes for high-class comic writing, spun from a desperate dissembling that both reveals and hides itself, all the while tying itself in ever more infuriated knots, railing against a world that threatens to uncover the real man beneath it all. Bitter Experience feels like the beginning of a classic English comic series.'
—NICHOLAS BLINCOE, *The Telegraph*

'His prose can include references ranging from Beckett to Buffy, and Santayana to Snoopy, without showing off. He is very funny, turning in memorably comic pieces about the previously mentioned toaster and sofa-moving, and about the hallucinatory after-effects of some herbal virility pills.'
—NICHOLAS CLEE, *The Guardian*

'This is a hugely entertaining book. Lezard is, as anyone who has enjoyed his writing as a critic knows, a perceptive chronicler of human strengths and weakness, and so he is with himself. His compassionate decency shines through – as he writes, "other people's troubles start bothering you almost as much as your own" – and buying this for a Christmas present is undoubtedly the most joyful act of charity that you can perform this year.'
—ALEXANDER LARMAN, *Observer*

'Lezard unashamedly takes his cue from Orwell's essay "Confessions of a Book Reviewer" with its comfortless picture of an ill-paid hack in the mid-1940s, scratching a living "in a moth-eaten dressing gown" surrounded by "cigarette ends and half-empty cups of tea". Regular readers will be used to dispatches from the Hovel, and encounters with the Beloved, and the Estranged Wife (one hopes that they are sufficiently anonymized). They will also know that Lezard frequently has "too much month at the end of his money", plus the hypochondriac twinges that borderline poverty and a sedentary lifestyle inevitably lead to.'
—BRIAN MORTON, TLS

'It is a sort of Bridget Jones for the middle-aged, freshly divorced, tenuously employed and borderline-alcoholic male literary critic.'
—KRISSI MURISON, *The Times*

'Lezard combines self deprecation with that spirit of irreverence and pride in rule-breaking familiar to those of us who grew up in, or shortly after, the punk years. There are belly laughs on every page.'
—LEYLA SANAI, *The Independent*

As a prose stylist, Lezard is the bastard offspring of a previously unsuspected union between P.G. Wodehouse and Samuel Beckett.'
—DAVID SEXTON, *The Spectator*

'Lezard is a magnet for misfortune — his finances, love life and domestic skills are equally disaster-prone, and he shares his book-infested lodgings with a variety of uninvited wildlife. Rueful and funny, this is a book to relish in the comfort of a tidy living room.'
—JANE SHILLING, *Daily Mail*

Nicholas Lezard is an English journalist and literary critic. Lezard has a weekly column, 'Down and Out', in the *New Statesman*. His book *The Nolympics: One Man's Struggle Against Sporting Hysteria* was published in 2012 by Penguin Books. Lezard's first volume of memoirs, *Bitter Experience Has Taught Me*, was published by Faber in 2013, and a second volume, *It Gets Worse*, was published by Salt in 2019.

FROM THE CASTLE TO THE HOVE-L

NICHOLAS LEZARD

FROM THE CASTLE TO THE HOVE-L

CROMER

PUBLISHED BY SALT PUBLISHING 2025

2 4 6 8 10 9 7 5 3 1

Copyright © Nicholas Lezard 2025

Nicholas Lezard has asserted his right under the Copyright, Designs
and Patents Act 1988 to be identified as the author of this work.

*This book is sold subject to the condition that it shall not, by way of trade or otherwise,
be lent, resold, hired out, or otherwise circulated without the publisher's prior consent
in any form of binding or cover other than that in which it is published and without a
similar condition including this condition being imposed on the subsequent publisher.*

This book is a work of fiction. Any references to historical events, real people
or real places are used fictitiously. Other names, characters, places and events
are products of the author's imagination, and any resemblance to actual
events or places or persons, living or dead, is entirely coincidental.

First published in Great Britain in 2025 by
Salt Publishing Ltd
12 Norwich Road, Cromer, Norfolk NR27 0AX, United Kingdom

GPSR representative
Matt Parsons matt.parsons@upi2mbooks.hr
UPI-2M PLUS d.o.o., Medulićeva 20, 10000 Zagreb, Croatia

www.saltpublishing.com

Salt Publishing Limited Reg. No. 5293401

A CIP catalogue record for this book is available from the British Library

ISBN 978 1 78463 351 6 (Paperback edition)
ISBN 978 1 78463 352 3 (Electronic edition)

Typeset in Neacademia by Salt Publishing

Printed and bound in Great Britain by Clays Ltd, Elcograf S.p.A.

To S.D.

And *in memoriam* Kevin Jackson, a.k.a. The Moose.

"Personally of course I regret everything."
—SAMUEL BECKETT, *Watt*

INTRODUCTION

THIS IS THE third selection from my weekly "Down and Out" *New Statesman* columns. I should at this point say that it is not necessary to have read the other two (*Bitter Experience Has Taught Me* and *It Gets Worse*). It would be nice if you bought them at full price from a shop or over the internet, but beggars can't be choosers. And while I am not exactly a beggar, I am still uncomfortably beggar-adjacent. That is the whole point of the column: to introduce the reader who, virtually by definition of being able to afford at least one magazine a week, is better off than me. Most of the left-liberal press, and I would count myself as a pretty left-liberal kind of person, has, for light relief, articles like "Your Ten Best Glamping Tents For Glastonbury" or "I Have Nothing To Say But I Am Married to the Editor". In each case, a relative domestic comfort is assumed. The authors do not have to worry whether they can afford to buy cheese that week, or if they're going to be homeless next month.

For those who want a recap, here it is: the series, and the column, began when I was asked to leave the family home by my then wife, not for any specific outrage but just because she had had enough. These things happen. Luckily, I found a place to live that wasn't too bad: a very wonky maisonette just off Baker Street, yes, *that* Baker Street, where I paid a just about affordable rent, under the table, to a friend of a friend who didn't want to profit much from the deal, but just to keep the place ticking over while he lived in the countryside with his family.

After exactly ten years of this very excellent arrangement, the leaseholders found out about it and booted him off the lease, and me out into the streets; this is, apart from a few introductory chapters to set the scene, more or less where this book begins. The place was called The Hovel because it was dilapidated, but it was still very much liveable in, if you weren't fussy. The place has since been done up and if you want to buy it, don't expect a lot of change from £2 million. (At 2025 prices.)

This book, containing about a third of the pieces I wrote between 2017 and 2020 (hence the many references to Brexit, B*r*s J*hns*n, etc.), deals with that exile, and its consequences; so it has more of a narrative than the other two, in which I was pretty much glued to the spot, although when your spot is London, W1, you don't really mind that much; but always there was a sense of precariousness; the situation was always non-permanent. Hence the drawing of the wanderer on the front cover.

Actually, that wanderer's path should be a little more complicated than it is. If you had attached a tracking device to me, the resulting map would look like one of those crazed diagrams cat owners boggle at when they try to find out where Tiddles goes at night. I was all over the shop. There were even diversions to Paris and New York for a couple of weeks (others paid for my tickets, in case you were wondering). But it meant I got to see more of the country – I try to look on the bright side, me – and some *New Statesman* readers wrote in to say that the column was all the better for it. I think I might be better for it, too, but I can tell you that at the time, it was pretty hairy. At the moment of writing, I am living in a small but well-situated flat in Brighton, from whose living room window I can see a small patch of sea, and the Rampion Array of turbines out in the English Channel: a fine view, and one I have been enjoying for four and a half years; five, touch wood, if all goes well, from the publication date of this volume. I like it here, but I am no wealthier than I was, except perhaps in spirit. It was my friend Caroline Gold, writer and comedian, who came up with the name "Hove-l", because although I live in Brighton, actually, I am only a few steps from the heavily patrolled and mined Demilitarized Zone that marks the Brighton/Hove border. A note on the title: I cannot tell you how long I have agonised whether or not to use the word "Hove-l" in it, particularly as, technically, the place I end up in in Brighton was never christened thus. In the end my publishers and I have decided on whatever we have decided on. But "Hove-l" is too good a joke to lose.

Well, that's enough for us to be getting on with, except to say that while my main purpose in life is to crack a joke, not everything is funny. The least funny things were the deaths of three of my friends, including the sudden one of my best friend, Kevin Jackson, aka The Moose. We would speak more or less every day; until, one day, we didn't. The others were not as close but also beloved: Deborah Orr, and Aileen Green, who is the supremely competent organiser I refer to at Bamff (NOT Banff), the castle I stayed at in Scotland. See inside.

The pieces here appear as they were written, not as they were published. There is a very good reason for this, but it is too boring to explain. Suffice to say that all typos are my own responsibility. My editors at the New Statesman have, twenty-nine times out of thirty, improved my pieces when they've had to make a change (see the Acknowledgments at the end of the book to discover these unfortunates' names) – correcting errors of fact and spelling and construction, etc. – but once in a while they say "we can't say that." A weekly publication operates under pressures that a book publisher does not, let's leave it at that.

We begin in London, in February, 2017.

FROM THE CASTLE TO THE HOVE-L

FROM THE CASTLE
TO THE HOVE-L

MY BEDROOM SMELLS of soup. This is how it happened. Feeling peaky but virtuous, I decide that I am not going to drink this evening. However, I also decide that I am not going to eat, either. Both decisions are made easier by the fact that there is very little to eat or drink in the Hovel. I could go over the road and buy a bottle of Emergency Jacob's Creek, but the last time I did that, when I chose a bottle with one of those little cardboard ziggurats on the neck offering the chance to win a ticket to the Australian Open, or an iPad, I got a bit excited, even though I am interested neither in the Australian Open or iPads, but you know, one can do with a change, I noticed on returning that the competition had closed last September. Another dream dies.

However (to return to the present), I need sustenance of some kind, and I notice a packet of Batchelor's Cup-a-Soup in a cupboard. I wonder whose it is. I have noticed it out of the corner of my eye for some time now; perhaps it has always been there. Perhaps the side of the packet gives details of a competition which offers you the chance to win a Mini Metro or a copy of Doctor Johnson's new dictionary. Not that this matters much. The half-life of powdered soup can be measured, I suspect, in decades, like Uranium-232, and this box has clearly been there, unopened, for some time. The expiry date of June 2016 is no help at all. After a time, ownership of items in the cupboards of shared houses reverts, or rather passes on, to those who have noticed them for the first time in ages.

Anyway, Batchelor's Cup-a-Soup. Did they name their company

that because the founder was called Mr Batchelor, or did they do so because they knew that bachelors would be constituting a significant portion of their customer base? I am a bachelor, say all the lonely men in the country at some time in their lives, and I am drinking soup from a mug. And how many brands of powdered soup can you name, off the top of your head? That's right. One. There's something funny going on here.

However, I have not told you the half of it. Well, I have actually told you exactly the half of it, for there are in fact two packets of Batchelor's Cup-a-Soup in the cupboard. One of them will not taste much like tomato and one of them will not taste much like minestrone. Reasoning that at least the latter will have some bits in it, and therefore will, when hydrated, have some kind of substance, I opt for that one. (I know now that these boxes are not mine. I would never buy tomato soup. There are many things about this country I like, but I draw the line at tomato soup.)

Get on with it, I hear my readers saying. We are all agog, they say, their voices dripping with sarcasm. All right, all right. But first, let me break off to reply to two letters – both food-related, so I am not utterly straying off the topic – which appeared in last week's magazine. To Karl Held of Birmingham: you're quite right, cream doesn't belong in a carbonara, and I don't know what I was thinking. And to the esteemed Keith Flett of London N17, pheasants cost £4 each these days and feed two handsomely, so it doesn't mean I am no longer down and out. I'll have you know that thanks to the annual financial car-crash that is January, I had £30 to live off for the last ten days, so the issue is raw for me.

Anyway, back to the soup. Well, now I come to think of it, the story of how my bedroom came to smell of soup is not exactly a three-pipe problem; I put the mug down carelessly on my bedside table and it tipped over. Odd how prepared foodstuffs, when misplaced, are so unappealing: I suppose it's because they look as though they have been vomited. At this point my decision to go for the more substantial soup looks very much like the wrong one. The only intriguing fact, and I am using the word "intriguing" loosely, is that I was profoundly sober when this happened.

I am too dispirited to do much about this immediately. "My bedroom is going to smell of soup," said the warning voices of duty and conscience. "So what?" I replied. "There are worse odours than soup, even Batchelor's Cup-a-Soup, and who else besides me is even going to come into this room? I mean, look at it." "Fair enough," said the w. voices of d. and c., and retired. Since then the soup has dried, the room has been hoovered, and the soupy smell remains. But for how long? And who the hell cares?

※

I can't remember where I was when I first worked out that I was older than Nigel Farage. You'd think that when that bombshell went off, you'd still be able to locate the crater. Anyway, there it is: the cut-price little Oswald Mosley is about a year younger than me.

I mention this not because I want to dwell on the nasty piece of shit, but because I have been having to face, at one remove so to speak, the problem of young fogeyism. It seems to be all around. And not only that, it's hoovering up women I know.

The first time it happened with B———. She was going to come round last weekend, but then cancelled the day before, because she was going to watch rugby - apparently there's some kind of tournament on, but it never seems to end - with her boyfriend. How ghastly, I said, or words to that effect, I'd rather die. She then made the Category One mistake of saying "rugby, cricket, all the same to me," with a cheeky little "x" at the end of it,

You really don't want to say that kind of thing to me. I replied thus:

"Rugby is a violent and brutal game (the coy term is "contact sport", which means you get to, indeed are encouraged to, injure the opposing team as often as you can, in the absence of any other tactic) loved by fascists, or, at best, those with suspicious ideas about the order of society with which I doubt you, B——, would wish to be aligned. Also only people of immense bulk and limited intelligence can play it. Cricket is a game of deep and subtle strategy, capable of extraordinary variation, which is appreciated across the class spectrum and which is also so democratically designed that even the less athletic – such as I – can play it. [I delete, for your comfort, a rant of 800 or so words in which I develop my theory that cricket is a bulwark against racism, and rugby, er, isn't.] "Both are dismayingly over-represented at the national level by ex-public schoolboys; cricket as a matter of historical accident (the selling-off of school playing fields under Thatcher and Major), rugby as a matter of policy. Have a lovely day watching it."

Two things to note. 1. This woman is not, by either birth or ancestry, from a part of the world where rugby is played. 2. You wouldn't have thought she was one of nature's rugby fans, as she considers that Jeremy Corbyn is a good person to be leading the Labour Party. (True, thousands of Tories think the same thing, but for radically different reasons.)

That's Exhibit A. Exhibit B is my old friend C——, whom I haven't seen for about five years or so but suddenly pops up from the past to say hello, how about a drink? I always liked C—— very much, largely because she is very funny and also, let's be frank about this, something of a sexpot. She is actually older than me but Lord, you'd never guess it. She seems keen to bring someone over with her who, reading between the lines like a modern-day Sherlock Holmes, I deduce to be her latest partner. The thing is, she says, she is not sure he can come, because he might be going beagling that day.

Beagling?

Well, she does come round, alone thank goodness, and she is looking even better than I remember, and even funnier too, and she shows some of the pictures she has put up on her profile page on some dating site, and they're not the kind of photographs this magazine will ever publish, let's leave it at that. (One of them even *moves*.) And, as it turns out, and it doesn't really surprise me that much, the young beagler she is seeing is a good thirty years plus younger than her, and his photograph shows him to be all ears and curls, like a transporter mix-up between Prince Charles and the young David Gower. He, like B———'s young man, is not called Gervaise or Peregrine but may as well be.

What on earth is going on here? Can we blame Farage? I can understand the pull of the void but this is getting ridiculous. Do they not quite understand what they're doing? Actually, C——— does, she's had her eyes open all her life, and B———, her youth and political idealism notwithstanding, didn't exactly come down in the last shower either. So what is it with these young wannabe toffs – one of whom isn't even rich? "You'd like him," says C———, but I'm not so sure. People who go beagling sure as hell don't like me, and I see no reason not to return the favour.

Well, I can't thrash this out here. C——— leaves, but not before giving me the kind of kiss that makes me wish Binkie Beagley, or whatever his name, is would just wink out of existence.

※

To Chelsea Harbour, and a dentist.

This is something of an adventure for me. The dentist part involves a free consultation, arranged for me by C———, who, you may remember from a couple of weeks ago, gave me that nice kiss. She has given me to understand that anything more exciting than that will not happen to me, at either her hands or anyone else's, if I do not get my gnashers sorted out. And she has a point: years of smoking and drinking red wine have taken their toll, and sometimes, when the lighting is in the wrong place, it looks as though my two front teeth have been knocked out when I smile. They're still there; just a little . . . *eroded*.

This being a private dentist, I entertain no illusions about ever being able to pay for such treatment as I will need, apart from an idle fantasy that not only will the dentist be a beautiful woman, she will also decide that I am so wonderful that she will perform her services upon me for free. This, I admit to myself, falls at the very far end of the range of possibilities, way beyond "unlikely", and indeed nudging the borders of "impossible". Still, I need something to motivate me to get out of the Hovel.

And getting out of the Hovel, and into Chelsea Harbour, is a drag. For one thing, I haven't been to Chelsea Harbour, to actually walk around it as opposed to clocking it while driving over Battersea Bridge, for about . . . God, it must be getting on for thirty years. More, maybe. I was with Deirdre Redgrave, ex-wife of Corin, mother of Jemma, sometime lover of Jeffrey Bernard, and in her own right one of the most beautiful women I have ever known. "Let's go and see my friend Lemmy," she said. "He's on a barge in Chelsea Harbour." I was terribly excited about meeting Lemmy, but he wasn't in. (There used to be a website called something like "Hall of Lame" in which people would post their hugely anti-climactic stories about meetings or non-meetings with rock stars. That story might be too lame even for them.)*

I wonder how I can avoid a whole area of London for so long. Well, getting there is fiddly; it involves getting on the right kind of District Line train, itself always an anxious process, and then, I discover, getting the Overground. Which is like a weird cross between a District Line train and a real train. I've been on them twice before in my life and on at least one of those occasions got horribly confused and agitated when it came to remembering whether one pushed the button to open the doors or not. They also come at very infrequent intervals, and you have to wait for them – the clue is in the name – above ground.

Travelling down there hauls me, somewhat painfully, down memory lane. A couple of days before I'd heard some of John Hurt's performance in *Jeffrey Bernard is Unwell*, and as I may

---

* When *The New Statesman* printed this, an enthusiastic sub-editor renamed it "Hall of Lamé", which is something else entirely.

have mentioned once or twice before, he and I had a little history. It was when I lived in Earl's Court; and I can date my departure from there to the day, because a few hours after I left, the 1987 Hurricane happened, and the fourth floor of the mansion block I'd been living in became the third floor; if I'd stayed one more night there, I'd have been killed by the masonry.

Anyway, I get to my stop, Imperial Wharf, and look about me, and I recognise nothing. Instead of what used to be there – that is, a visible stretch of Thames, with boats on it – all I can see now is some kind of sanitised Ballardian mall, fake Georgian architecture nestling up to more unapologetically modern stuff, and in front of me an utterly typical car park. Such traces of individuality as the area may have had have been erased. It is remarkably dispiriting, and I have to call the dentist three times to get my bearings and point myself in the right direction, even though Google Maps told me they were only three minutes' walk away.

Well, as it turns out the dentist is not a lady keen on giving herself and her dental skills to me, but a nice man in (I suppose) his 50s with a picture of what looks like Stirling Moss in his Maserati 350S at some point in either the 1956 or 1957 Mille Miglia. I cannot tell for certain because the photo has been taken from behind. I am also distracted because I have been totting up the costs that would be involved in making my teeth sexy again. It comes to about a grand; and the chances of finding a spare grand are remote; as remote as finding a time machine that will take me back to 1987, or the keys to a Maserati 350S in the car park downstairs.

※

I am downstairs, in the living room, while Marta, my heroic, patient and kind cleaning lady, tackles my bedroom. Occasionally, a sob or a shriek pierces through the Henry's wail of protest. Henry vacuum cleaners, as you probably know, arrive from the factory with a smiley face painted on them. This, of course, makes vacuuming so much fun that sometimes I do it for the sheer giddy joy of vacuuming. However right now, Henry and Marta, sounding almost like one of the couples from *Who's Afraid of Virginia Woolf*, are at it alone, and I am leaving them to it, but if I were to go up there now and look at Henry, I would bet that that stupid smile of his had been wiped off his face, and, at the very best, be set in a line of grim determination.

And the reason for this? It must be pretty momentous, given that since last November I have been, with regret, barring Marta ingress to my bedroom on the grounds that it's just too ghastly. You know how it is. You lose your last vestiges of self-respect, you let the place slide a little, and the next thing you know you are having to walk on books, like stepping stones, just to get out and go to the loo. Underneath is a sea of dirty clothes, empty packets of Frazzles, and Lord knows what else. And one week turns into the next, and Martha raises a pair of enquiring eyebrows, and I shake my head in mute refusal. Did I say "the last vestiges"? I meant "almost the last vestiges". Those last vestiges are what is keeping anyone else from looking at the pigsty.

However, the week before, I finally tackled it. Myself. It was a three-hour job, involving playing lots of motivational music (I find that a pounding beat helps), and two sacks for the recycling and two more for the rubbish. I even got round to scraping off most of the tiny little hoops of pseudo-pasta that come inside a sachet of Cup-a-Soup from the carpet. (See a previous column.)

And the reason I did that? Go on, I'll give you three guesses. Yes, you've got it. I have a Date. Capital D. Things are at the very early stage yet, but it's definitely a Date, and although it is unwise to jump the gun, or jinx things, you never know. The last time anything like this happened, which was in April 2016, and came as a bit of a surprise to be honest, I deliberately did not tidy the bedroom on the grounds that to do so would be to invite the Fates to have a good laugh at me. Well, they were always going to have a good laugh at me, but at least this way I got out of tidying my bedroom.

Meanwhile, the butterflies have arrived, and settled in the stomach. They've actually been in residence for some time: the first Date was postponed about a week ago. I had promised to cook a *daube* of ox cheek but the main ingredient had to go into the freezer, along with my hopes. Recently I started reading Mick Herron's series of spy novels: his spies have screwed up, left a classified document on a train or something, and have been sent to a place called Slough House where they perform tasks so demeaningly useless they eventually resign, or go mad. Every single one of them lives with a heavy sense of failure, and every one of them lives, emphatically, alone. It didn't take me long to sniff the aroma of despair and recognise it as one that had become deeply to familiar to me. And here was something that, like romantic Febreze, promised to clear the air. Is that not spring I smell, just around the corner?

Well, it turned out in the end that tidying the bedroom and then having it cleaned professionally did the trick: there was another cancellation. As the circumstances of how the Date arose are so improbable in the first place, far too good to be true, this should have come as no surprise. Good things do not stroll into one's life like this, or if they do, they stroll out again straight away (I'll show you my file on April 2016 if you like) and besides, Mick Herron's books have made me suspicious of human motive.

But I refuse to be driven to despair, or to impugn her good intentions. How long can a fool live on hope? How long have you got? Still, this waiting is getting me down, and I am beginning to know how Vladimir and Estragon felt. I am also beginning to wonder what the feminised version of "Godot" might be. Godotte? Godette? And I think I can hear a noise, just within the limits of my hearing: it's the Fates, slapping their thighs, and telling their mates to come over and watch this, it's hilarious.*

---

* The Date eventually arrived, my braised ox-cheeks with pappardelle were a complete success, but alas, it was a one-off. We are, though, some years on, still friends, but chastely.

The big news around here is that I bought four new shirts yesterday. This might not sound like big news to you but round here it most certainly is. You probably go around buying shirts all the time, with your fancy disposable income and all that. Men's shirts, ladies' shirts, it's all a big, frenzied carnival of shirt-buying round your way, I'll bet. In the Hovel, though, it's a very different story.

For a start, shirts are not bought new. They are bought from the charity shops, because they are cheaper. If I do not see one in a colour I like – which means white, cream, or pale blue – I don't buy a shirt. A woman from France once sent me a red shirt c/o this magazine, which was very kind, and I wore it on the day of Thatcher's funeral. But that was a special occasion.

So what happens is the collars of the shirts wear out, and I end up looking like more of a wreck than ever. I have been told that one can go to a tailor to get the collars turned, but doing so would, I suspect, entail an expenditure not too far from the cost of a second-hand shirt in the first place, and although one likes to give local industries a shot in the arm, one does not like to walk in and announce one's threadbare existence to a larger audience than necessary. And everything is threadbare right now: my collars, the majority of my socks, my mind, and there is a hole developing in the front of my 501s which is only a few millimetres away, at time of going to press, from provoking a charge of indecent exposure. (Why *there*, I ask myself? It's not as if the region is prone to undue pressure in the course of a normal day.)

But my mother said she would get me some shirts for Christmas, only I should choose them myself and tell her how much they cost and then stand menacingly over her until she writes me a cheque for the amount. So now I am the proud possessor of four TM Lewin shirts, one pale blue, the others white twill, cotton, with a rather nifty cutaway collar and a double cuff so that I can drive myself into a frenzy trying to put the cufflinks in should I go anywhere posh. I am wearing one now, as it happens, and I am wondering whether what I am smelling is new Shirt Smell, or whether New Shirt Smell is actually the absence of Old Shirt Smell.

Buying them was quite fun, if we are going to use the word in its loosest sense. The last time I bought shirts from a shop they came with pins in them, but I gather this hasn't been done since the days of Cool Britannia and the first Blair administration. I had to ask in the shop, though, and by asking that I may as well have added, "because I am old, and broke, and have never really got used to decimal coinage." Earlier on I had been invited to try on a demonstration shirt, to check the fit and the collar size: it came in blue and white stripes, of the kind which used to be favoured by the more appalling sort of banker in the 80s, and may well still be; looking at myself in the mirror gave me the odd impression that I had slipped into an alternative timeline, one in which I had embraced the Big Bang of 1986 and gone into the City to become a wanker. (And in the unlikely event that someone from the City is reading this and feels moved to say "we're not all wankers", forget it, pal, because you are.) It was a sobering minute, and probably accounted for my request to the assistant for a slightly wider collar, on the grounds that I have a fear of tight collars (true) because one of my ancestors was once hanged (not true, as far as I know).

Well, I have now spilt red wine over the shirt I'm wearing – not now, last night; even I don't drink while writing – and I marvel at the fact that I can go for years without spilling wine on any number of crappy old shirts but can't quite go six hours without doing so on a brand new one. It is all incredibly depressing.

Still, it keeps my mind off what the next instalment will be of the cliffhanger I left you all with last week; you know, the one about the Date. I imagine there may even be a few of you who want to know how it went, or if it happened at all. Well, it happened all right. As for the details, though, I would remind you of the old gentleman's adage that one does not bandy a woman's name. But one might buy a new shirt or two.

I am lying in bed, as is my habit, nude, for the weather has turned, and firing up the laptop in order to write this column, when I hear above me and to my left a noise which is either a far-away motorbike, or a nearby wasp. I would much rather it was a motorbike. However, as I am on the second floor, and the sound is coming from above me, it can't really be one, and I look round and there, doing its menacing hovering thing, is a big, fat wasp. It really is a whopper. I don't think it's a hornet because I think they're much louder and a bit bigger than this specimen, but it's big enough to scare the bejesus out of me. I hate and am absolutely terrified of wasps: nothing else scares me, apart from heights, but at least heights don't make an extremely sinister buzzing sound and suddenly veer towards you, or make drinking outside a misery in late summer. You can tell me all you like about wasps' ecological importance, the beauty of their nests, etc., etc., but they terrify me, and they must die.

However, this is not late summer, it is early spring – March 29th, as it happens, the day Theresa May signed Article 50. I have lived in the Hovel for nearly ten years now, and I can recall only one other time a wasp entered my sanctuary. Believe me, I would have written about it. My attitude to wasps being what it is, I know exactly where the tin of No More Flies is, and I grab the dressing-gown and run downstairs to get it. I had been feeling a little dopey and sluggish beforehand, but fear has given me wings – although while trying to keep an eye on the wasp and run in the opposite direction, I overbalance; it is a moment of panic, and the dignity of my comportment for which I am so well known deserts me. It is well, I reflect later, that I am alone; the women I have known have looked at me in a new and not very flattering light when they see me freaking out and madly dancing about when plagued by any of the Hymenoptera. Show me a mouse or a spider and I will blithely ignore the former and humanely rescue the latter, but show me a wasp and I am unmanned: a child again, beset by terror. That I am naked makes things all the worse, and a dressing gown is not really much help: there are too many loose folds, places where a malevolent insect can insinuate itself and wreak havoc.

It is not, though, an unreasonable fear. The pain of a wasp sting is, I feel, unnecessarily great. I mean, really, a simple pinprick would be sufficient. "Did he who made the lamb, make thee?" asked Blake, raising the matter of the tiger's place in creation, suggesting a divine inconsistency; but you have to wonder, if you believe in a creator God, what the hell He was thinking when he made the wasp. Did he say to his minions "make me an evil fly that hurts like buggery"? About the only thing you can say in the wasp's favour is that it abandons its business at nightfall, and sometimes I wonder whether I could live on a planet where they flew about at night.

So I find the tin of No More Flies (I do not have a problem with flies, as long as they aren't there in numbers large enough to form a cloud - "my uncle Toby had scarce a heart to retaliate upon a fly," says Tristram Shandy, "—Go—says he, one day at dinner, to an over-grown one which had buzz'd about his nose, and tormented him cruelly all dinner-time,— ... I'll not hurt thee ... —I'll not hurt a hair of thy head:—Go, says he, lifting up the sash, and opening his hand as he spoke, to let it escape;—go poor devil, get thee gone, why should I hurt thee?—This world surely is wide enough to hold both thee and me."), and I empty about a quarter of it at the insect, and watch with grim satisfaction is it writhes, and sinks, and falls, with an audible thud to the sill.

The big worry is this: it is far too early for wasps to be acting like this, unless there is a nest of them nearby. And that would be a disaster. Living next to a hive of these vicious, mindless, parasitic vermin, whose only purpose is to confuse, disrupt and alarm, who care nothing for humans except for what they can plunder from them - why, that would be a nightmare, the exact thing that one does not want, and I consider that it is no accident that this omen of pain and disaster should occur today, when a similar intelligence has consigned this country to confusion and despair.

It has been a grim week. First, we edged a bit closer to nuclear war. Then Teresa May did you know what. People of intelligence and sensitivity like me have been staggering under the repeated hammer-blows of political fortune for nearly a year now.

So let me tell you a happy story.

As some of you already know, I have a happy and beneficial relationship with the branch of Majestic Wine down the road. The staff rotates, but slowly, like that aboard the International Space Station, so there is always time to get to know them. And, like the astronauts manning the ISS, knowing that the boys (there used to be a girl; but she has gone now, alas) are there, even when one is not, contributes somehow to one's peace of mind. I once went in there and, seeing that (a) there was a queue and (b) a bottle on the shelf from a case of six I'd paid for previously, I grabbed it, and walked out, indicating to the Wine Guy behind the counter what I was doing, so he could cross it off my account. (I collect my wine this way now, as the cardboard boxes they come in by the half-dozen had started to crowd me out of the Hovel. When I removed the empty ones in the winter, the temperature in the Hovel dropped by three degrees centigrade.)

The Wine Guy muttered, as I walked out, "yes, because you're so important."

The next day, because if I collect my wine by the bottle it always is the next day, I came in and he apologised. He was hassled; it had been a long, hard day.

"Don't be silly," I said. "I deserved that, and it was also hilarious. I should be the one apologising. In fact, I do so now."

Cut to last week. I go in there and see a rather hideous but unambiguously celebratory trophy placed slap in the middle of the display shelf in front of the tills. It is far too big to ignore when one is anywhere in the shop, and it bears the legend: "Team of the Year 2016-17".

"Is this yours?" I ask, stupidly.

Wine Guy (the same one) breaks into a proud half-smile.

"It is indeed. Did you know," he goes on, "that you can fit a whole bottle of wine into the cup bit, without it overflowing?"

I peer into the bowl. It scarcely seems possible.

"Anyway – well done!" I say, and maybe shake his hand, take some wine, and go. A few steps down the street, I turn around and go back in.

"Do you mind if I take a picture of this and share it on a social medium?"

"Be our guest."

The responses come in thick and fast. There is a general theme, summed up in my friend D——'s words: "Without you they would be nothing." This is a slight exaggeration, but one sees what she means. I have been drinking between a bottle and a bottle and a half a day of their cheapest drinkable wine, whatever it is, from that branch alone, for the last nine and seven-twelfth years. That adds up to rather a lot of wine. I think I've missed out on about two to three weeks of those years, due to illness or travel, but it's still plenty. Majestic Wine has over two hundred branches in the United Kingdom, and of all those 200 plus branches, guess which one wins the trophy? The one with my boys in it. (And the one girl.) Coincidence? I think not. I remember the time I went to the Casa Becci, the excellent little local Italian restaurant, and they were all having a dinner in the back room, and when I walked past them to go to the loo they all cheered. They knew who had paid for it. Another one recently made me a very good Bloody Mary when I walked in early one Sunday afternoon.

I went in there the other day. Yes, I know, funny, that. The trophy is still there, as it should be, for the rest of the year.

"Do you want to come in when we fill this up with wine?" basks Wine Guy.

"Why, yes," I say, blinking back the tears.

Evil walks abroad: it controls the world in its clammy, hideous hands. Its talons pierce the flesh, its breath reeks in our nostrils. But in one corner of Marylebone (and, who knows? 200+ other corners too), there is also Truth and Beauty and Kindness.

This article has been written without any assistance, financial or otherwise, from Majestic Wine, who seem not to be getting the memos.

※

The children have been with me quite a bit lately: they are all going to be, by the time you read this, on their travels, and the Hovel is a useful staging-post for the start of their journeys. Staying here means an extra hour in bed when you have to take a coach from Victoria, or a plane from Stanstead, or, worse, Luton.

Their company never fails to delight, which is not how I imagined things would turn out. I was a surly clock-watcher at my own parents' home, counting the days until I could cast off the oppressive yoke of having my meals cooked for me and my laundry done. That was how it was back then. Nowadays parents try to close the gap between themselves and their children, or, even if they don't try, the gap seems to be closing anyway.

I suppose not being *in loco parentis* for ten years, on the ground doing the daily heavy lifting, helps. I am not the monstrous, Freudian oppressor-figure: I am the messy layabout with a certain weird kind of authority but not one who assumes, automatically, the moral high ground. But here they are, or were, and as they get older they get more and more interesting, more pleasing to be with. And the interesting thing is that they now have skills that I can learn. The traffic of instruction is not one-way.

My daughter worked, for a while, in the kitchen of a restaurant in Berlin. She already knew how to cook, and get along with people, but there she also learned how to sharpen knives. I thought I did, but I didn't, not at all. When you see a father – it is invariably a father – zinging a honing steel along the blade of a knife prior to carving the Sunday roast, he is not doing anything useful apart from establishing a sense of theatre, which is of debatable utility anyway. He might think he's a cross between Zorro and Anthony Bourdain, the rather cool New York chef – there's always a certain flourish in the wrist action – but the trained chef will raise an eyebrow.

Now, for some reason my children have often given me sharp things as presents. For my first Christmas in the Hovel they gave me a Swiss Army Knife, which I still use, especially the corkscrew; one birthday they gave me a pizza-cutter in the shape of the original Starship Enterprise – which I still use; and last birthday the boys clubbed together to get me a proper kitchen knife.

I had hitherto resisted the notion of getting one, despite the fact that I like cooking and also know how important a good knife is. Here is Bourdain himself, writing in his *Les Halles Cookbook* (the only one I ever use these days, having more or less memorised Elizabeth David): "Your knife, more than any other piece of equipment in the kitchen, is an extension of the self, an expression of your skills, ability, experience, dreams and desires." I suppose this was why I put up with rubbish knives for so long: my dreams and desires were second-rate, and the rest of that list third-rate. I was cooking on an electric hob, mostly for myself; besides, I wasn't going to be here forever. What the hell was I going to do with a decent knife? Also, I have a healthy respect for sharpness, and whenever I cut meat up with a good blade, I imagine that blade cutting into my own weak flesh, and see vividly, in my mind's eye, the wound it makes.

But a good knife needs to be looked after, and my daughter, who was given a Japanese chef's knife as a parting gift from her fellow-workers, learned how to use a water-stone, and last weekend taught me. It is fascinating, and soothing, sharpening a knife: you have to gauge the correct angle at which to place the blade against the stone; you have to feel, with the pads of your fingers, the sharpness of the knife itself, and the burr that results on one side of it after a few dozen passes over the stone; one is aware that sharpening is about removing steel, of shaving it off, almost as if it were by molecules at a time, a process that has no theoretical end, except when, one day, the knife itself is sharpened to invisibility. I am reminded of the fabled measure of eternity: the bird who sharpens his beak against the rock of a mile-high mountain once every hundred years. When the mountain is worn down, a mere day of eternity will have passed.

Meanwhile, my daughter passes the knife across the stone; dips her fingers in a bowl of water, sprinkles it over the stone, and repeats the passing. The father sits there, absorbed in her skill, wondering at this inversion of the traditional learning process.

"Here," she says, handing over knife and stone. "You have a go."

I was walking down the road at about 11.30 p.m. last night when I was given an enormous pizza. What was I doing out so late? You may well ask. Whatever you like to imagine, if it helps. A drug deal gone wrong, say, for dramatic effect. I got into a twitter fight with Peter Hitchens a few days ago which is still, as I write these words, still rumbling on. This is about a review I wrote of his rotten book on drugs FIVE YEARS AGO. (Almost. October 2012, to be precise. He is a stickler for the facts, when they suit him, and was particularly aggrieved when I mistook the Daily Mail for the Mail on Sunday, and has used this confusion as one of the load-bearing planks in the scaffold from which he plans to hang me.)

For reasons only he will be able to explain, he picked out something I said in this column and started calling me "Mr Lysergic Acid". Desperate to stop being the grown-up in this exchange, an experience I found bizarre, unsettling, not to mention unprecedented, I said "that's Mr Lysergic Acid Diethylamide to you, if you please", but it has not abated his indignation. In fact, everything I say seems to inflame it. I suppose now is not the time to say that I have not taken that drug for over twenty years now, and the last time I did, I was so helpful, so considerate a father, a house-husband and a lover that my wife asked me, after a few days, whether I had been on drugs. I said no, how dare you, but with a twinkle in my eye. But that's another story for another day.

Anyway, I have learned one thing: never get into an argument with the humourless. One should, indeed, pity them; or even marvel: they are like those people you hear of who are born without a brain, merely a thin layer of brain cells wallpapering the inside of the cranium, yet who, with some help and care, manage to live reasonably normal lives, and sometimes even get invited to appear on Question Time. *On the panel.* You may expect, and I will put money on this, a letter from Hitchens Minor to arrive in time for next week's correspondence page.

Sorry. I have drifted off the point.

As I was saying, I was walking down the street at about 11.30, and someone gave me a pizza. It was from the new quasi-artisanal pizza emporium that opened a couple of years ago, and was *mahoosive*. If you had put the box on top of a 1960s Mini Cooper it would have overhung the edges. The man carrying it had come up to me in the dark, and said "do you want a pizza?"

I first explained that I had not actually asked for a pizza, and although I have not asked for a pizza to be delivered for even longer than I have not taken LSD, I assumed the form was that they delivered to one's door. One does not say, for example, "I will meet you on the corner of Junky Street at 11.30. The code word is 'pepperoni'." he explained that it was a pizza that was, and I paraphrase here, no longer fit for purpose, a couple of slices having been consumed, for form's sake, and now being touted around the streets in search of a good home, and someone who might fancy a spot of pizza.

Being a Londoner, and not as daft as I look, I asked: "What's the catch?" They might have put Rohypnol or something on it, you see, and then, once I had passed out after eating pizza, had their wicked way with me. These things happen.

He assured me this was not the case, and although I had already dined – on a nice *smorgasbord* of methamphetamine, crack, and mescaline, all of which can take the edge off one's appetite – I accepted the pizza, for who does not like a pizza, and took it back to the Hovel, which was only a short distance away.

I bore it with some sadness, though. The last time I had eaten the wares from this chain it had been when I was going out with A——, who pronounced the pizza serviceable but overpriced, and with ideas above its station. (She had a dirty pizza habit, in that she actually preferred *pizze* from the bottom end of the gastronomic edifice, such as the ones you get in the freezer cabinets of corner shops which Italians would not even give to their dogs. A remarkable woman. With a full memory, everything reminds you of something else.)

Well, the pizza is heating up in the oven now for my lunch. If you do not hear from me again it is because I have, after all, been poisoned. Which I suppose is Peter Hitchens's cunning plan.

We now skip ahead some months, to the greatest catastrophe to befall me since my eviction from the family home: my eviction from the Hovel. I was unable to write about this directly: it would have got the person I was sub-letting from in trouble. My thanks to Guy [redacted], for the 10 years – to the day – that he let me stay there, at a rent which barely covered his costs. A true gentleman. We resume first, though, with a melancholy but tender memory a few weeks before the dreadful event.

Some people have drug habits; some a gambling addiction; some, illicit sex. What I do, though, when I want to distract myself by spending money I can ill afford to spend, is go to second-hand bookshops, and buy something old. Glamorously old.

I have a seventeenth-century edition of St Augustine, in French, bought in Toulouse for Fr. 100, or about a tenner (oh, the second-hand bookshops of Toulouse! Hard by the cathedral, the weight of its million bricks pressing down on the city like the brutal hand of history . . .). I have my 1720 edition of Thomas Creech's translation of Horace's *Odes, Satyrs and Epistles* ("On the Luxury of the Age": "Our Squares still rise, our Fields decrease,/And now the Ploughs must rust in Ease . . ."), bought from Fosters on Chiswick High Road (£35); and a late-nineteenth-century edition of Tennyson, its stiff boards encased in leather and stamped, in gold, with the livery of Christ Church, Oxford, smelling like the inside of a Rolls-Royce (£30 or thereabouts); it was awarded as a prize to some scholar, but I cannot remember who now, as I gave it to K—— for her birthday last year, as it was the only thing I had of value to give her. In Paris, I now have to deliberately avoid the *bouqinistes* whose stalls line the Seine, for I will end up doubling the weight of my luggage with, e.g., multi-volume editions of Verlaine, or du Bellay's *Regrets*, which are only going to make me sadder than I already am.

My favoured bookshop – and it's actually bookshops, though how two of them managed to exist in such close proximity – are in Bell Street, off Lisson Grove. Supremely shambolic, with teetering piles everywhere, and in the basement a piano, gap-toothed and chaotically tuned, but just about good enough to try out a piece from the stacks of music sheets surrounding it.

A good second-hand shop is the deep memory of an area. A location served by one is blessed. In it lie the fragments of a civilisation, shored up against its ruins. It is both a testament of decay, of oblivion, and also a kind of limbo; not true death, but a place where the minds of people long dead can be made to live again in someone else's. They draw the lonely, the bored, the idle, the mentally unstable; oh boy, do they draw the mentally unstable. I feel myself going a little batty when I enter one. I mean really, what am I going to do with a copy of Volume I of *Don Quixote*, date and translator unknown, as many early pages are missing? Or indeed my 1681 *Soliloques, Manuel, et Meditations* of Augustine? "Delivrez-moy, ô mon Dieu, du neant du peché, comme vous m'avez tiré du neant de l'estre": deliver me, oh my Lord, from the void of sin, as you drew me from the void of being. (And yes, the accent on "neant" is not there in the original, in case you were wondering whether I or the subs had slipped up.)

So there I am, walking up Lisson Grove, my mind more troubled than it has ever been since the end of my marriage, for disaster I cannot write about has struck, and I think: at least I live within walking distance of these shops. My income has been reduced by 60%, but I have a little cash left in my account, saving right now is futile if not impossible: I'll buy myself a beautiful old book.

The astute reader will have worked out the punchline by now. The shops have gone. In London, everything is going. Venerable businesses are being forced from their premises; people are being forced from their homes. When the price of the tiniest, seediest London property reaches such absurdly high figures then it is a marvel more people aren't simply being murdered, to save on legal fees. People are talking, quite rightly, of the Sixth Great Extinction, by which humans are exterminating countless species apparently just for the sheer giddy hell of it, or because they can; this is another kind of extinction, caused by money, doing it because it can, and because, in many people's hands, it can do nothing else.

Anyway, there I am, already at a low ebb, and feeling emotionally labile. And these two modest sanctuaries have gone. Well, who needs them, apart from me, the dozen or so other lunatics who browsed in them, and the people who ran them? It's not as if they were providing anything like a useful service, such as a betting shop, or an estate agency, or a branch of Starbucks.

I am getting tired of this world. The list of good things in it is getting shorter and shorter. And I write about one of its most affluent corners. Imagine how much worse it is everywhere else, and how much worse it's going to get. Sorry about the gloom this week. But that's all there is.

⁂

The first beggar was walking, but still wretched. Probably in his early twenties, clearly ravaged by more than just alcohol, he made a beeline for me, as if he had an appointment. He was not to know I was in a mood from hell, although the look on my face would have told him, if he'd been in any kind of state to register it.

"Excuse me, have you got ten pee for . . ."

"No." And I walked on.

Why? I am almost invariably a soft touch for this kind of thing. But as I said, I was in the foulest of tempers. Also, this was East Finchley. For those who do not know London, East Finchley is a northern suburb, which at one end hosts the wealthiest street in the country, the Bishop's Avenue, where multimillionaires tear down houses and erect others even uglier than the ones they have replaced, and at the other end a typically seedy, dull collection of terraced houses. The main supermarket is called Budgens, a name so ugly that it could only have belonged to a real person, either too proud or unimaginative to think of something else. (It did, although I cannot vouch for Mr Budgen's pride or tin ear.) But what, I asked myself, was someone this wretched doing in East Finchley? And what was I doing, dismissing him with maximal curtness – and not caring?

The second, further up the street, I met the next day. Much older, and clearly mad rather than chemically poisoned. He asked how I was doing.

"Not so well, as it happens," I replied.

"Would you like me to say a prayer for you?"

"Why not?" I said, and he placed a clenched fist to my forehead and made a brief incantation, something like an exorcism, and then kissed the large white plastic crucifix hanging from his neck. I half expected to feel a jolt of faith, some kind of divine restructuring. This time I gave him money: a pound coin and a fifty pee coin, but then later I thought: why didn't I give him more? I'd been doing some tidying earlier and had retrieved a heavy pocketful of change; I could have given him a generous handful.

The third was in Shepherds Bush. I knew him from the days when I lived there: a skinny middle-aged black guy who would occasionally stop and rant in a friendly way at me, just sane enough not to ignore. That was ten years ago. Now, he was raging at everyone, accusing the teenagers queueing in the kebab shop of being batty boys and saying "bloodclaat" a lot. (Batty boy: homosexual. Bloodclaat: tampon. Probably used.) The people he was addressing thus were also black, and knew perfectly well what he was saying. They shrugged it off. I got on the bus; so did he, and the whole bus knew about it. He had finessed his insanity to present itself as not quite violent enough to get him thrown off. The driver and passengers on the 207 took it in their stride, the limits of their patience tested.

That's it, I thought. I'm getting out of London. I've had it with this place. Luckily, my great friend S— had asked if I could catsit for her in Brighton. I know her cat, and I know Brighton. Also, I know about a dozen people there who I keep meaning to see; why not? London was making me ill, and possibly a bad person. So S——— invited me down a couple of days before she was due to go on her holidays, and I packed hurriedly and took the first train I could.

And now I find myself sitting on a sun lounger in a tiny but cute back yard, in a charming house just abutting North Laines, and the mood is palpably different to the capital's. It is like a city ought to be: compact, diverse, and funky. There is no reek of High Capitalism. It is healthily decadent. It would appear to be full of people who thought, in London, "sod this for a game of soldiers", and made a congenial space for themselves. The very hairs went up on the back of my neck with pleasure.

So this is what it's like, to fall out of love with the city of one's birth. What most surprised me was the speed and force with which it happened. I'd made my mind up over a nice lunch my friend N——— was buying me, to cheer me up.

"Don't you have to stay in London? You know, for book launches and things like that?

"I don't go to fucking book launches anymore," I said. Once again, I found myself taken aback by the furious vigour of my reply.

I am only going to be here for ten days but I have plenty to do, plenty of people to see, and dozens of memories, all good, to bump into. I'm already feeling better.

The BBC says it's 3°C out there, but that's a filthy lie. It's much colder than that, up here, at the foot of the Cairngorms. Were it that balmy, then everything wouldn't be covered with ice. Last night I made the mistake of going out for a goodnight smoke in leather-soled shoes rather than my knock-off Timberlands and went down like an early slapstick actor on a banana skin. At one point I was, I swear, upside down.

Luckily there was no one to see me, not at that time of night. People go to bed and then rise early here, still a knack I have yet to master. But who can go to bed early when the nights are so glorious? One of the reasons I went arse over tit last night was because I was gawping at the stars, instead of looking at the ground. There is no light pollution here and once the eyes adjust the cosmos becomes gloriously manifest. A carpet of light stretched across the sky. I stagger about the place, going "wow". And other senses besides sight become enhanced: one hears, in the distance, the lowing of the cattle, the hooting of owls, and the gentle, rhythmic sobbing of vegetarians.

My children, in correspondence with me, have noted that I have taken surprisingly well to rural life. How could I not? There's a pick-up truck, and they let me drive it into town. Try and imagine, gentle reader, the thrill of being an effete metropolitan softy given the keys to a machine like that. Hot dang! I murmur to myself. All I need is a hound dawg, a barrel of home-distilled whuskey and some loco weed and my inner redneck is finally allowed free expression.

Maybe less of the "redneck". Scotland is, in many ways, a more civilised place than its southerly neighbour, whose name I forget. I went into the local town the other day to pick up a prescription. As I was leaving I remembered that there had been something incomplete about the transaction.

"Oh, I pay for my prescriptions," I said.

I might as well have said: "I have three legs." There were looks of bafflement all around, and then the penny dropped. At which point files were fetched, tills consulted, heads scratched, and they still couldn't work out how much I was meant to be paying for a prescription faxed over from an English surgery. (England! That's the name of that bigoted little country to the south.) In the end I just left a tenner with them and told them to put the change in the charity tin.

It is a far cry from London. My last evening there was spent in the Seven Stars, the wonderful, venerably old pub in Carey Street, next to the Law Courts. It was a weekday evening, and by about ten o'clock I had the place to myself, apart from the bar staff and the pub cat, Mr Peabody. (Named after the name of the estate where he was found.) I was warming myself by the fire and wondering how I was going to tear myself away from this idyll when in walked a very noisy young group of – it soon became obvious – lawyers. They had been on a pub crawl which involved drinking pints very quickly in each one. They were clearly reaching the end of the evening. Oh well, I thought, they'll just be staying for the one, then they'll sod off.

They did not sod off. They sodding well stayed there. And my sweet Lord, I did not know until then how objectionable a group of young lawyers could be. Well, I suppose they weren't all bad. One of them even tried to make conversation. He had noticed the copy of *Private Eye* I was reading.

"Private Eye," he said, "ha ha, it's very funny, isn't it?" It was as if he had made a great discovery and was anxious to pass his wisdom on to me. He burbled on for a bit. I tuned out. I was mainly worried that someone was going to step on the cat.

"Actually," I said, just to put a natural stop to the conversation, "Ian Hislop's a mate." (He's not exactly a mate. But every so often we run into each other and he says "hello, Nick", and I say "hello, Ian", and we swap a few words, and this pleases me mightily.)

I flush to recall this line. At which point does the solitary middle-aged man in the pub start looking like the solitary middle-aged fantasist? I would imagine at the point where the man claims friendship with the country's most famous magazine editor, that's when.

As the lawyers downed their pints, and ordered replacements, and talked with every atom of arrogance and privilege at their disposal, I edged my way out, and thought, happily, of the seven billion stars, as opposed to the mere seven, I'd be seeing the next evening.

※

I am trying to think of anyone who had a happy, prosperous and serene 2017 and no one springs to mind. Come on, there must be someone. I know some people who had an appalling time, much worse than me, and I lost my home and my main source of income. Don't tell me that's a walk in the park (letters printed here which have expressed sympathy were greatly appreciated at this end). If I tell you that paying off a ten-year tax bill was actually one of the year's groovier moments maybe that will give you an idea.

Of course, if I had a girlfriend all this wouldn't have been that much of a problem. I would be at her place, or, if her place was my place too, our place. If we'd been kicked out of that, we'd be able to pool our resources and find somewhere else. Probably. Or maybe we would be entering a vortex of despair and recrimination, our relationship fraying and disintegrating as the fierce and bitter winds of the world toss and buffet the frail bark of our love. Then there would be heartbreak on top of everything else to deal with. So maybe it is just as well. It is important to look on the bright side. That's what keeps me so cheery.

Still, 2017 has been taking the piss, that's what it's been doing. The lack of companionship in bed makes me particularly cross with it. I used to think that a night not spent in the company of a beautiful woman was a night wasted and I still think that, only this time I prefer not to dwell on it. Basically, I had sex twice this year, and one of those times was a birthday present. I should also point out that I am told that I am good at it, but a fat lot of good that seems to be doing me. Are any of you lot getting the hint yet?

But my friends . . . oh man, have I been done proud by my friends.

They have been righteous. Offers of places to stay have been coming in from all over the world, as far west as Los Angeles and as far east as Delhi. And these are serious offers, not grudging offers whose deeper meaning is that under no circumstances am I to show up with a suitcase and a meaningful glance at the sofa. There have been more than I can take up, and it is getting to the point where I feel I may be causing offence by not accepting them. However, there are only so many spaces one can occupy at the same time.

But one lives from moment to moment, out of a suitcase; or, if travelling light, my Slazenger cricket bag. This Christmas one of the presents I was given was a candle in the shape of a wine bottle, and I marvelled at the tactlessness involved: for a candle in the shape of a bottle of wine weighs as much as a bottle of wine, but with the significant handicap of not actually containing any wine, and, as with space missions, minimising weight is a priority when one is in a condition like mine. Then again, who can really imagine another's life? The person who gave me this present actually has two homes, so his dilemma, had he been given a candle of his own, would have been which one to put it in. "Burn time 120 hours", it said; I rarely live somewhere for 120 hours at a stretch these days.

I wonder, as we all do, what the new year will bring. I remember 2016 being pretty appalling but that was a soothing back rub compared to 2017. If 2018 turns out to be worse (I write at the end of December 2017) then that's going to be a bit of a problem. The nadir was actually yesterday, as I lay in sickness in my childhood bedroom, desperate for sleep, while my mother pounded on my door, informing me, in a powerful and penetrating voice, of my many failings as a son, swear words included. Rescue arrived in the shape of an invitation to Penge from K——, the one with the dog who loves me, as you may recall. I was spectacularly unwell but nothing short of actual death – a possibility, as yesterday was largely occupied by thoughts of self-immolation, and the best way to go about it – was going to keep me in East Finchley for a second longer. It will be some time, I fear, before I set foot in that place again. It is quite a journey from Scottish rural splendour to Penge but I have at least discovered the taproom of the Southey Brewery, which is the most Hovelly pub I have ever been to - a garage with some chairs, basically - and my new spiritual home. The beer is first-rate, too.

But travel beckons. I have gone from being a totally sedentary man to one who dots about all over the place. I even had a few days in Latvia last month - but that's another story for another day. I seem - and this seems to be the ongoing theme for me - to have run out of space.

So it's farewell to Penge, and the new friends I made there, but London's maw refuses to let me go. I lasted one night at East Finchley to see if things would get any better there. They didn't. So after putting out a distress call on a social medium I took an Uber across North London at the invitation of K—— (another K——, not Penge's K——). I grew up in North London but this journey, cutting across east, exposed me to parts of it I had never seen before. In London, if you rely on the tube, the journeys are all in-out, not side-side. The pattern is repeated across, or up and down, the country. (A quick note on Uber. Like many of the metropolitan elite, I expressed a certain amount of solidarity with Sadiq Khan when he announced that Uber's licence to operate in London was to be revoked, due to unfair employment practice. My position on them has shifted somewhat, since having to rely on them to carry me and two not very light bags across town rather regularly. Sorry.)

I passed through Crouch End, Hornsey, Harringay, West Green. Unlovely names for unlovely districts, scantily served by the tube. And then to Stamford Hill. The name rings a bell. I knew not that I was going there. I thought I was going to N16, which I only know as a district of London called Stoke Newington. This is an area notorious throughout the capital for being absolutely inaccessible by any means of public transport whatsoever. (Residents of Stoke Newington, fiercely proud and about to fire up their laptops in indignation and tell me and this magazine's readers about the many bus routes serving the postcode: I exaggerate for comic effect.)

But here I am now in Stamford Hill, and as I struggle with my bags and a bottle of wine for my host (three bottles, the last of the Château Batailley 2000 I bought *en primeur*, when I was in funds, have vanished from their storage in East Finchley; their theft, if theft it is, represents a loss of some £150 at current prices, and is a further insult to my situation), I am passed by a Haredi, his shoulders hunched, as if in horror at the modern world.

Stamford Hill! It comes back to me now, and as my hostess reminds me, it is home to the third largest concentration of Haredim in the world, after Jerusalem and New York. As I go up the stairs to her flat I am pleasantly assaulted by the smell of baking *chollah*, and wonder whether I have committed a floater by bringing her, along with the wine, ten slices of excellent *mortadella* which, I suddenly realise, is made almost entirely of pork.

But I need not have worried: although, as she says, she could Pass, she is not Jewish, and we settle down to our feast – and, later on, to pepperoni pizza scored from the Sainsbury's down the road. Is there, we ask ourselves, any other kind?

The next morning I go for a walk to pick up the latest *Viz* and *New Statesman*. I am struck by so much . . . orthodoxy. "The only living goy in New York," I hum to myself, but I too could Pass, and, as I am wearing a thick black coat, black trousers and boots, and wearing glasses to boot, I wonder if at some point I am going to be accosted and asked why I have forgotten my beard and my *shtreimel*. I marvel at the rejection of the modern world which exists, in the same people, with their living in it. Does the fact that they dress almost identically – the women too – mean that greater stress is laid upon the individual character, or less? Was the young man I saw the night before scuttling away in panic from the burden of his own personality, or towards it? Yes, I think at one point, if I adopted the gear, I'd fit right in here; but then I wouldn't, not really, not with my disinclination to join any tribe - citizen of nowhere, indeed - my unholy urges and desire to read other works, almost any other works, than the Torah. I would also like my fondness for mortadella and pepperoni to be taken into consideration. I am also extremely uneasy about Netanyahu's policies, but perhaps that is a can of worms it is unwise to open in this column. Well, I think to myself, at least this is not a place in which I will get up to much mischief, so I find myself surprised, on my first evening here, to be propping up the bar of a most delightfully *louche* den called the Mascara, opposite the Morrison's, at one in the morning, chatting to the regulars and the landlady, a most splendidly tough Irish woman called Maggie, whom I have gathered during the course of the day is something of a well-known character round here. Ten years I lived in Central London and I never found a place like this. And yet here is one of the great bars, as if a chunk of New York had materialised in N16.

"Do you mind if I write about you?" I ask. I get the feeling that it is wise to ask her permission. Very possibly to do anything.

Morning now: I head off, on a bus, to the British Library - to visit the tribe of scholars, as it were, a tribe I have been exiled from ever since the Guardian sacked me last summer. Best not dwell on that. But a bus! That's how you get around town in these parts. It is another world here. To think I have lived almost all of my life in this city and yet found so much of it I did not know.*

---

* This is not how the column appeared in *The New Statesman*. My editor did not like the bit about the young man and his personality. Quite understandably. And they corrected my original "Hassidim" to "Haredi", also correctly, which shows how much I knew. So I keep one correction and ignore another.

And so farewell to Stamford Hill. It got better. One night the craic at Maggie's (see last week's column) lasted until seven in the morning; Sunday night was quieter, with me striding home at 5 a.m. on Monday morning. Everything in moderation, that's my motto. For those who think that this was a drunken debauch, let me assure you it was not: my bourbon was topped up only hourly; this was about the conversation, not the alcohol. (Maggie herself is teetotal.) It was also cheap: Maggie's being a legit place, no money changed hands at the end of licensing hours. This was invitation only, and I was proud and honoured to be invited. I was also particularly pleased to be introduced to Maggie's husband of twenty years, an incredibly cool Jamaican with a wide-brimmed hat and an awesomely natty double-breasted suit. Were anyone to ask me for an example of a gentleman, he would be the first person I would be pointing at, if pointing were not rude.

And then the travels begin again. I now find myself in an attic room in Shepherd's Bush, not two hundred yards from the family home. The room I am in belongs to my great friend L——'s daughter I——. This is yet another example of time having a little joke at my expense. I have known I—— since she was a small child; she has since then been through university and came back yesterday in order to look up some stuff in order to do her taxes. That she is not only grown-up enough to have to do her taxes, but grown-up enough to do them, all by herself, is itself remarkable, but then there has always been something remarkable about her.

She is one of those people I keep bumping into, beyond all likelihood, and by far my favourite. One of the others is ok, but a bit of a bore, and with tiresome political views; the other, whom I shall not name either except to say that he once starred in a television adaptation of the *Just William* books, is a weapons-grade, ocean-going twat, pompous, affected, and weird, and, thank God, I haven't seen him in years. (But when I was at school with him,

I had to see him *every sodding day*.)* The last time I saw him was in a flat whose owner had made the design decision to turn all her books' spines to the wall. She was a wealthy woman, as it happens, and there was a lot of wall.

That was depressing enough; and then Toby Young walked in. We all know what we think of Toby Young, but at least I know him well enough to call him an arse to his face, and can derive a little innocent pleasure from doing so. And then in walked Once William. It was, by some margin, the Worst Dinner Party Ever, and only the presence of H——, the Best Girlfriend Ever, saved it: she didn't know Toby Young from a hole in the ground, and still managed to find fault with just about every aspect of his educational policy when she asked him what it was. Never have I been prouder to go out with anyone.

Anyway, back to I——. I have met her, by accident, at: Moorgate tube station, en route to THAT VERY DINNER PARTY; sitting opposite me on the last train from Cambridge to London on a summer's Sunday night; on the anti-Trump march last year, a million-to-one chance given how many other people there were on it; and one other time, which I have forgotten, maddeningly, but you'll have to trust me on this.

Watching the young grow up is one thing; seeing it only at well-spaced intervals is another. One is reminded that one progresses not only at a snail's daily pace to the grave, but by leaps and bounds.

* I saw him again a year or two ago, in 2023 I think, at a lunch given by a magazine I write for occasionally; was even its theatre critic for a few months, until Covid closed the theatres. My editor said, "... and you'll remember..." and I didn't catch the name, because the place was noisy; and I didn't catch the face, because he had gone bald, and he looked completely different. He said "oh, we go way back," and I thought, "is he insane?" Halfway through the lunch, during which he had been giving me lots of strange looks, I realised who he was. I didn't admit my mistake to him, because I don't like talking to him much. I wonder when we'll run into each other again.

Yesterday I took advantage of my proximity to the family home to take my youngest son to the Uxbridge Arms in Notting Hill Gate. That pub has changed hands – the inimitable and unconquerable Linda has left, alas – but it still hosts its Sunday evening Quiz there; next time I'm in the area, on a Sunday, with funds, and a working brain, I'll go in there and have another go at winning the fabled pot.

But my son behaved with humour and grace: it is important to tell the younger generation not only about the importance of pubs, but the importance of behaving well in them. It is nice to know that the baton is being passed on. I have seen more than enough evidence to suggest that the future may well be in safe hands. I mean, just think about it. People roughly my age: Toby Young, Nigel Farage. (But at least the only life I've screwed up, or made more miserable, is my own.) People roughly my children's age: my children, and I———. I think that says it all really, don't you?

It's the little things going wrong that can do the most damage when you're homeless. Top of the Worry List right now is the left arm of my glasses. The hinge went the other day and the arm now dangles limply. It is, I fear, only a matter of time before it drops off altogether. I went to the opticians in the O2 centre on the Finchley Road and they wouldn't touch it. "Hand me the screwdriver," I said, and performed some surgery which gave some temporary respite, but now, we are back to the *status quo ante*.

In the old days, i.e. when I had a home, I would have gone to the local branch of the famous optician chain with the amusing adverts and they'd have fixed me up in a jiffy. But right now, with funds tightening at the end of the month, I can't just swan into the place and get a spare pair. At time of writing, I have twelve days before I can even think of doing so, and I'm not even sure these specs are going to last to the end of this column.

But do not fear for me. I am at the moment lodged in Olympia, in an extremely *bijou* ground-floor flat. Let me put it this way: I think the sugar bowl earns more than I do. (I am in a coffee-drinker's apartment, hence my familiarity with the sugar-bowl. Coffee, as they say, should be black as night, as strong as death, and as sweet as love.) I have certainly been seeing all sorts of places lately. For some reason all the people who have been putting me up for the last few months have been women. Can that be right? There must have been at least one bloke who's done the decent thing. If there has, and I've forgotten him, and he's reading this, please accept my apologies. In my defence, this is not a period of my life which I will want to remember very much. "I hope you're taking notes," said L—— in Shepherd's Bush a couple of weeks ago. "I don't want to," I said, and she nodded in understanding. She had also raised a concerned eyebrow at my alcohol intake and the effect it might be having on my health, but I had said that my circumstances had prompted a certain short-termism in my outlook. Again, she sympathised.

As it is, I have found myself drinking not quite so much lately. Don't worry, I'm still well in excess of government guidelines, but not as much in excess of them as I was. One of the side-effects of being of No Fixed Abode is a continuous tiredness, and when you spend as much of your time in the British Library as I have been lately, you don't want to be tired. As I have written here before, it is all too easy to pass out in the reading rooms, and if you snore, this is frowned upon. I eye the long, padded benches by the lifts and sometimes see a young student stretched out on them. For some reason it's ok for a young person to snatch forty winks in a public bench but I suspect that if I tried the same thing I'd be hauled off to the local nick.

So the last couple of days have been spent revelling in the use of a bed ALL DAY LONG, and I have forgone the library. Gentle reader with a roof over your head: do not take the existence of a bed of which you have the use for granted. And here's another thing about my hostesses: three of them have let me use their bed. Two of them have decamped to the couch, although as they explained to me this was not so much out of self-sacrifice, but because they really liked their couches, what with them being handy for the telly. The third of them, though, likes to have me in her bed while she is in it at the same time too, and that is a most welcome development. Then she goes off to work, and I play with her cat, and prepare dinner. Yesterday was devilled kidneys and mushrooms. (I cook this dish so well, if I say so myself, that even people who profess to loathe offal have come away as converts.) Have you any idea how hard it is to find kidneys in W14, if you have been foolish enough to look for a butcher's instead of going to the Waitrose at the end of Kensington High Street first? It's not hard to find them – it's impossible.

It did feel odd going into a Waitrose again. It's been four months since the last time, and I was beginning to wonder if they'd let me in again. I'd had a haircut a few days before so I wasn't looking completely mad, but the glasses hanging askew on my face told another story.

So here I am in sole possession, for the next seven days, of an extremely chic flat in West Kensington, cat-sitting. The cat, a black Persian of venerable years, is called Mrs Peel. How could you not love a cat called Mrs Peel, nor respect the person who named her that? I have been told that woe will betide me should anything happen to this cat, but as I have cat-sat for a 15-year-old cat (also black, by an odd coincidence) within the last few months with nothing to show for it but the cat's undying esteem, I am not very worried.

I am a bit worried, though, about the flat. As I mentioned last week, even the sugar bowl makes me feel like something Mrs Peel dragged in, and the sugar bowl is by no means the swankiest item in the place. The meanest object is the TV, a purely utilitarian artefact that occupies, when viewed from the sofa, roughly the same arc of vision as a business card held twelve inches from your face. This shows the right priorities. I have banned myself from using the fancy plates and assorted crockery, and am already, at one p.m., in a sweat about holding a glass of red wine, unsupervised, anywhere near the cream carpet this evening. The Hovel's carpet was of such a colour that you could tip any amount of red wine onto it and the only way anyone could tell you'd done it would be to get down on your knees and smell it, or feel for dampness. This carpet is not like that.

I wonder what could possibly go wrong. The mind reels. Immediately after B———, Mrs Peel's owner, left the building, I turned on the main overhead light and somewhere within the exquisite art deco chandelier a light bulb went BANG. Well, that's a great start, I thought. I have spent the next couple of hours just sitting carefully on the sofa, while somewhere underneath it Mrs Peel makes odd grunting noises in her sleep. At least that means she's still alive. (Mrs Peel, I am pleased to say, has developed what looks like a deep affection for me, but this might be only to make B——— jealous and teach her a lesson. "Divide and rule," says B———, "that's her policy."

So at some point I am going to have to go outside. I will, of course, be terrified of leaving my keys behind, or leaving them somewhere else; I am also worried about everything that can happen to me. A few minutes ago I looked at the most drenching rainstorm I have ever seen in London and thought: I'm not going out in that, I'll get swept to sea. I am also worried that I will get on a bus and have to hear the new safety message that goes: "please hold on, as the bus is about to move off". Those of you who do not live in London now have another reason to be glad you do not. Whenever I hear this announcement, which on some of the routes I take can be over twenty times, I feel my hair turn a little greyer, my blood a little more pressurised, the valves of the aorta a little more constricted. The thing is, you want to say, either everyone on the bus is sitting down, so they don't really have to hold on to anything, or those that are standing up are so wedged together that there is no room to fall. One wonders if the pavements will one day be equipped with loudspeakers reminding us to put one foot in front of another when walking, or to remember to obey the laws of gravity. (I called the Transport for London press office to tell me if they had any figures for people who had been killed or injured by failing to hold on when the bus moved off prior to this announcement's adoption, and they said 4,900 odd a month, but they're not sure how many of those were injured because they weren't holding on. The trial, thank goodness, will only last a month, and may even be over by the time you read this. I am also taking that figure with a pinch of salt.)

Or I will have to take a train or a tube anywhere in the country and be forced to listen to the anti-terrorist announcement that ends with the words "See it, say it, sorted", and I will run amok on the platform, screaming incoherent curses in rage and beating random members of the staff and public about the head with my man-bag, until I am restrained and placed under protective custody under the provisions of the Mental Health Act 2013, and who will feed Mrs Peel then?

※

I am sitting with my wife on the bed, watching University Challenge. A small family of chimpanzees sits on the bed with us, grooming each other. There are also a couple of gorillas, one of whom has taken a liking to me, and she holds my hand gently. I am worried, though: I have heard that the great apes can be violent, and the phrase that keeps popping up in my head is "ripped his face off", from a long-ago news report, and that was just a chimp. Lord knows what a gorilla could do.

"How long are we looking after this lot again?" I ask.

"Until around midsummer," she says.

"*Midsummer!*" I yell, and suddenly it's the radio alarm clock, and John Humphrys on the *Today* programme.

My dreams have been getting weirder lately. I will spare you the worst. I wonder if it's where I've been living. I am under strict instructions not to open any windows – apparently the cat is an escape artist. I am not so sure about that but orders are orders, and the lack of fresh air is doing things to my subconscious.

A more interesting explanation is that it is the area I'm in. Olympia is in an interesting part of London. If you wanted to make someone a present of Hammersmith, Shepherds Bush, Kensington and Earls Court, Olympia would be where you put your finger on the knot to tie up the parcel. And yet it is also weirdly difficult to get to: you have to use the Overground, which is basically a train, and although there is a tube station, it only works at weekends. Don't tell me that isn't an inversion of the natural order. In the morning I can stand in the kitchen in my underpants and watch gouts of commuters leaving the Overground every fifteen minutes. As often as not it's been raining, and I watch with pity.

But the area is liminal, on the threshold between worlds. Turn left out of my door and you are in a part of the world where JK Rowling has her London pied-à-terre, and where Jimmy Page and Robbie Williams have furious rows about the latter's proposed basement extension (I am so with Jimmy Page on this one). However, turn right out of my door and before about sixty yards are up you can be staring, as I was, at some of the grimiest and most depressing housing that this country has to offer. It is remarkable to think that, within stone-throwing distance of Holland Park, there is housing like this. The exteriors may be Victorian (in West London, the bricks are yellow – they're called the London stock brick, made from the local clay – as if the road to Oz has been torn up and used to make houses) but you can tell from the state of the net curtains what it's like inside, and the mental picture is not a pretty one. Then again, who am I to judge? Right now, anyone with an interior they can stay in or return to for the foreseeable future is in a better state than I am.

Carry on up Holland Road, and you get to Shepherds Bush station, and from there it is but a fifteen-minute walk to the family home, where the wife and I raised our chimps, I mean our children. She is after a divorce, understandably enough, and keeps calling me to check that I have done my taxes. I'm doing them, I'm doing them, I say. (It is my financial condition that is giving her demand for official separation some urgency. I completely understand this.) As I write, it is the last day for filling in tax returns before fines start to build up, and I am being beset by anxieties. I have not filled in a tax return in my life; I have always got someone else to do it for me. Now I cannot afford to pay anyone else to do it, and I am unmanned. In fact, I cannot afford anything that costs more than £5.13, for that is all the funds there are remaining to me in the bank account. Things keep dropping out of it mysteriously, and I run the risk, if I take the tube to the British Library, of not being able to take it back, and it is a long walk.

Meanwhile, I am waiting for some Albanians to give me the advance for a book they want me to write about a part of Albania. Rereading that sentence makes me realise it may be unwise of me to base any future financial decisions on this advance.

So I suppose that wraps it all up nicely. What with the air, the psychogeography, and the sense of looming disaster, no wonder I'm dreaming of primates, sitting around me on the bed, waiting to tear me apart.

Back in Brighton, looking after Laurie Penny's flat while she travels the world, saving it. The last time I was here I was, to start with, unaccountably depressed. These days I am cheerier, although that may be down to a growing acceptance of my condition. Whether this is a good thing or not I don't know. "Why don't you get a job?" was one unhelpful comment I was subject to not too long ago, but how does one go about getting one of them? The last time I had a job, as in one of those things one gets dressed and goes on public transport in the morning to do, Margaret Thatcher was Prime Minister, and not looking like she was going any time soon, either. Anyway, I already have lots of things to do, which, if I were doing them, would take up all my time. I have a book about fiction in translation to write, another book to organise, and a script that is meant to be my ticket out of here. So I have enough on my plate. The day goes a bit like this:

> 7.45 – 9.00 a.m.: Wake up (variable).
> 7.50 – 9.05 a.m.: Have a look around.
> 7.51 – 9.06 a.m.: Pick up a book, start reading in bed.
> 7.52 – 9.07 a.m.: Fall asleep again.
> 11.30am: Wake up. Panic. Make tea. Read some more. Maybe even write something, if there's a deadline.
> 1.30 p.m.: fall asleep again.
> 4.00 p.m.: wake up, feeling dreadful. Eat something. Make tea. Pick up book.
> Etc. Until 6.00 p.m. Wine. Bedtime comes around 1 or 2 a.m.

As you can see, we are not exactly in the realm of The Seven Habits of Highly Effective People. The person who made the suggestion that I get a job had herself done a lot of hard work to turn herself into a teacher, for which achievement I have nothing but admiration, but she did so in the knowledge that whatever happened, she was still going to have a roof she could call her own over her head. Not having a roof one can call etc. makes the slightest effort at self-improvement daunting, and you don't have to google "psychological effects homelessness" to work that one out.

One thing I do is pay a lot more attention to the rough sleepers I encounter during the course of the day. Shelter, the charity I started giving to the moment I got thrown out of the family home, says there are about 4,500 rough sleepers in the UK, a figure I find somewhat at odds with my own observations, although I am prepared to take their word for it. (It works out at about 21 per square mile, but that doesn't account for the fact that you're not going to be sleeping rough in the Highlands, or Exmoor, etc. Then again, it didn't account for the fact that there were usually around six rough sleepers between

Baker Street station and the Hovel, which indicates a somewhat higher figure than the one provided.)

So nowadays I do what I can. I give change when I have it; when I don't, I ask them what they want and go to the nearest shop to get it. (Last week involved a personal financial crisis, and I was unable to help in any way apart from curling up next to them, but I'm not a *saint*.)

One thing this does is bring home the gulf that exists between the pavement and borrowed accommodation; but then again, that gulf has narrowed, for until I start making rather a lot more than I'm earning now, a room of my own is an impossibility. It has always struck me, and now strikes me even more forcefully, that in contemporary society, one of the most fundamental of human needs should also be one of the most expensive. Start thinking like this and you become prey to gloomy imaginings, like: what if they decided to do the same with food, and make a loaf of Mother's Pride cost fifty quid? There seems to be no reason why not, in principle, and it does seem to be the way the world is going right now.

I apologise for going on about this, week after week. What I really should be doing is, in 800 well-chosen words, considering the place of Flaubert's *Education sentimentale* in the canon, and persuading people to read it in translation, and then doing the same for many other novels, but it is damn hard to concentrate on anything else. Although today has been one of the better days. For which, as I believe I have said before, the last time I was in her flat, you can thank Ms Penny, who, as I also said before, walks the walk when it comes to rescuing flotsam. Although she wants me to put up some shelves. It's a blue job, she says.

Every so often, over the last few weeks, I have thought of giving out some tips for those of you who aspire to be thrown out of their home and have no fixed abode. Some of this is instinctive: keep your chin up, travel light, don't stay at your mother's, that kind of thing. No need to say any of that. But I think I now have something worthwhile to say. Sit down and read the following story.

I had been to the Foundry in Brighton with my great friend S——. I have mentioned the Foundry before. It is a pub lit largely by candles and with basic furnishing and bare brick and tongue-and-groove wooden walls. It is, you could say, literally groovy. I love it. It was enhanced this evening by a wood fire roaring away in the fireplace. (Which is where, after all, you want a wood fire, or indeed any kind of fire. This is not, as you will see, an irrelevant observation.) The beer, as always, was excellent. The bar staff were attentive, intelligent, amusing, and in both the man's and the woman's case, extremely good-looking. So what with one thing and another, S—— and I didn't want to leave. We got chatting to a noisy poet who recited one of his poems, even though it was rather long. He looked like a student but was a landscape gardener. It was that kind of evening.

Eventually, though, I made it back to Crickhollow (Laurie P's adorable name for her demesne not.) I had, on the way, picked up some fish and chips, or, strictly speaking, fishcake, batter sausage and chips. Something had happened to the sausage on the way back. I'm pretty sure I would have remembered eating it.

Still full of the joys of the evening, I settled down with a glass of wine and sat down to catch up on *Star Trek: Discovery*. The *ennui* which had been plaguing me for months seemed to have lifted.

Well, you know how it is. One episode of *Star Trek: Discovery* turns into two, and before you know it you've only got two left, and you've promised to watch those with Laurie when she gets back, so you start watching *The Day of the Jackal*, which is even better than you remember, and then suddenly it's about three in the morning and you're hungry all over again, and what you fancy is something like cheese on toast, in fact, what you fancy is *exactly* cheese on toast. So you cut some bread and put it in the toaster – the very toaster you bought Laurie last time you were here, because she hadn't yet bought a toaster, so you bought her one as a flat-warming present, and told her that it had a name, and she must address it as "Nick".

A few seconds later, and I am looking blearily at the flames roaring out of the toaster. They're not meant to do that, toasters, are they? I turn it off at the mains, dampen a tea-towel and spread it over the top, then lift it off to see whether it has magically doused the flames, and it hasn't. Eventually they do die down, and I discover that every socket in the flat is now non-operational. I spend the next ten minutes looking for the fuse-box. It is not a large flat, and ten minutes' searching covers it twice. I go to bed with a book.

In the morning I look again for the fuse-box. I go to the shared hall and look inside the big cupboard of Really Scary Fuse-boxes. I prise open the one to Laurie's flat and look at a whopper of a 60 amp fuse. I'm out of my league. I call the emergency number on the laminated card on the wall. As it is a weekend, the charge for a visit will be £100.

£100! I could have spent that on the greatest debaucheries known to humanity. But I bite the bullet. I have copy to file, and the router is dead.

Hours later, the electrician arrives. He looks barely old enough to drive. He has a look around. After three seconds, he looks up, and says "ah." I follow his gaze. It is resting on the fuse box, in a corner of the ceiling where one would normally only expect to find cobwebs.

Let us pass over the rest of the visit in silence, except to say that he had arrived in a white convertible Mercedes. Well, of *course*. I hand over his cash, weeping a bit.

"I'm in the wrong line of work," I say.

So here is my advice. Become an electrician.

A couple of months ago, I got into an argument about shoes. People

I knew, whose opinion I had hitherto respected, were talking about some new fad that promulgated the desirability of going around the place barefoot. OK, I said; I can see the point of this if it's all about toughening up the soles of the feet, but really? In London? The pavements are most unsavoury, my dear.

No, they said, this is about being connected to the earth. You what? I said. They went on to claim some nonsense about earth energy being transmitted through the soles of the feet. Wear rubber-soled shoes, they said, and you are depriving yourself of a source of vital something or other. You are more or less giving yourself a death sentence.

"What about these?"

I said, pointing to my leather-soled boots.

"I suppose they're not so bad," I was told.

I thought of these halfwits last week in Brighton, as I stood on a damp pavement and felt a faint sensation of moisture in my right foot. I knew what this meant: it was time to get the Chelsea boots resoled.

I had bought them, with the aid of a grant from the Royal Literary Fund, in Brighton, the last time I was there; since then, they had seen more or less continuous wear, apart from during the icy conditions in Scotland, where I was obliged to use my fake Timberland walking boots, which have thick rubber soles and so I suppose are the equivalent of smoking 900 cigarettes a day while eating a block of lard the size of your head every hour.

Shoes are important. This was brought home to me forcefully by A———, who went out with me for a while even though she was almost 20 years younger than I was. An important factor, she said, was that most men her age didn't know decent, stylish footwear from a hole in the ground. The worst kind, she went on, were men who wear those pointy shoes that are now thankfully out of fashion, but persist in some benighted areas (there is a scathing reference to them in *Brighton Rock*, if I recall correctly). My shoes - Loakes Chelsea boots in the winter, tan suede desert boots in the summer

– passed muster. In the end, everything north of the shoe failed to pass muster, but that's a story for another day. (We're still friends.)

But the expensive shoe is an expense that keeps on going. The leather sole not only allows for some vestigial contact with earth energy, it transmits vital knowledge about the surface one stands upon. Let the soles wear down thin enough and you can tell whether a coin is heads or tails just by standing on it. Yet once a hole appears, you have to do something about it, or the whole shoe is ruined. And this becomes a big problem when you are in a town with only the one pair of shoes. They take a day to mend and you can't wander around without any shoes on, not even in Brighton, whatever people may say.

So then I remembered that my friend S——, who lives in Brighton and is a tall woman, has the same size feet as me, more or less. I asked her if she had a pair of shoes I could borrow while the Loakes were being fixed and she handed me a pair of silver Doc Martens. They weren't exactly Doc Martens: they were vegan Doc Martens. Brighton, she pointed out, is the place where you can get vegan bondage gear.

So for a couple of days I wandered about the town wearing silver pseudo-DMs. I posted a picture of myself on a social medium and they caused a sensation. Gentle reader, imagine if I had been in any British city other than Brighton. I don't think I could have got away with them even in Bristol. The mind boggles at the comments I might have drawn had I been in Liverpool, or Newcastle. I do not mean to impugn these fine cities. I just suspect that their attitudes as to correct male footwear are a little more conservative than Brighton's.

And did the thick rubber soles make me feel as though I had lost touch with Mother Earth? Not really, but the design did make me rather fancy the man at Timpson's who resoled my Loakes.

I asked if I could come in the next day to see him fixing my shoes. (He had been referred to, in the other branch, as Timpson's "shoe guru". And yet he seemed so young!)

"I don't think we pay enough attention to the way our shoes are made," I said feebly.

He looked at me a bit oddly but said that would be fine, and indeed, I was deeply impressed by his sole-repairing skills. But when I put my repaired boots on again the spark had gone. I was straight again. What was all that about?

※

By the time you read this it will all have gone: the snow, that is. Mais où sont les neiges d'antan? indeed. Well, if you must know: they're here. I'm looking out of the window at them, the snows, and very pretty they are too.

It would be wonderful to go out in the snow and frolic. But these days, frolicking is largely out of the question. And frolicking in the snow more so. Walking the roughly hundred yards from the bus stop to the family home, where I was scheduled to keep an eye on and cook for the youngest Lezard, involved me in about three close encounters with mortality: that is, slipping on the snowy ground.

Forgive me. I am going to have to go on about shoes again. But when the weather's like this, or when it was like this, you know, last week, you have to give serious thought to your footwear. As it happens, my faux Timberlands are excellently equipped to deal with snow: they have the proper soles for ensuring grip and confidence, such as that which was once enjoyed by people who had superior dentures, or toupées. (One never sees adverts for these products anymore. Do no-one's teeth fall out anymore? Are the bald condemned to shave their heads, like Prince William?) However, these boots are in East Finchley, a long way from here, and going there to pick them up would involve exposing myself to the risk of falling again. Which would rather defeat the object.

For those new to this column, this may strike you as odd. "Why doesn't he," you ask yourself, "just go into the place where he keeps his shoes, and dig them out?" Because, dear new reader, my belongings are scattered among various locations. This makes picking a wardrobe for inclement weather rather difficult. "Britons prepare for cold snap by already having coats and houses", said a headline in the satirical online publication, *The Daily Mash*, but this rather ignores the plight of those who do not have a house, or even a home. And for those of you who say "well get one then", all I can say in reply is: you try getting one when you are earning two-thirds as much as a nurse.

It is for this reason that I have been looking meaningfully at the family car. This is a fine beast, a Mercedes C 180 which is about twenty years old, bought second-hand at a reasonable rate because it is of a lurid turquoise colour, better suited, perhaps, to a cheongsam than a family estate, which no other car manufacturer has ever duplicated. (Strangely enough, Mercedes painted a few this peacock's-tail shade around 1997, and I've seen a couple of them, but then those were strange days, the nation losing its mind over Tony Blair and Princess Diana; anything seemed possible, and usually was. Also, everyone was on drugs.)

When I say the car is twenty years old, do not think it has been lovingly tended and polished at weekends. Each wing mirror is held on with gaffer tape; to see behind you on the left-hand side you have to crouch down so your head is slightly lower than the steering wheel. Moss grows freely within and without it; it has a cassette player but no CD player; someone poured acid or something over the bonnet a couple of years ago so it looks like something from *Mad Max*, an impression heightened by the purely decorative bicycle rack on the roof, and when you're on the motorway other cars give you a wide berth, because someone who has a car that looks like that is capable of *anything*. We are not a million miles away from the Jag in *Withnail and I*. It even has only one windscreen wiper, but in this instance that is deliberate.

Well, it seems that its time has come. It still runs fine – it's a Mercedes. But the estranged Wife's parents have decided that, due to their infirmity, they are going to part company with their car, and they are going to give it to her. Which means farewell to the post-apocalyptic Merc.

The children and I are devastated. This car has driven us to Scotland in the North and the South of France in, er, the South; and has never broken down. But it probably can't be sold for any more than £150.

And then it dawned on me: even I can run to £150, and if I don't drive it around that much - it does tend to drink petrol like I drink wine - well, it's big enough for me to sleep in, to carry around all my shoes, plus a few clothes and a fair number of books. It might be a bit parky in this weather but I can put on an extra jumper if necessary. And if I get peckish I can nibble on the moss. You see? 2018's looking up already.

※

It is about half past eleven, and I am smoking a goodnight cigarette on the porch in Olympia. For some reason, this part of London affords much in the way of street theatre at night. Or maybe it is the promise of it, such as the way the look and layout of Earl's Court promises great seediness and debauchery. (Although it never delivers.) Here, though, things do happen. There was the woman singing an evangelical hymn who stopped to have a chat. The woman with the cutest dog in the world. The Deliveroo guy smoking the strongest spliff I had ever smelled. It is all heightened by the tracks opposite, which carry both freight and passenger trains, allowing one to meditate on the transience of both human and other cargo, and make one feel as though one is in a Tennessee Williams play, or something. In other words, it is a good place for atmospheric brooding, and a sense of possibilities.

Anyway, I am halfway through my cig and I hear a "BANG-flap-flap-flap-flap", and see a very swanky Mercedes S-Class slowing down and pulling into the kerb on the other side of the road.

Well, what would you do? I suppose there are some of you who would say "none of my business", stub out the fag, and go back inside. Others would say this is too much like the beginning of that 90s film (or was it late 80s?) whose name I can't remember but involves a nice yuppie type who gets involved in an increasingly nightmarish spiral of misfortune because he sticks his nose in at the wrong time.* That, though, is precisely what the doctor ordered, as far as I'm concerned, so I flick the ember off the rollie, put down my glass and stroll over to the car.

Yes, it has an impressively flat tyre. I am surprised, frankly. I thought Mercedes car tyres simply didn't *do* that, and besides, — Road is hardly a warzone, and people don't even chuck bottles into the street. The driver and another man have got out and are contemplating the tyre. The driver goes to the boot and pulls out a jack that looks as though it would have trouble lifting up a Dinky Toy version of the Mercedes, and a wheel wrench that looks as though it could, just about, break a wine glass if you really gave it some welly.

At this point I become really, really worried that the driver is going to start using the jack to lift the wheel off the ground before using the wrench. This is a very, very bad idea, because what you are meant to do is use the fact that the wheel is fixed to the ground so you have greater purchase on the nuts fixing it to the axle. So at this point I break my silence, and volunteer to try and shift the wheel before he starts using the jack. (I should point out that it is also raining a bit, and I am not wearing a coat. I am *that hard*.)

I'm handed the wrench and start having a go. This wrench is not only feeble, its handle is not at right angles to the business end, so it's even more useless than it has to be. And the nuts are stuck on fast, as if welded. Because I have the best boots on for the job (see *Down and Out, passim*), I try kicking the handle, but the wrench just bounces out of the socket, and clangs to the pavement.

By this point I have started making conversation with the driver and the passenger, who he says is his brother. The accent is . . .

* *After Hours*, dir. Martin Scorsese. I must watch it again some time.

well, let's just say it's exotic, and contains the thrilling promise of adventure.

The driver is extremely grateful for my help, even though I have done nothing helpful, and as he waits for his back-up we talk. I bring him a cup of black tea, two sugars. He talks about his now war-torn home, his ethical position ("I will not kill. I will not steal"). He says he is delighted to see that there are still gentlemen such as me around, and we swap phone numbers, because he says if I ever need any help with something, he will see what he can do. "I am very broad-minded," he adds.

I cannot begin to tell you how much these words move me. OK, he won't kill or steal, but then I don't want anyone killed or anything stolen. But I imagine that were he to turn up at a door or two I could think of with a meaningful expression and a wrench rather more impressive than the one he has, then I imagine that certain areas of my life would become smoothed over rather rapidly. He wouldn't even have to do anything. Sometimes you just have to stand there with A Look.

We part with handshakes. I think of *Androcles and the Lion*. Or is it *Goodfellas*?

So, it all went a bit weird last night and I'm still trying to process it.

The first weird thing is that I went to a dinner party. That may not seem like a big or strange deal to you, but it is for me. As I might have explained before, I don't like dinner parties. I don't like the idea, I don't like the execution. I am not sure, also, whether I am wholly sympathetic to the kind of people who give dinner parties. I certainly don't get invited to them anymore, but whether this is because of my shrieks of protest, or my reputation as a surly or over-boisterous guest, I do not know. That's my problem at these affairs: I either talk too much, or not enough. And whatever I say, it never seems to be *the right thing*.

But A———— was most insistent. I told her all my objections, but she wasn't having any of them. She told me that her friends were lovely and I would find them all delightful. Well, you would say that, wouldn't you? You don't say, "of course, soandso's a jerk, and we're only inviting wossname because we really want to borrow a huge sum of money off her, thingummy's a complete waste of space, and why we invited Toby Young no one seems to know."

However, I gave in. I'm back in Stamford Hill for a few days, and A————'s is only a short bus ride away, and I can always escape to the Mascara Bar, and, crucially, I am also very fond of A————. I also remember that the last time I went to her place, her husband had poked all the bits of fat out of the *saucisson sec* they were serving as nibbles. I've never seen anyone do that before and I very much wanted to see it happen again.

"I will come for you," I said, "but only if your husband pokes all the fatty bits out of the salami." (I mentioned this in an email to someone, and she said "is that a metaphor?" As in, I suppose, chewing the fat or something like that. "No," I replied. "Maybe in his head it's a metaphor while he's doing it, but *he really does do that*.")

It turned out not to be too bad at all. That was weird. I was definitely on the talking-too-much end of the spectrum, and I think I probably overstayed my welcome a bit, but I blame that on the consideration of my hosts and the presence of Cosmo Landesman, an old colleague of mine from way back whom I generally find rather amusing, as he does not take himself too seriously.

So, while that part of the evening was weird for me, because I enjoyed it, you can't really flag it up as an experience that anyone else would find weird. (The husband didn't poke any fat out of the salami, alas.) The weirder stuff came later, at the Mascara Bar.

For those who haven't heard me go on about this place before, the Mascara Bar is a New York-style bar on Stamford Hill which stays open till two or three in the morning, depending on the whim of Maggie, the superbly tough Irish cookie who runs it. For some reason I got into her good books the last time I was in this neck of the woods, and this pleases me greatly, for this is my kind of place.

So, after having cadged a lift from the last guest at the dinner party, I strolled into the bar in the manner of a conquering hero returning from his campaigns. And it was wonderful – as wonderful as I remembered it.

I started chatting to the man next to me. And then I stopped. Also, everyone else sitting at the bar did a double take. I use the phrase deliberately, for this man was, basically, my double. The same build as me, the same, er, salt and pepper hair (with the emphasis, as with me, on the salt), the same kind of accent, and – this is where things started getting spooky – exactly the same outfit. A cream linen jacket, more or less matching chino-ish trousers, and brogues. I was not wearing brogues, because I can't go around carrying shoes all over the place, what with being without fixed abode and all that – but in an ideal world, I would have been wearing the same style shoes as him.

He was a couple of years older than me; I'd settle for being in that condition at his age. However, he also knew my work, here and from that newspaper I used to write in every week whose name escapes me.

As it turned out, I liked him. But I couldn't stay. Everyone likes to think they're unique, or original; but all of a sudden I felt like a *type*. Or, at that time of night, a faded photocopy. And *de trop*. I made my excuses and left.

"I am bored," writes my friend the Moose. "Tell me something funny."

I struggle to think of anything funny. This morning saw me, for no particular reason save the usual ones, in a particularly glum frame.

"I did fifty push-ups today," I reply, "in batches of ten, each batch interspersed with a lie-down and a coughing fit." He has not replied, but then he sent his message a couple of hours ago, when I had gone back to bed in disgust with the waking world.

"Why are you doing push-ups in the first place?" you may ask, and well may you ask. Two reasons. The first is that I dimly recall a poem by Kipling in which he recommends mild physical exertion as a cure for the blues. In one sense this is the worst poem ever written, but in another sense there may be some good advice lurking in there, on the grounds that the relief of not doing push-ups will be desirable in itself.

The other reason is that I need to get fit for a cricket match this weekend, and at the moment I look like an egg on which someone has drawn sticks for legs and arms. Unless, of course, I hold my stomach in.

I have been working on my legs, though. This is thanks to the bike. I'll get back to this. For those who missed last week's announcement, my adventures now see me in Oxfordshire, cat-sitting for my friend A—— who has gone to Japan to see her son, whose jumpers caused such a sensation in last season's *University Challenge*. The cat is called Tybalt, which I think is an excellent name for a cat, but the cat himself looks on me with a mixture of horror and outrage, dropping in only to eat his Crunchies, look at me with a shudder, and then stroll off again to the greenhouse, where he maintains his *boudoir*. (From the French *bouder*, to sulk.)

Much friendlier are the neighbour's dogs, and at least two of their three cats. But it's the dogs who are the best. These beasts – one looking a bit like a Staffie, the other a bit like a terrier – have decided that their lives are bereft without me, and they prop themselves up on the fence and whine and bark piteously until I come over and let them lick my hands. Boy, do they like licking my hands. It is as if I secrete some kind of drug that dogs are particularly fond of. I wonder which one it is. I learned, the hard way, that I am mildly allergic to dog saliva, so have to break off every minute or so to rinse it off, which perhaps compromises the flavour, but the dogs don't mind.

The village I am in is a little isolated, if you don't have a car. I don't have a car. I do, though, have a bike. This bike is somewhat challenging, being one of those whose tyres never quite pump up enough, and whose derailers keep slipping, especially when you are trying to go uphill. The nearest village with a shop in it is a mile away, which you'd think was nothing on a bike, but it is on this one, especially since that mile is up a hill which is imperceptible to the eye, but agonising to cycle. The agony is compounded by the fact that it doesn't even *look* like a hill. I have now done this route, there and back, about a dozen times, and I have not noticed the slightest improvement to my leg muscles.

I find, at the village shop, that my reputation precedes me. "Are you Nick? A——— said 'he likes his red wine,'" says the lady at the counter. "He does," I reply. This is actually quite a good village shop, as village shops go, and it even stocks this very magazine. The thought that this column is now sitting, read or unread, inside the very village shop I am writing about, is something that makes my head spin a bit. I think the French term is the *mise en abîme*.

But I must not complain about the blues. The weather here has been glorious. Even when every single neighbour for a mile around got out their angle grinders to trim their lawns on Bank Holiday Monday, things were not spoiled. The day before, also Power Tool Day in rural England, saw me wheezing off on the bike to watch a bit of village cricket and check out one the two pubs it boasts. May I recommend The Star in Stanton St John? (It's very near the village shop.)

I have now dug out the Ordnance Survey map and, after writing this, plan a little hike over the fields. We are, basically, in the Shire, as imagined by JRR Tolkien. If anyone can think of a better place to be on the planet in clement spring weather than the English countryside, with spectacular views of the Chilterns, do write in, but I bet you'll be stumped. Meanwhile, I will have to think of something funnier to tell the Moose. Maybe if I sprain something.*

※

And so to Scotland again. I write this on the train. I do not normally like writing on trains, or any kind of public transport, unless it is an emergency. But as my laptop refuses to let me connect to Virgin Trains' Wi-Fi and today is Filing Day, I might as well get cracking. The best bit of the journey is over: the view of the sands as we hurtle north after Berwick. Other good bits, earlier and later: the view of Durham cathedral,[†] Edinburgh Waverley (how wonderful to have a station named after a novel!), and, of course, the destination itself, but that's not for an hour and a half or so. (I am also very fond of Leuchars, but that is because of the name, which strikes me as even more Scottish than Inverkeithing, also on the way. I have never got off at Leuchars, but golly, what a name.)

Meanwhile I contemplate my fellow passengers in the Quiet Carriage: the sunburnt young man with an unusually irritating sniffle who put his feet on the seats; the woman who reminds me of P——, who is in a relationship with a weirdo who happens to be a minor celebrity, when she could have been in one with me; the woman with the peroxide hair who found my quarter bottle of Virgin plonk when it rolled down the aisle as the train took a sharp curve. I am forever in her debt.

SNIFF, goes the young man, liquidly. There are gurgles in that sniff; listen carefully, and you can hear the mucus, beating like surf against the membranes.

I am dying for a cigarette.

---

* The Moose, aka Kevin Jackson, died suddenly in May, 2021. His memory is more than a blessing, but I will miss him forever.

† During Covid lockdown, Durham became a very special place for me, but that's another story for another day.

There is also a dog. I am not sure about dogs on trains but this one is extremely well-behaved. It is certainly making less noise than my typing. As to whether my typing is more irritating than Mr Sunburn's sniffle, that is not for me to decide. I like to think my typing indicates a mind at flow, whereas his sniffles, a nose mindlessly at flow. It could be a lot worse. In the next carriage down are two of the worst-behaved children I have ever seen, one of whom is either called Romaine, after the lettuce, or Remain, after the vote.

SNIFF.

Anyway, I am going back to Bamff, where the beavers roam, and where pick-up trucks are not an affectation. Once again, I have had enough of London. I went to a party in That London last week and I realised that there were more people there that I wanted to avoid than that I wanted to meet, and I wanted to meet quite a few people To be fair, the people I wanted to avoid also wanted to avoid me at least as badly. I also have to avoid distractions, and I realise if you are going to rebuild a career then it helps to have a body of work to present to people. A couple of weeks should do it. It doesn't have to be too big a body. But I have learned that I can do a lot in two weeks.

Also, I missed the countryside too much.

SNURRFFF.

I have a dim memory of something like this happening before, but on a plane. A man with a hipster beard and extravagant, tattooed biceps. Even at some years' remove, Mr Biceps' sniffing makes my current neighbour's look amateur, or a piccolo to his entire wind section. I asked the stewardess for a napkin, and then offered it to my neighbour, who turned it down.

"You sound awfully ill," I said solicitously, doing my best to provide a hint. I gave up, and decided to drink myself to death. Maybe everything else since then has been my death reverie. It would explain a lot.

And yet what was that I said earlier about the best bit of the journey being over? Am I nuts? We are coming up to Kirkcaldy, and the views of the sea and the Firth have been amazing. In about thirty minutes or so (we're stuck behind a slow train) we are going to be going over the Tay Bridge itself, and there are few more thrilling views from a train than that. You feel as though you are flying over the water, while at the same time being mindful of the disaster immortalised by MacGonagall.

KSNURRFKLE, says Mr Sunburn as we pull into Kirkcaldy, and with that, he leaves. Will I miss him? I doubt it. The sniffing I can forgive, for we have all been there, but putting even one foot on the seat is a deal-breaker for me. Will I remember him, I wonder? Well of course, now I will, having written about him. That's what writing is for, even this. No one forgets the Tay Bridge Disaster, because it was fixed in the mind in legendarily bad verse. Which will be remembered for a very long time, if I may quote the bard himself. Lord, how we giggled, or were invited to giggle, as schoolboys, when presented with that work. And yet who has the last laugh? MacGonagall, that's who. *Exegi monumentum aere perennius*, he could have said, after Horace, if that's how it goes, and I don't even have the internet to check up on it. There are worse legacies, alas.

༺༻

The rain rattles against the window like gunshot; the wind, whipped into a frenzy across the Atlantic, howls like the wolf. Welcome to Caledonia in June. "It's nice in Scotland," says G———, the son of my host. "You don't have to put your jumpers away in the summer." Yesterday evening a young couple, here to observe beavers in the wild, had their tent collapse on them, and they were invited in to share our bread and salt, and to stay under an actual roof.

This place is very much about bringing succour to waifs and strays. Last week's, and indeed this week's too, is a fledgling jackdaw found lying by the side of a path nearby, looking very much the worse for wear. Under the care of G———, he has flourished, but we are very worried about his left leg, which dangles uselessly as he or his gammy leg has recovered enough to prevent the rest of her or him being eaten by something. As I sit on the lawn, I fancy I hear Kutkh calling from the branches.

And there has been quite a bit of lawn-sitting. Yesterday, in Alyth's chip shop (it is, officially, the best one in all of Scotland) the boss and I looked up at the TV screen we both boggled at the weather forecast, indicating that today the temperature in our area would be twenty-nine degrees Celcius. I wondered if it was a misprint; he said "what's the world coming to?" Earlier in the day, I had driven in to Blairgowrie to fill the pick-up with diesel and I bought sunglasses. *Sunglasses.*

I also had to buy some basic stuff for my living quarters. The previous inhabitants had stripped it bare. They hadn't quite taken all the lightbulbs but that might have been an oversight. I thought they'd left the fridge but, after I noticed that things that I put in it went all hard, it turned out to be a freezer. They also left the rawlplugs in the wall that used to hold up the mirror above the loo, but unless I find a mirror with exactly matching holes, they're not much use to me. Living without a mirror has been much less painful for me than I thought it would be. I am both unusually vain (oh! Those gentle brown eyes!) and undeceived about my physical failings (oh! Those gentle brown teeth!), so on the whole my desire to gaze, as Molesworth puts it, on my strange unatural (*sic*) beauty is cancelled out by my desire to spare myself the sight of a once-young man sliding fast down his fifties.

Also: no curtains, tea-towels, oven gloves, cutlery, or bog roll. That last one took me somewhat by surprise. I mean, I can understand taking away your curtains if you bought them yourself, but bog roll? Also also: the toilet seat had been unscrewed from the bowl, but what that was about I don't know. Were they going to make off with that, too, but were disturbed at the last moment by a knock on the door? We shall never know.

I mention this to the master of the house, who has, it must be said, a somewhat impish sense of humour. (He introduced me, one evening at dinner to his guests, who included his own sister and brother-in-law, as the Suffragan Bishop of Mayfair. "Marylebone," I corrected him. We maintained this *ad hoc* subterfuge all evening.)

"Ah well," he said as I expostulated on the removal of the bog roll, and speculated as to what kind of people did that, "the thing to remember about the previous occupants of the flat is that they are *English*."

"I'm only a quarter English," I said, much in the way that Withnail insists he is not from London.

But I am beginning to feel very much at home in this country. There's something about driving beneath a sun-dappled canopy of trees with road signs saying "red squirrels" (when I was here with the children a couple of years ago I saw one sitting by the road, bold as brass). Also, social interactions are conducted with a breezy geniality which is most cheering. And then, of course, there is, or are, the politics. When I think of England now and set it alongside Scotland, it suffers by comparison. If there is a figure in Scottish public life the equivalent of, oh, let's pick some names out of a hat, Boris Johnson, Nigel Farage, Michael Gove, Paul Dacre, William Rees-Mogg, then I haven't heard of them. (I've actually done some research on this. I googled "repulsive Scottish public figures" and absolutely nothing came up of any use.)

If there is a downside, it is the isolation. I do not want for company, as there are plenty of people around the place, and the chickens have welcomed me here again with open beaks. I throw little bits of bread at them from my window, and practise my bold, fiery flights of oratory on them; we will, one day, become a force to be reckoned with. (The cockerel, though, is frankly not exactly the brains of the operation, despite being called Enkidu, and finds himself being outsmarted every time by the hens when it comes to finding the little bits of bread; I had hitherto thought "henpecked" was a purely figurative term; it is not.)

But I am aware, very much so, of the distance between me and my friends. I try to persuade them to visit but it's a tall order. I invited the woman who introduced me to this house in the first place to visit, and she said she'd dearly love to, but added "I won't be going anywhere near the place while you're there," which is a strong contender for the nastiest thing anybody has ever said to me. I asked her which dates she'd like to come, and I'd absent myself, but have yet to receive a reply.*

But the worst thing is being so far away from my children, the youngest of whom turned eighteen yesterday. Good God, I miss my children. I thought that was the kid of thing only mothers said; but apparently not.

※

Has it really been a month? By the time you read this it will have been. A month in the country, and me a born and bred Londoner, 450 miles from the place.

I am, perhaps, beginning to go a little nuts. This is hardly surprising when, in my echoing quarters, the noise my chair makes is as startling in its way as the sound the chair makes in Keir Dullea's room as he eats, aged and alone, at the end of *2001: a Space Odyssey*. I lack, though, his *gravitas*, and the deep wisdom that going through the Stargate has given him, and have taken to burping extravagantly after swigs of the Lucozade that keeps me going during the working day. We Lezards are talented eructators, and my brother can scare cats from three doors down with his burps, which sound like something between a chair being scraped along a wooden floor and a shotgun going off. I rebuke him when he does this in company, but I have none, so who cares. My eldest son also has this gift, and I tell him off, too, when I catch him at it. Otherwise, how will he find a mate with whom he can make other, better Lezards?

* We're friends again, which makes me very happy.

Meanwhile, there are my friends, the chickens. One cockerel called, as I have mentioned, Enkidu, after Gilgamesh's great friend, and six lady chickens. The hens are difficult to individuate but long association with them has taught me how to do this – the trick is to look carefully at their combs – and their names are Peter Theodore Alphege, Mary Anne Charlotte, Thomas Wentworth Somerset Dunstan, Anselm Charles Fitzwilliam, Alfred Wulfric Leyson Pius, and Sixtus Dominic Boniface Christopher, which by an amazing coincidence are exactly the same names that comedy MP Jacob Rees-Mogg has given his children. (It is also all the more amazing when you bear in mind that hens are, by definition, female.) I throw little bits of bread out of my window at them, and one of them crapped on my windowsill in excitement. The chickens, that is, not Jacob Rees-Mogg's children.

Meanwhile, I contemplate England's forthcoming football match against Sweden. By the time you read this, it will all have been over, but right now, the morning after a somewhat crapulent evening watching us squeak past a nasty Colombian side (I seem to have demolished two and a half bottles of wine during the course of the evening, which is a lot, even for me), I am in the mood for murder. Not literal murder, of course, but I crave my vengeance against the nation that took the Best Girlfriend Ever from me for five years. During the course of those five years I have come to loathe our Swedish neighbours, from their overpriced Volvos to their disgusting meatballs and their ludicrous flat-pack furniture, which not only do I hate as much as fascism, but was also invented by an actual fascist. What I want to happen is for the Swedish team to be crushed – to have been crushed – like bedbugs, and for the very word "England" to make every Swede born and as yet unborn sob with shame until the end of time.

I am doubtless tempting fate, of course, but as I say, with Sweden, it's personal, which is why whenever I run into a Norwegian I buy him or her a drink, and when I tell them it's because they're not Swedish they laugh and say they know exactly what I mean.*

Ah, here come the chickens again. One of the interesting things about chickens – some would say the only interesting thing about them, but not me – is that they eat pretty much anything with some kind of food value, including – and this is where it gets weird – eggshells; which here are the shells *of the very eggs they have laid themselves.* When I mention this to some people they think I am pulling their legs, but I swear, on the lives of Peter, Mary, Thomas, Anselm, Alfred, Sixtus and Enkidu, that I am not. It is a disconcerting sight the first time you see it, admittedly. But once one has got over the shock of what can almost be called cannibalism, they are soothing things to have around, with a surprisingly wide vocal register, and especially comical when seen running, from behind.

However, I am uncertain as to the length of my stay. The rent has been fixed at a rate which seems suspiciously low, i.e. I can just about afford it, but whether this is a temporary arrangement or a permanent one I do not know. I think the idea is that I am to stay here until I have written a novel, or a TV script, or a collection of short stories, or all of these things, but given past form this could mean that I will be here for as long as Keir Dullea was in his room, and with about as much to show for it. Then again, once one has driven to the Co-op, played with the chickens, thought dark thoughts about Sweden, and practised one's burping, there is little to do here except write. I have, though, noticed a harmonica in my luggage. I have never learned to play the harmonica. Maybe now, with all the wild acres of Perthshire in which to practise, is the time to start.

Tragedy: three of the chickens have disappeared, and some feathers by the path strongly suggest a fox is to blame. The cockerel, Enkidu,

---

* England beat Sweden by two goals to nil. Not nearly enough, but it had to do.

and two of his harem, so whimsically named by me in last week's column after Jacob Rees-Mogg's children. To think that I maligned Enkidu, insinuating that he wasn't the smartest chicken in the coop. His diffidence in picking up the bread I cast for him may well have been nothing more than selfless concern for his hens. And now he and two or maybe three of his wives have gone to the great coop in the sky, not that I believe with all my heart that there is such a coop, but saying so brings a little comfort.

"The thing to do," said P—, their lord and master, "is to be happy for the fox," and while one salutes his pragmatism and ability to draw something positive from this loss, you could tell he was upset, and now the remaining hens are imprisoned within a nettly area the size of a smallish garden. There's plenty of room but it's not the same.

This slaughter set me off on gloomy thoughts, and when I noticed that (a) all the sheep seemed to have disappeared and (b) that noise which had sounded like a distant but massive crowd, and for which I could not account, turned out to be coming from an enormous shed, and to be being caused by the bleatings of several million extremely anxious sheep. And the worst thing about it was that it went on for *days*. And then it stopped.

Look, I've read *Watership Down*, I've even written the introduction for the Penguin Modern Classics edition ("this book is, inescapably, about rabbits"), I know nature and the country life isn't all fun and games, but this really rattled me. I remembered Clarice Starling's little speech explaining why the story she was in was called *The Silence of the Lambs*, and even though the sun was out, and I was in a perfectly sober frame of mind, I started considering vegetarianism. I do this every so often, until I remember that the only vegetables I like are chips and spinach; everything else is more or less a chore. (Although I can cook cabbage in such a way as to make it fairly tasty, believe it or not.)

Later on, I mentioned the business with the sheep to my hostess, or for the time being landlady, and she said, "they were being shorn," and when I next looked at the fields, I noticed they were once again dotted with sheep, only now they looked all nude. You can take the boy out of the city, but you can't take the city out of the boy.

And yet I am happy here, happier than I have been for months, if not years, despite suffering, right now, from a bout of nausea that kept me up all night. Funny thing, nausea; when you're in the grip of it you can't think of anything else, and when it's extreme you really begin to accept that death is the only release. it's a rather philosophical feeling.

This particular bout though, is entirely of my own making. One of the things they don't tell you about homelessness, presumably on the grounds that it's too bleeding obvious, is the fact that you find yourself doing very much less cooking than you used to. This is even true in my kind of homelessness, which is not to be confused by the kind of homelessness that means sleeping on the streets. My homelessness involves me being allowed to take up space in other people's homes, which is psychologically wearying after a while, for all concerned, but not nearly as bad for your health. But when it comes to cooking you find that you are far less inclined to, because you find yourself asking questions like "where's the colander?" so many times that in the end everyone concerned decides it's too much bother, and you end up ordering a succession of alternating curries and Chinese takeaways. (Which I adore anyway, but it's not great for the bank balance.)

Here, though, I have my own kitchen for the first time in ten months (apart from a two-week period in December), and I've had to stock it myself from scratch, which keeps me reminded of a question that was asked on some cookery show ages and ages ago but which has haunted me ever since: what's the most essential non-essential item of kitchenware? (Do write in. It sounds like an almost nonsensical question, but you get the point. At the moment I am managing without a tea-strainer, which you may think isn't much of a privation, but it is when you insist on drinking leaf tea.)

So the thing is this: I seem to have forgotten basic kitchen hygiene. Also, there are many flies and insects about the place, because the good people here do not drown the land in pesticides. (They're farmers, but not in the way that characters in *The Archers* are farmers, if you see what I mean, and they are ethically committed to good ecological practice.) So I leave food out, the flies do their business on it, I eat it, and then, well, you get the picture.

Well, I am going to have to relearn the business of wiping surfaces and putting stuff away. (I could do with a larger fridge, and am saving my pennies. This one is a barely knee-high cube.) I am expecting a visitor here, and I do not want to make her sick.

I am having to begin to think properly about setting up home here in Scotland. I left London in something of a hurry so arrived here with only three shirts, two undershirts, two pairs of trousers and no hat (it's a baseball cap bought in Antigua, and it says "Antigua W.I." on it, and when I play cricket wearing it I hope to fool at least some of the opposition into thinking I have played for Antigua, and that the stains on it are faded blood, and not red wine). I have two pairs of shoes: the knock-off Timberlands that are essential for walking around here, and a pair of ancient brogues, older than me possibly, one of which has split up the back and so is technically more of a slipper with laces than a proper shoe.* However, they are comfy as heck. (I once got refused admission to the Pavilion at Lord's because of them, and their battered state. You only get one shot with the security at Lord's and I didn't quite have the chutzpah to say, with a tear in my eye, "these were my father's shoes", largely because they weren't. So I went in through another door.) My suede desert boots, long an essential part of my summer plumage, are too far gone in decrepitude to be much good here, so I didn't take them.

Anyway, as I said last week I am expecting a visitor and I would

---

* What happened to my Loakes Chesea boots? I could have sworn I had them.

like to give her the impression that I am actually a civilised man, and not some kind of ape who has been trained to dress himself in a fashion comically like that of *Homo sapiens*. During the worst of the heatwave I bought a 50% polyester short-sleeved shirt from the charity shop for a quid but it's now too cool, weather-wise, to wear; also, it is not quite the garment with which one impresses a lady. I drove to the nearest Big Tesco, the kind that is big enough to sell clothes, but they didn't have a shirt I liked – I need a darker one, all-cotton, because I have learned that wearing a white or pale blue shirt isn't the cleverest fashion statement when you're lighting a coal fire every evening – and the smallest-waisted trousers were 32", which is a couple of inches too big for me. Plenty of trousers with my inside leg measurement, but their waists suggest different bodily proportions to mine, and I will have to eat a lot of haggis before I fit into even the slenderest of them.

Meanwhile, Scotland continues to entrance, and if I said before that I have fallen in love with the country that was nothing. This is the Real Thing. News from south of the border, and indeed from the rest of the world, makes me feel as though the best place to be right now is sheltering under the protection of the Cairngorms. Also, as the internet noted, the Scots have the best anti-Trump slogans, and they also voted Remain. I love them and although sometimes the accent falls somewhat heavily on my ears – I had to ask for three repetitions from a passerby who had kindly informed me that the pick-up truck's bonnet wasn't properly shut – I get by, and no one mocks or disparages me for mine. I am also having to start checking myself from saying "aye" instead of "yes", in case anyone thinks I'm taking the mickey. I am not. I have noticed, by the way, that drivers are considerably more courteous here than in the South: when pulling over to one side to let another car pass on the windy hill roads, there is always, always, an exchange of waves between the two drivers, friendly almost to the point where it seems we are about to stop, get out and exchange phone numbers. I also like driving the pick-up truck because it makes me look as though

I have a proper job here, something manly like timber management or fence-mending, instead of writing book reviews and whimsical accounts of my shenanigans for a venerable left-wing magazine.

Oh, and the beauty of the place. This is what Heaven must look like; well, maybe a little further north than I am, but it's only a short drive. The trick is persuading people to come up here. I can't say "this is how you find out who your friends really are" because only the strongest of motives could get someone to spend £150 on a return train ticket, or make an eight-hour drive up here, however much they will realise it was worth it when they arrive.

Actually, it so happens that I have recently met someone who is prepared to make that journey, and I am, I must admit, getting all in a tizz about it. A very pleasant tizz, as it happens. I have yet to give her a nickname appropriate for use in this column - it is early days yet - but I have a feeling that the auguries are good. After all, you don't spend nine hours chatting on the phone to someone you won't get on with once she's stepped out of the car. (I bet you haven't spoken to someone for nine hours on the phone. Well, it's a record for me.) So cautiously, and without wanting to jinx anything, I can at least say right now that I am happier than I have been for years.

I write to the sound of a Henry vacuum cleaner being pushed around the living room. Love takes many forms, I suppose, but now I come to think of it, the spectacle of a woman taking a look around my living quarters, wherever they may happen to be, and deciding, like Edward VIII, that Something Must Be Done, is not an unfamiliar one. I remember A——, who looked at the Hovel with something approaching awe; when, some months into the relationship, she decided to sort out the bookshelves and was still going strong at midnight, I decided that enough was enough (we are still friends).

"I'm not doing this for you," she says, "I just can't bear it anymore."

However, this tidying-up operation stings me mildly, as, before the arrival of the Welsh Enchantress, for that is what I have decided to call her, I had spent about eight hours intensively tidying up two months' worth of detritus. Living alone in an echoing, barely furnished space gives one the impression that there is no real urgency to the decluttering project; in fact, one feels that one could actually do with a bit more crap about the place, in order to make it look, you know, lived in.

It was actually horrible. I don't think I've ever worked so hard in my life. For a start, the washing-up had been largely conducted on a need-to-use basis, and if you know what that is a coy euphemism for, then your vision of the sink at the beginning of *Withnail and I* is not a million miles from the reality. Also bear in mind that there is a lot of coal dust about the place; the resulting footprints look as though . . . look as though . . . well, the only simile that can do it justice is to say that it looks as though the lino has been stomped on by someone wearing boots whose soles are impregnated with coal dust, which isn't a simile really, because that's exactly the reality.

The rest of the tidying we shall pass over in horrified silence, except to say only that unloading the empties into the bottle bank took about half an hour. (To be fair, this was, as I say, about two months' worth of bottles, and this included the empties from a luncheon party the previous weekend, at which there had been forty guests.)

But I wanted to please this woman; we had corresponded and spoken for long before her arrival, and she seemed of an extremely pleasant and accommodating disposition. Asking if there was anything that she could bring from her home in Salisbury, I replied, in a sentence which I doubt has ever been written before in the English or indeed any other language, "just bring the tea-strainer and the thigh-length boots." We have been speaking frankly and at length, you see.

There was considerable apprehension on both sides before her arrival. Photographs can be manipulated; expectations and hopes can put a filter on the lens. A 475-mile drive to see me in my new abode bespeaks considerable commitment; which can lead to a sense of obligation, not necessarily a good thing in this kind of situation. Also, I had been agonising somewhat over the ethics of a romance with a subscriber to *The New Statesman*. If it all goes wrong, does she get a free subscription or something?

So when an extremely attractive blonde woman drove into the Alyth market square in a black Audi TT and a pair of LK Bennets, I was considerably relieved; and so was she. (LK Bennets may not be the most appropriate footwear for rural Scotland but they don't half make an impression when you step out of a sports car.)

I am pleased to report that everything has been going swimmingly. The life of a writer is, to her, an unfathomable mystery; as, to me, is the life of someone doing her best to survive in a massive bureaucracy. I can't say I disbelieve her when she says she gets around 600 emails a day to do with work, because the look on her face, and the sound of her voice tells me she is not exaggerating. (Oh, and the voice. Welsh, as you may have spotted. From the South, so less guttural than, say, Cerys Matthews's, another beauty from Wales; but I could listen to it all night, and in fact, on one occasion, did. Seriously, until the dawn.) And where, when and how did the foul libel that blondes are unintelligent arise? She is smart as a whip. And last night we sang along to every word of *Rubber Soul*. That's a deal-sealer.

And so now begins the odd business of accommodating oneself into another's life. I have been allowed to run wild, as it were, not only over the last eleven years, but particularly over the last two, and one becomes, in one's habits, how shall I put this . . .? Personalised. Or as if a team of social scientists had decided to see what would happen if a man had been allowed to live free of all external restraints. It did not take her long to realise that I am deeply eccentric, albeit with certain redeeming qualities which I might blush to list here. I am reminded of the old conundrum: (a) good sense of humour (b) good in bed (c) lots of money. Pick two. But so far this is great.

And so life keeps moving on. I wrote about the ancient Mercedes that died; and now Jaffa, the cat I wrote about a few months back, has died too. That pitiful miaow she employed to extract food from the soft-hearted was probably saturated with pain; her liver was collapsing, and her life was becoming unsupportable. The eldest son, who was the family member she was closest to, held her while she was put down. His mother couldn't face it, and stayed in the vet's waiting room. I can't blame her. I don't know if I'd have had the character to do what the son did.

So I invited him up here; he'd have been alone in the house otherwise, and I know how unsettling that can be after a beloved pet has died; you keep seeing it out of the corner of your eye.

Lord, it was fun. If someone had told me, around the time my wife was nagging me to get her pregnant, that I would end up actually pining for the company of my children, my reply would have been terse and sceptical. And if they had dared to suggest that they, in their turn, would enjoy my company, it would have been even more so. But so it has proved.

The important thing for a father in the autumn of his life is to show his children how grown-up he is; to offer a model of maturity, and wisdom. So I ask the Welsh Enchantress, who has been here a couple of days, if I can borrow her Audi TT to pick the boy up from Dundee station. What I want to do, I explain, is try to shock the Eldest Son. He knows I'm driving a pick-up truck, and while he would think it cool, it would not be a surprise. A black sports car, though, would. He is normally a master of the poker face, as deadpan as Jeeves; I want to see that eyebrow of his raised a quarter-inch.

The EW and I go back and forth on whether I ought to borrow the car. She let me drive it back through the Highlands, after a trip to Braemar, on the kind of roads that are used to advertise precisely this kind of car; but this time I would be driving it on my own. It is also a little rainy. In the end we agree that it would probably not be a good idea, especially as I would be driving into Dundee, a city I do not know well, without a map or a satnav. But fate forces our hand: the pick-up is being used. So I take the car. For added effect I am dressed all in black. I suspect I look like a complete *wanker*. But the important thing, I remind myself sternly, is to wind up my son.

I park behind the permanently-stationed police van outside the station and call my son, to ask when he's getting in.

"What car are you driving?" he asks, for practical reasons.

"Um, I'll be standing up. You'll see the *Discovery* on the other side of the street when you get out of the station; just turn right, I'll be a few yards down the road." I think I have dodged the question successfully.

As he approaches the car, we both try to keep our faces straight but it is impossible. Broad grins are exchanged.

"Where did you steal this?" he asks. The last time he saw his father, I was sleeping on the sofa of the family home, at something of a low point in my life.

"Long story," I say. "It all begins with the Novichok poisoning of the Skripals in Salisbury."

To where the WE returns the next day; but I am glad her and the ES's visits overlapped. That the boy is with me stops me from feeling too bereft.

We settle into a routine. I get up before him, and make him sausage, bacon and eggs for a late breakfast. Then I show him how grown-up writers behave, by filling him in on all the latest details of an ongoing feud with Rod Liddle. This involves some background explanation.

"Rod Liddle is someone who used to be quite an interesting figure in journalism, but he made a face when the wind changed and is now mainly known for writing columns which wind up liberal lefties like me, and for having cheated on his wife during his honeymoon. Oh, and for accepting a police caution for common assault on his then-pregnant girlfriend. Apart from that, he's lovely. I read an article in which he said that 52% of the populace – yes, he said 'populace' – voted for Brexit and I corrected his error. The next thing I knew he sent me a private message saying 'you really are a talentless piece of shit', and it all sort of escalated. The last thing I heard from him, he's going to sue me, but on what grounds I'm not sure." Later on, in the queue at the Co-op in Alyth, I listen to my voicemail.

"George Carman here," says one message. "There's a fire here, and we need to put it out." I nervously leave a message, before reflecting that George Carman's voice sounds awfully like my friend John's, and also that Carman died in 2001.*

I wonder how all this goes down with my son, but he's playing it cool. Unlike his father.

※

And so to London. The dog returns to his vomit, as the fool to his folly. I agreed to cat-sit for my baby brother, who is going off on a little holiday to celebrate his 50th birthday. You may remember I have written about this cat before: it's the one I let out by mistake some months before, which drove my brother into a rage the like of which I had never seen from his before.

Anyway, now I am here for a week, looking after the mog, and a very fine mog it is too, and a very fine house I'm staying in, although I don't know where they keep the pepper. Tony, if you're reading this: where do you keep the pepper?

Anyway, That London. I thought it would be nice to go back, see old friends, maybe haunt an old haunt or two. But I haven't. Instead I find myself paralysed into inaction by the sheer horror of Neasden.

For those who do not know it, Neasden is a suburb in the northwest of London. It has a tube station which can get you there, and, more crucially, whisk you away from it. This, I have discovered, is the only good thing about it. Apparently Twiggy grew up here but she had the good sense to get out, and there is also apparently a temple here but as I am not a Hindu it is of purely architectural

---

* George Carman, QC (1929–2001) was an leading barrister during the 1980s and 1990s.

interest only and not, for me, worth the two and a half-mile round trip (on foot; my brother hasn't been able to find the time to put me on his car insurance).

I have learned many things about Neasden since I have been here, and the burden of my research is that it has always been a shithole, but the demolition of pretty much all the pubs here has made it progressively worse. One enters Neasden, if a pedestrian, via the pleasantly unassuming 1930s tube station, which is above ground, and if you want to enjoy your time in the suburb, my advice is to stay on the platform with a picnic and maybe a good book, and then when you're done get on a train going back the way you came.

If you must go out, cross the road and take the path by the railway tracks. Have a good look: this is going to be the nicest view you're going to get on the walk to my brother's house. You will pass one shop on the way: it sells a wide array of Polish foodstuffs, which is nice, as I am half-Polish, and like this kind of stuff, even their slightly weird cheese. The rest of the stock is not exactly a gourmet paradise. You will find two kinds of pasta, if you look carefully: spaghetti and macaroni. You will search in vain for any fresh vegetables beyond the cucumber, or any fresh fruit beyond the lemon and the lime. (Although they get a tick in the margin for selling limes.) I think it sells tomatoes, but I can't be sure. Onions, no. My time in that shop is limited to buying Casillero del Diablo Cabernet Sauvignon at £6.99 a pop (I've seen worse deals) and large bags of cheese balls. Then, to get to my brother's house, you have to cross the worst road anywhere outside Los Angeles: a place where you have to stand and wait until about 11.30 at night for a gap in the traffic. It is at the bottom of two hills and the cars scream down from both sides, and if by some miracle a gap emerges it is only for a car which has been waiting at the junction of a rat-run to dart in.

Will Self once invented the game "East Finchley", in which players to take turns naming London suburbs, with each player having to name a suburb more boring than the last one. The loser is the player compelled to say "East Finchley". After having been here five days, I think the game needs some fundamental revision. Will Self and I both grew up in East Finchley, and just as you cannot imagine anyone's parents being more gauche and boring than your own, so you cannot imagine anyone else suffering greater privations in a boring, ugly North London suburb. East Finchley it was for us, so East Finchley it had to be.

But oh dear, Neasden. East Finchley is a Shangri-La, a downtown Manhattan, a twinkling fairyland of hopes and magic compared to Neasden.* Dreams don't come here to die: they never lived in the first place. If you want to accuse me of snobbery, go nuts. I have nothing but the deepest compassion and pity for the people who are forced, by circumstance, to live here. No one likes living here: it is the price they pay for living in London, but in its bleak isolation, its poverty of life and amenity, its miasma of tedium and scant resource, it strikes me that Neasden is very much a vision of post-Brexit Britain, and I'm not kidding. I haven't left the house that often because even with the promise of a swift tube ride into town I still have to cross that road, breathe that air.

And so there we are. It turns out that I have abandoned, or renounced, my citizenship of London. I miss Scotland, badly.

Back in Scotland. Neasden saw me off, via East Finchley, by giving me a stinking cold and a sense of deep failure and regret. This wasn't helped by having to unpack about a hundred books that had been sent me by various publishers keen to press their wares upon me.

---

* A couple of years later, having driven with my Eldest Son back from the North Finchley hospital his grandmother was recovering in after a fall, he said: "After North Finchley, East Finchley is like *Rome*." He has a point.

New readers may not know this, and maybe old ones don't either, but I used to be a book reviewer for the *Guardian*, specialising in giving the kind of books that rarely get a chance (small publishers, obscure authors) a chance. Unpacking book after book and knowing that, in an age governed by how many clicks you get, these books were mostly doomed, was a dispiriting experience.

As was the journey north, which seemed to take for ever. I have to go back to London in September to judge a literary prize and I am beginning to wonder if there isn't a better way than a nearly six-hour train journey. Someone suggested flying which might shave a couple of hours off but then there's the whole getting to and from the airport business, which is something that I don't think I am psychologically robust enough to handle right now.

No, there's no getting round it: I live a really long way away, or rather, you do. Funny how the more often one does the journey the longer it seems to take. I suppose it's frustration. When I got here, I spent the first couple of days being too ill to move, but yesterday I rallied a bit and went into town for a haircut and a visit to the butchers, whose profits must have dived while I was away. The butchers and I have a special relationship. I asked them a couple of weeks ago if they had any smoked streaky with the rind on and they said No, they didn't, but they could cure some for me by the weekend. They could what? This is accommodation of the customer to a high degree, the kind of thing you only read about in cookery books by long-dead authors. A modern cookery book which contained the phrase "ask your butcher to . . ." would have to end with ". . . and you will be met with a blank refusal." Anyway, this lot – and I am happy to name them as Ewarts of Alyth, with a few branches spread over Tayside – produced some of the best bacon I have ever eaten, and I have eaten a lot of bacon. I was worried while I was away in London that they might have thought I had forsaken them, or become a vegetarian, or, even worse, Found Another Butchers, but when I came in and spread my *largesse* about the place it was as if I'd never been away.

"We can close early today," they said. (The hairdresser was happy to see me too, and gave me the Senior Citizen's discount for my short back and sides, on the grounds, she said, that she didn't have that much to cut off in the first place. Hmm.)

Things have changed a bit up here, even in the relatively short time I was a away. You don't notice this when you're holidaying somewhere. The market square is being dug up; they're putting ports in for electric cars, which is great (or would be, if there were any round here), but also chopping down trees, which is very much not great. And the weather has turned: it may be warm down south for the softies, but here there is a chill in the air, and even though the hairdresser said some of her customers claimed there was going to be another heatwave, she pointed out that their sources were no better than the more hopeful parts of the internet. This colder weather is fine by me as it means even more of an excuse to light a fire; and also it intensifies the experience.

And like the character in Martin Amis who craves a cigarette even while he's smoking a cigarette, I crave more Highland-y stuff even while I nestle beneath its folds. Last night, in front of the fire and with a succession of steaming hot toddies by my elbow, I watched, on Netflix, *Calibre*, a film set in the Highlands (one of those cheery little numbers which is like a cross between *Deliverance* and *Shallow Grave*; I'd give it 3/5, but 5/5 for the scenery), and, on another media platform, *Troll Hunter*, which is set in Norway, most of which is so far north it makes Scotland feel like Tuscany. I've seen this four times already, but I felt that I couldn't get enough of watching people driving at night through pine forests, being scared.

And then the lights started flickering and a noise came from the kitchen very much like a cricket ball being tossed around in a washing machine. This, after watching the films mentioned above, was rather alarming. The simplest, most rational explanation, it seemed to me at the time, was that I was entertaining a poltergeist, but it turned out that the fridge had gone kaput. But as these days the kitchen itself is a giant fridge I probably don't need to get it fixed until June. Which makes me think: how long am I going to live here? Is this it, the place? I've even got a letter asking me to register to vote. Crivvens.

※

And it begins again.

The partner of a friend alerts me to a post that Roderick Liddle, the newspaper and magazine columnist, the one who ran off with another woman on his honeymoon, has placed upon a social medium. In it, he describes being accosted, while carrying some shopping, by a man with "a fine ginger beard" who says "Nicholas Lezard is a stupid . . ." Well, I blush to repeat the word that this man closes his sentence with, for it has no place in this column. Mr Liddle then says that he replied "a very stupid . . .", and then the unrepeatable word again. He then says, and I paraphrase, that the encounter cheered him up no end for the rest of the day.

Leaving aside the question of Mr Liddle's veracity, it least it gave me an excuse to get back to him. He'd sent me a message a week or so beforehand which I hadn't had the energy to reply to, but which contained some interesting claims which I probably shouldn't air here, just in case *The New Statesman*'s lawyers operate on a metered basis. But I thought it best to let the whole matter drop, because I have better things to do with my time.

As it turns out, I don't, because this is too much fun. Actually, I have several better things to do with my time, such as get on with some work, put on a laundry, buy some more milk, and practise my burping, but I am an expert at procrastination if I am an expert at anything. So I replied to his previous, unacknowledged private message with an assertion which would certainly have this magazine's lawyers running around, flapping their hands in panic were I to mention it here, and he replied, "you heard wrong." He then suggested I had raped an owl (?), but I don't think I'll be taking him to court about that, as I don't think he really meant it, and also it is considered, or used to be considered, very bad form for journalists to sue each other for libel.

However, the issue has gone live because the day before yesterday I received an invitation to the *Spectator*'s writers' party. (Don't make that face. It's not against the law to write for both magazines, and anyway I only write for their civilised and erudite books pages.) I have to be in London next week; should I go early and so go to the party, and have a show-down? I could at least get a column out of it. A couple of friends are going too, one of them a good one, and it would be nice to see them again. They could also form a bodyguard, lest Roderick, whose youthful membership of the Socialist Workers Party may have taught him some street smarts, decide that this is an argument best solved with his fists.

On the other hand, this would leave me at a loose end in London for a week, although I could always go to Salisbury to meet the Welsh Enchantress. This is a compelling argument, except that another friend is coming from Los Angeles to stay up here and I'll already be missing three days of her visit as it is.

So now I have a major organisational dilemma. Do I go down to London in order to be pounded into a jelly by a columnist whose position on immigration is, to say the least, problematic, and then to be tended by a lovely woman, and disappoint someone who has flown five thousand miles to be here? Or what? Then there is the matter of seeing my children. I would have to see them before Mr Liddle rearranged my features, because no one likes seeing their father hurt, and the timing would be tricky. It seems I cannot fix matters without disappointing *somebody*.

This is the odd thing about modern life. It gives one the illusion of connectivity; I can have an amusing feud with a fellow hack whose immediacy of exchange makes it feel almost as if he's next to me; and yet there is no getting around the fact that if he wants jump up and down on me in hobnailed boots I'm going to have to be there in person so he can get on with it. I know I mentioned this last week, but the sheer distance is inescapable, which places a strain on one's conception of Britain as a relatively small island. Well, it isn't. There's loads of it. (In fact, there's so much of it, especially round here, that there are people who claim, *pace* certain columnists, that we need more immigrants in it, rather than fewer.)

Gentle reader, forgive me for going on about this man again. But it helps me to feel part of a vibrant journalistic scene. The surprising thing is how news of our spat has reached the streets of Blairgowrie, where I do my big shops. In fact, only the other day, while I was crossing the car park at Tesco's, a man with a fine ginger beard, an armadillo on a leash and a splendid pair of antlers growing out of his temples, came up to me and said "Rod Liddle is . . ." Oh no, wait. I have a feeling I may have dreamed that one. One must, above all, have a solid respect for the truth.

※

So, in the end I didn't go down to That London in order to confront Rod Liddle and slap his face with a white kid glove, demanding satisfaction. For there have been more interesting developments here. For hark! Bzzt! The doorbell goes. It is A——, the supremely competent and smart woman who runs the office here, telling me that a new sofa is being delivered tomorrow, at eleven, and that I will be in receipt of the old sofa, which it will replace. She is at pains to remind me about the time, perhaps because I have a reputation as a late riser. I try to contain my excitement.

"At eleven," she says, again.

I am not kidding about being excited about this development. I know this sofa well: in fact, I helped carry it up from a storeroom to the Library. (Yes, this place has storerooms large enough to contain sofas. And has a room which is full of books and so is called "The Library.") It was – is – a splendid sofa, a bit battered by the years but a lovely deep blue colour and about the size of the QE2. And it is comfy. I have succumbed to its deep embrace only a few times, as the Laird has assumed *droit de seigneur* over it, as is his prerogative, and likes taking naps on it.

But tomorrow, at eleven, it will be mine. And I think that may be that for me. I will never move again, for it is going to be set in front of the fireplace. And every evening I light a fire, and I sit in front of it in a nice battered old armchair, and it gets later and later, but I cannot bring myself to go to bed, for there are few things nicer than sitting in front of the fire with a glass of wine, or maybe two. The room doesn't need it: there are functioning radiators, but why use them when you can have a fire? Well, yes, pollution, I know, but it is not a very big fire and when you place it in the grand scheme of things it is even smaller. And outside, the trees are festooned with lichen, which only grows where the air is clean, and that's good enough for me.

There are only two problems with it. One is that it needs to be cleared out, almost every day. It's a coal fire, which means that it produces a lot of clinker. This, I learn from Wikipedia, is good for nothing except perhaps making pavements. Steamships used to dump it over the sides. When I think of the amount of clinker I produce, I think of how much of the stuff there must have been back in the days when everyone had a coal fire. What did they do with it? I put it in the rubbish bins in straining black bin-liners, but I come over all giddy when I think of that being multiplied by several millions.

The other problem with having a fire is that I am forced, every so often, to buy the *Daily Telegraph*. Those of you with experience of fireplaces will know why. Others may be a little mystified. I have to buy this newspaper because it is the only one big enough to open out and spread against the chimney-piece, or whatever you call the hole where the fire is. You do this so that the fire draws nicely without having to faff about with bellows and stuff, and the tabloidisation of all newspapers save the *Torygraph* means that only the *Torygraph* will do. Well, the *Sunday Times* too, but I never seem to find myself in a shop on a Sunday.

Anyway, you can imagine the problem I have buying the rag (I see it has a cryptic crossword called "The Telegraph Toughie". Look, if you're going to be conservative, do it properly, ok?). I like to think that people will think well of me, and one of the things I don't want is for people to think I am a Tory. (I was going to say that it doesn't go down well in my neck of the woods, being a Tory, but a quick check reveals that my MP, Pete Wishart of the SNP, whose voting record seems ok, held his seat in 2017 by an astonishingly tiny 21 (twenty-one) votes, out of 50,000-odd who did vote. The Conservative candidate came second, after a 9-point swing. Terrifying.) I already have an English accent, so maybe it's assumed I'm a Tory anyway, but am also enough of a familiar figure in the Co-op for the staff to say hello to me, which means I am on their radar, and they may be speculating about me. So when I buy the paper, should I say, "I hate this paper, it's for the fire"? Or should I buy a copy of the *Guardian* for balance? (I'm not a huge fan of the *Guardian* these days, but that's personal.) Or should I drive miles out of my way to get the paper from different shops? All of these options are, of course, nuts. The whole business causes a degree of anxiety that goes entirely against the spirit of sitting in front of the fire with a glass of wine in one's hand. Then again it's quite satisfying using Boris Johnson columns to light fires with.

For the last few days one of those anxiety-induced boils that have not been plaguing me for months started brewing again. I will not go into any further physical details because my editors have gently let it be known that going on about them is a bit ick, a point of view I quite understand. However, the question arises as to why I have it in the first place. My love life has taken a marked turn for the better, I have somewhere to live until December, and possibly April, and I am picking up work, touch wood (to all three).

Then I realised: it's the travel. I have been doing rather a lot of it over the last week. Scotland to London; London to Brighton; Brighton to Salisbury, Salisbury to London, and tomorrow, assuming the trains are running (on the day of writing this column, they are not), London to Scotland. These have been for essential things like important family meetings, a literary prize panel I'm on (the Goldsmiths'; I am this magazine's representative on it, and deeply honoured), taking the Youngest to Sussex University with his mother, and seeing the Welsh Enchantress. I list in increasing order of pleasure, with a very small gap between the last two, as seeing the Y is always a pleasure, and his mother and I didn't fight, not even a little bit. (Although she's a nervous passenger, and in the small stretch of road she let me take the wheel for, I made her scream about five times, but then nervous passengers always make one's driving worse, don't you find?)

But I'm really getting fed up with this travelling lark, especially when I know that the finest sofa on God's green earth is pining for me back in Perthshire. Lee Marvin's "I Was Born Under a Wandering Star" was one of those records I heard as a child and never forgot, and I always thought that being born under a wandering star would be kind of cool if you liked that kind of thing, but at my age it gets awfully tiring. I am travelling light, but with my laptop, a venerable Lenovo T410 which comes in at just under 5 lbs (or two pounds more than a MacAir), and four or five books I want to scrutinise more closely for the Goldsmiths, I am using the word "light" loosely. I also have a spare pair of undercrackers, a few socks, a spare vest; everything else I am wearing, like a budget airline passenger trying to avoid luggage surcharges. It's all packed into the fetching manbag a previous inamorata gave me, and believe me, whoever sold it to her on the grounds of utility and robustness wasn't pulling her leg. It is doing (again: touch wood) a terrific job under the circumstances; it is holding up better than me.

The big mistake was to travel with a fleece and a heavy coat. These are necessary in Scotland at this time of year; in balmy southern England, not so much. So, I stepped off the train at King's Cross already sweating with distressing freedom, and people on the tube were glancing at me anxiously, as if I was one of the first people infected in a new terrible plague. (Also, such a tan as I picked up in Scotland has now largely gone, so I looked paler than everyone else.)

I wonder if I am the lightest packer in the world. My great friend, the late Robert Lockhart (subject of Louisa Young's wonderful book, *You Left Early*; read it), would go off to Paris for a month with only the clothes he stood up in; his travelling companion/minder bought him a toothbrush when she discovered he hadn't even thought of taking one; he managed to lose it before they even got to the airport. Since he has gone, I might have to take the crown. Take the laptop and the books out of the equation and I think I am. People marvel at this. The WE is grasping quickly how deeply unusual I am so little surprises her now, but I think even she was impressed, and not necessarily in a good way, by the fact that I only took one shirt for a week's travel.

I wonder if what I am doing is trying to pretend that I am only nipping out to the shops, instead of travelling the length and half the breadth of the country. Everything has been about change for the last eleven years, and I am not wild about change, unless it's for the better. So, while recent developments have been most satisfactory, I crave a time when no further developments are necessary. When, I wonder, will I again have a place I can truly call my own, for good? That December deadline isn't getting any further away. Could I move in with a certain person? The thought is appealing for many compelling reasons, but I think I may have become too feral for a normal person. How did I do it, the whole living-with-someone-else thing? Is it a skill, like riding a bicycle, that you can pick up again? I have a feeling it isn't. I am now an object that is never at rest. My life is in flux; and I remember, with a start, that "flux" is another word for what comes out of boils.

Another journey like that and I am done for.

It could have been worse, though. I could have decided not to buy the ludicrously overpriced snacks from the artisanal food market outside Kings Cross station. £4.50 for a bagel! £4 for a few slices of chorizo wrapped in a paper cone! But if I hadn't . . . it doesn't bear thinking about.

It became clear that something was wrong when I got inside the station, and I saw all the people staring up at the departures board in a way suggestive of great and increasing anxiety. I'd decided to take the 14:00 train. A comfy seat, a sandwich, maybe a couple of those little bottles of wine, sleep all the way to Edinburgh. Who travels at 14:00? I thought. (A second consecutive night of insomnia had ruled out the 11:00.) Well, everyone, it turns out. When the platform was announced, a scant two minutes before the train was scheduled to leave, people *ran*. It was like being transported back to some grand wartime narrative of displacement and loss, and I half expected to see forlorn children in flat caps carrying battered suitcases and with labels tied to their coats, bearing the names of rural destinations.

I managed, in the end, or rather at the beginning, to find a nice little spot against a door, by the toilet. A woman who needed a stick to walk commandeered that, and good for her. I can fold up quite small, like one of those bicycles, so at least until Peterborough I had something like a seat, if you call the floor a seat. I drifted off. At Peterborough an angry little man with grey hair, about my age, shouted and swore at me while he made his escape. Dazed, I was a little slow for his liking, but he got off the train in plenty of time, which he used to turn to me and swear some more. I couldn't think of anything to say back to him, which is probably just as well. Meanwhile, several slices of chorizo rolled out of my pocket and onto the floor. Have you ever looked closely at the floor of a train by the toilet? I mean really closely? It's not very nice.

At Newark things got a bit worse and now it was standing room only, as a man called Shane carrying a huge bag got on. I know he was called Shane because he had it tattooed on the back of his neck. (It seemed pretty safe to assume that Shane was not the name of his lover.) Shane had had a little argument with one of the railway staff on the platform; Shane had asked if there were any seats in first class, and the guard had answered his question with a question, viz. Did he have a first-class ticket? The question was clearly rhetorical, expecting the answer "no", and Shane wondered aloud, as he squeezed into the last available space, whether he should have decked the railway employee. I like to think I am good at sizing people up and even from our scant acquaintance it looked as if Shane was extremely well practised in decking people, so I decided that while we were crammed up against each other the best thing to do would be to make friends with him.

Shane got off at Doncaster, freeing up quite a bit of space (he was rather wide, but in a way suggestive of muscle, rather than fat), and I was able to fold myself up again, but not before looking up and down the carriages and noticing that it was standing room only everywhere else, and that it would have been impossible to get to the buffet car even if I'd wanted to. As I returned to the floor it started, amazingly, to rain on me; the window had a leak. Is this, I wondered, what Brexit is going to be like?

It thinned out at Newcastle, enough for me to get a seat. A real seat. I used to work as a copywriter, and my mind drifted back to the days of slogans. "You know what?" I text the WE. "Seats are hugely underrated. So gentle to your bum."

We got into Dundee an hour late; it was dark; the taxi driver grumbled a bit about the trip to Alyth, and I spent all my last money on him. I have to remember that when I travel to and from here, it's not just the £150 return ticket, but an extra £100 in taxis and snacks and drinks and what have you. I meant to go back down to London in the middle of October, and then again at the beginning of November; I really don't think I can face it.

Several days on, and I am beginning to recover from the experience, although my bank balance is going to have to wait until tomorrow. Meanwhile, I wonder if the experience truly was a foretaste of the collapsing infrastructure. If so, at least people comported themselves with good humour (Angry Peterborough Man aside). But the experience has left me with a terrible apprehensive phobia of train journeys. I mean it's one thing to experience that kind of discomfort, and another thing entirely to be charged to the point of ruin for the privilege. LNER now stands, in my mind, for "Let's Never, Ever Return"; but I have to.

So, the other day I got a text from A Certain Woman asking if I'd grow a goatee. For her. Well, that was an easy question to answer: "no", I said. I have several reasons: 1. Facial hair is itchy. 2. It indicates a certain male vanity 3. It makes me look older than I want to look (I know this flatly contradicts reason 2, but there you go) and, most importantly, 4. My little brother has one.

I am fine with him having a goatee. It suits him (Bertie Wooster appeals to Jeeves by saying that David Niven has a moustache, so why can't he have one, and Jeeves replies diplomatically that "his moustache is very becoming to Mr Niven"), and helps people differentiate us, in the way that Spock in the parallel evil universe has a goatee, and his our-own-universe incarnation doesn't. So the thought of my growing a goatee and having him smirk inwardly, or very probably outwardly, and thinking or saying "I thought of that first" makes me shudder.

But after getting back from London ten days ago I was too enervated to shave for a few days, and then after that, I thought "why not? Let me do something for this most excellent woman."

For a while, all went well. It was disconcerting when I emerged from the bath still stubbly, for I always shave in the bath, so I would have the odd feeling of being unwashed even though I had just thoroughly washed myself. Then the hairs continued to grow, and from occasional glimpses in the mirror I noted the Stations of the

Beard. First, there is the "haven't shaved today" look. Then there is the "modishly unshaven" look. After that things go downhill rapidly. For there then follows the "gentleman of the road" look, and then the longest stage of all, which I am still suffering, the "wanted by the police for a string of crimes too disgusting to mention in a family newspaper" look.

It is funny how something which is literally no effort can be so effortful. I remember having most of 1970 ruined by a Peanuts strip in which Linus, the cartoon's conscience and moral core, suddenly announces that he has become aware of his tongue, its continuous and disconcerting presence in his mouth. His sister Lucy says that this is the dumbest thing she's ever heard, until she, too, becomes aware of her own tongue and finally says, in very large capitals, "I oughta knock your block off!" Well, I am now aware of my own beard. During the summer my friends in the South would ask me about the midges up here, and I just said that I laughed them off; they weren't so bad. But growing this blasted beard has been like having my own personal cloud of midges living on my face. I am being driven mad, and although the upside is that at least, having been unable to think of anything else for the last few days, the subject of this week's column has been ready to hand, I really would like to think about something else now, even Brexit. *It's that bad.*

How did beards get so popular? Also, just as you don't see any baby pigeons, you don't see anyone walking around with my Sex Criminal's Stubble. You either see nothing, or something full and bushy. (Actually, now I come to think of it, I did see someone at this mid-stage, and it was none other than Christopher Hitchens, and I felt emboldened enough to ask him what the hell was going on with that beard, and he mumbled something about his son having dared him to, or wagered he couldn't, or something like that. I felt sorry that I'd raised the matter. I think it's the only time he was ever lost for words.)

But the popularity of the hipster beard is, I think, more than just a yearning, ironic or not, for the fashions of the past. It is about an ideal of commitment: the notion that one is in this for the long haul. I am reminded of my occasional attempts to write a novel: the first three or four thousand words are a breeze, it's like running downhill with the wind at your back, and then on day four you look at it and realise it's rubbish. The beard-wearer, on the other hand, is announcing to the world that he *perseveres*.

Maybe this is what accounts for the fact that, bizarrely, quite a lot of women like them. But it is one thing to be twenty-four years old but looking much grander and more mature (supposedly) because you have a beard, and very much another thing to be fifty-five and looking like a seventy-year-old who has just got out of, or is just about to go into, a penal institution.

Ah well. In between the end of that paragraph and the beginning of this one, I have had a bath and shaved off the fungus. I don't know how I am going to break it to the woman who asked me to go through this ordeal. Even though I am revelling in the fresh play of air about the lower face, I can't help feeling that I have let her down somehow. Maybe I should quote Meatloaf at her. "I'll do anything for love, but I won't do that."

Autumn hits Scotland sooner and harder than it does the southern regions of the British Isles, and the last week has been alternately dreich and wild: miserably drizzly and cold, and then, for the last three days, a relentless wind, all day and all night, the night-time wind unsettlingly insistent, and making me feel as if I were on board a sail-ship rounding the Cape of Good Hope rather than inside a castle, which, after a while, I started imagining was actually rocking. The wind was exciting at first, but after a couple of days it begins to mess with your head, a roaring as if the biggest gas ring in the world had been left on, and I felt that the shifts and imbalances of meteorological pressure were beginning to affect me at the level of the synapse, and that I was entering a phase of what seemed like a precursor to insanity: I felt like Lear on the Heath, with pauses in the turmoil not helping me that much: then I started feeling like Macbeth. Which is at least more geographically appropriate.

But today it is gorgeous: mild and sunny, and even though all the leaves have been blown off the chestnuts (I fear the work of the leaf-miner moth; the conkers beneath them that I saw were pitifully small, the largest not much bigger than an acorn), the rest of the landscape was picture-postcard perfect, a glorious gradation of reds and browns. The woods are lifting with mushrooms, although they're getting on a bit now, some of them the size of soup-plates and with their caps aged to concavity. But in the sedge by the side of the lane I heard a cricket chirping, and there are still butterflies. How they survived the last week is something of a puzzle.

The season gets to me. It always has, but even more so now that the deadline for my removal from the apartment approaches. I have about six weeks, and although Plan A involves my relocation to the newly-vacant cottage a hundred yards up the lane I am not sure that the work that needs to be done to it is proceeding quickly enough. At the moment it is semi-derelict, and looks from both the inside and the outside like the kind of place that the Scooby gang would hole up in, to the detriment of their nerves, Shaggy's and Scooby-Doo's in particular, as if they had forgotten the lessons that they had been taught in the previous week's adventures. A friend rang me up on the computer the other day and asked if I didn't feel terribly isolated up here; not really, I said; there's always something going on here, and there are ancillary staff doing the myriad jobs that need to be done to keep the place ticking over. It's like a little village here, or a benign *Gormenghast*, although last week I had the place entirely to myself, and when there was a power cut, probably due to a tree being blown down and knocking out a power line somewhere (it happens up here from time to time), I got properly rattled, and got a taste of what life before electricity would have been like, with the major difference being that in those days, people would have known where the candles were. Should I move to the

Scooby House, this is a mistake I won't be making in future. But I wonder whether moving up there will actually make me go mad, or madder. It could be fun.

Meanwhile, *Doctor Who* has started again, and the Laird and Lady invited me to watch the first episode with them, with dinner afterwards (cooked by me. Rabbit. "Who would have thought the old man to have so much blood in him?" I thought to myself as I took the skinned carcass from its packaging). This was rather poignant. I had been hoping that my daughter, back from Amsterdam for good now, it seems (and living with my mother; god help her., i.e. my daughter), would join me for the new season, but as it turned out I was playing the part of the child, sort of, my hosts/landlords being just about old enough to theoretically be my parents (well, the Laird, at least).

It is always a bit tricky watching a TV programme one wants to concentrate on in the company of people one does not normally watch TV with, and I suspected that my landlady was the kind of person who feels unafraid to do a live commentary during even the tensest of dramas. Actually, she is one of the wittier and more articulate and intelligent people I know, so her conversation is always a delight, but there are times when one wants a *continuo* along with the action, and times when one wants to catch all the nuances of Jodie Whitaker's take on the venerable Time Lord, so I radiated a kind of pained silence throughout, like a sulky teenager, until they got the message. I feel a bit bad about that. As someone whose English roots are in Lancashire, I was a bit vexed that she was from The Other County, but then you can't have everything turn out just the way you want. Wasn't she good, though? And great to have the show back. Ideal for dark and stormy nights.

So, the WE is coming tomorrow, which means I have to swing into action. The last time she came, you may recall, she took one look at the place and demanded to know where the Hoover was kept, and then started using it. This is a damning reproach to my ability to tidy a place up, but then I am under no illusions about my inability to tidy a place up, or ability to mess it up. I simply don't see the things ordinary people see, as if my eyes see a different wavelength to everyone else. So to this end I have hired a cleaner.

Those new to this column may wonder what on earth I am doing with a cleaner, or how on earth I can afford one, but a tenner a week or so isn't going to break even my bank; and also, boy, do I need one.

So Kelly, who works at the castle, has been assigned to me, and so far all is well. As I learned with Marta, the first cleaning lady I dealt with, in the Hovel, the trick is not to tell them what to do, but to learn what they are prepared to do and not to do. It takes one a while, for instance, to grasp that they're not going to do the washing up. At first I thought this fell under the rubric of "having a dog and barking yourself", but I eventually grasped the fact that washing-up is considered *infra dignitatem*, and rightly so. I tried it with Kelly – leaving the dishes in the sink – and was told after her stint, pointedly, that the dishes were still in the sink, "steeping." Fair enough. She has enough on her plate as it is.

She's only been twice, but the second time she looked around the place and asked: "how do you get it into this state?"

"I don't know," I said. "It's a gift."

But the true gift is hers. How does she, anyone, do it? She had a go at the place yesterday and after less then an hour the place was transformed. And yet, twenty-four hours later, it looks as though it had been de-transformed, and we are back to square one, and I swear that all I did for the rest of the day and the evening was sit on the sofa, doing nothing except maybe having the occasional sip of wine. And yet it looks as though eight teenagers have had a party, and run away before doing the tidying up. And these aren't the modern kind of teenagers, who eschew alcohol and look with contempt at their parents' dissolute generation: these are old-school teenagers, who have firm ideas on how to have a good time. So Kelly's maybe coming in tomorrow to have another go.

Of course, the very idea of having a cleaner puts the guilty middle-class person into a bit of a fix, contortions of guilt, and I imagine that there are plenty of readers who are right now firing up their laptops preparing to give me a piece of their minds. Well, by all means do so, but bear in mind that Kelly needs the work, I pay her over the odds, and also give her lifts into town and back. (During these journeys, the conversation flows freely, and I have learned quite a lot about her, not for these pages, as they're her own business. But one thing I have learned that a really good way of shutting down a conversation, with a wide range of people, is answering "I'm a writer" when people ask me what I do. It is as if I had admitted to a hugely embarrassing habit, like compulsive masturbation.)

Meanwhile, since writing the last paragraph and this one I have managed to do something incredibly painful to my back, simply by standing up. I had always, until about five seconds ago, been rather smug when listening to my peers complain about their lumbar pains: well, not smug exactly, for I feel for them, in very much a there-but-for-the-grace-of-God way, but conscious of the fact that my slight build relative to absolutely every other man I know might have something to do with it. Only the other day I was thinking about how much healthier I am than I deserve to be; and now I feel I have taken a great leap forward in the direction of the grave.

The timing could not be worse. As I write, the WE is packing her Audi for her drive up here; she is bringing wine, beef cheeks for me "to work your magic on", and a fluffy towel dressing gown I coveted when I last stayed at her place. (When a woman lives in sole charge of a place, you can be guaranteed two things, bathroom-wise: a really impressive set of shampoos, and a fluffy dressing gown. Bliss.) The thing is that she expects a certain, um, liveliness on my part, and right now I don't know, now that I have sat down again, how I am ever going to move from this position without howling in agony. And as for finishing the last bits of the tidying up, putting on a laundry so that the sheets and duvet cover are clean (unwashed since her last visit, in August), I have no idea. Reader, pray for me.

Work continues on the Spooky House I will be moving into at the end of November. It actually has a name: the Grieve's House, Grieve being a Scots word for a bailiff, or farm overseer. Having always considered myself more of a poacher than a gamekeeper this is quite the turnaround, but then when I first came here, about five or six years ago, I started daydreaming about giving up the London literary scene, and becoming a sort of apprentice groundsman or gamekeeper here, occasionally retiring to a shed to write an exquisitely poised feuilleton about the simplicity of rural life or some such poppycock. Now I don't think living in the Grieve's House will actually involve any duties as such, I won't be collecting rents or pointing a gnarled stick at someone and saying "you there!", but the thought hangs in the air, and it makes me smile.

As for the work that continues, it would seem I am being asked to do some of it. Last weekend the Lady of the House got me and young R—— to move a heavy rolled-up carpet, and then a heavy wooden table, from a utility room to the House, and by "heavy" I mean both "very heavy" and "unwieldy". Carrying the carpet was a nightmare but moving the table was worse. As we turned it round to get it through the door its drawer fell out, and out popped a dusty copy of an old *Escort* magazine from 1994. I didn't recognise it as being from 1994, my knowledge of this soft-core grumble mag (rhyming slang too rude for me to explain) being even scantier than the women's clothing therein, but I checked it out later, purely in the spirit of sociological enquiry. Actually, sociological enquiry, as it turns out, is all it is good for, for although one does not want to be ungallant, the women in it are not of the most enticing. In fact I am amazed that anyone, even in those days when lonely men were not as spoiled for choice as they are now, could have been aroused by the contents.

Anyway, I have no need for any such entertainment, as the WE joined me again for the weekend. Again, she drove up nearly 500 miles to see me. (And yes, it does make me think of that song.) I cannot begin to say how touched that makes me. Seeing how she was putting herself out for me so much, I agreed to a request from her, which involved me popping into Boots in Blairgowrie because what she wanted me to get was not the kind of thing I wanted to get in the nearest chemist, because the nearest town is about the size of a hall carpet and once I bought what she wanted me to get, word would get about, and people would point at me and snigger, even though there is no shame in this (well, ok, quite a bit) and I do not, as it happens, have a problem in that particular area. It's just that I'm not as young as I was, and sometimes I drink ever so slightly more wine in an evening than the government recommends I should, so a sort of belt and braces approach is, I was told, advisable.

So I gave Kelly a lift back into town that day and she asked me what I was up to in Blair (that's what the town is called here; I like saying it too, as it makes me feel like a local), and I said I had to go to the chemist, and then I realised that she was giving me a look which was roughly along the lines of "but there's a much nearer chemist", and so I stammered something about the chemist in Alyth not stocking what I wanted, which was blatant garbage, so I made things rather worse for myself, but not as bad as I did when I went into Boots and found her standing at the prescription counter myself. I ran away, but not before she waved at me. I went in the next day, wearing a false moustache.

I tried this thing I was asked to get for the sheer hell of it, even though I do not have a problem in that particular area, and one of the more remarkable side-effects it had was, and I can put it no better than this, an increased flow of blood to the brain. The WE drove back on the Sunday morning and I was left at something of a loose end, so I actually started writing something, which is unusual for me on any day of the week except filing day for this magazine, and even then it's sometimes unusual, and by the end of the day I had about 2,500 words down, not all of them bad. I repeated this feat (not the words, the feat) the next day, and the next, and what with one thing and another I ended up with 8,000 words of prose, every one of them a gem, which, I have just learned, has been accepted for publication by the first people I sent it to. Whether I can put it down to this thing I got at Boots I am not sure. I wonder if it will help me at picking up tables, because they are bastard heavy things, tables. I shall stick to writing, and being a Grieve.

※

As I write, it is about half past one in the afternoon, it is twilight outside, and rain is lashing the windows of my bedroom. I have just come from the kitchen, where the view is much the same, and rain is lashing its windows too, which is quite something, as the kitchen window faces east and the bedroom window faces south. If I had north- and west-facing windows, I have a hunch that they, too, would be being lashed by rain.

Well, you may say, that's Scotland in November for you, you knew the risks. But hey, I'm not complaining. Because I've gone back to bed. I mean, look at it out there. Would *you* go for a walk in that?

I've been spending quite a lot of the last few days in bed. I think I've given you my schedule before, but it's been revised. The day now goes like this: noon-ish: wake up. Ablute, make tea, go back to bed. The bed, as ever, contains a small library on one side of it, so there is plenty of reading matter. I am alternating, right now,, at about half-hourly intervals, between the LRB, a 1951 book by RS Fitter, *The Home Counties*, published to coincide with the Festival of Britain, both poignant and thrillingly written (the general editor of the series was Geoffrey Grigson, so this shouldn't come as too much of a surprise), an incredibly scabrous novel about the music industry in the 1990s by John Niven called *Kill Your Friends*, a collection of our very own Dr Phil Whitaker's "Health Matters" columns called *Chicken Unga Fever* (you won't need me to tell you how good it is), and Adam Mars-Jones's sadly neglected novel, *Pilcrow*, which is about the size of the *Bismarck* but incredibly well written. (The Niven was posted to me by my friend the Moose, and I wonder how shredded his delicate sensibilities must be after reading it. It is *unspeakably* sordid, and I had to read it twice.) There's also a copy of *Nicholas Nickleby* but pp 5-12 are missing so I'm stalled there.

This keeps me going for a couple of hours, and maybe I have a little nap, or another cup of tea, or some toast. I then muck about on the internets for a bit (I don't turn the machine on until lunchtime.) At about five o'clock I get up and have some more tea and wonder what I'm doing with my life, and then at six make a fire and open the wine. I then chat with friends and/or family, make a solitary dinner, and then, around 1 a.m., curl up on the sofa, the blessed sofa, while the fire burns itself out. I then wake up at 4 a.m. and read for another two or three hours in the hope of falling asleep again, which I do, eventually. And that's why I wake up at noon.

It's perhaps not an ideal routine, and one which perhaps owes something to mild depression. (The schedule is very different when I have a serious deadline.) The cycle generally is generally 48 hours long, that is, I alternate between days of interior gloom and days where things seem fine. Trips to London, I have discovered, generate waves of anxiety and inner panic which take days to get over. (During my last trip, I had to cancel, or fail to meet, at least three people I very much wanted to see, and I was only there for three days. At least one of these people has not taken it well, and that doesn't make things any better at this end, conscience-wise.)

At this point I have to acknowledge that I am at least in a position where I *can* stay in bed as long as I want to, or admittedly, on occasion, longer than I want to. I do not, like so many people with insomnia, wake at 4 and realise with mounting horror that I will be having to get up to go to work in three hours whether I like it or not. For that good fortune I will forever be grateful, and my heart goes out to those who do not share it.

Of course, I have plenty of other things to wake me up at night, and keep me awake. Lately I have been having a run of (relatively) well-paid employment, but the problem is that the payments have not been made yet, and, already living on short commons, was dismayed to learn, in London, halfway through it, I had £15 and whatever was in my pockets to last me until the end of the month. Luckily, a cry for help on a social medium resulted in some loans I will, thank goodness, be able to pay back. (Two return tickets in one month to London holed me below the waterline. I am beginning to realise that if I want to go to London again, I'm going to have to find another way than the train, but the idea of spending 12 hours on a coach does not appeal.)

I wonder how many people are in a similar situation, bed-bound because psychically rather than physically nailed to it. I can't even escape it in fiction: the narrator of *Pilcrow* is, at the point I'm at, a bed-bound young boy, and reading it is like looking into a hall of mirrors.

※

Olympia, Stamford Hill, Brighton, Shepherd's Bush, Manchester, Salisbury, East Finchley, Perthshire: 2018 has, rather like 2017, been a year of dotting about the place. This is actually my last week in the castle, where I have spent the last six months; I then move to the Grieve's House down the lane. Without those last six months I wonder if I would have gone mad. My gratitude to my hosts-cum-landlords knows no bounds. Their son G——, the one who rescued and tended Kutkh the jackdaw, is back for a few days: he has been to Kamchatka, donning a heat-resistant suit and throwing people's regrets into a live volcano. Yes, you read that right. People emailed him their regrets and he printed them out and chucked them into a volcano. I forget which one.

My regret was not giving H——— my business class seat on the way back from our trip to Antigua all those years ago; it really has haunted me. (Yes, I once travelled in Business Class to Antigua. It was a freebie. And I learned not too long ago that airlines don't like it when you change seats, because they use the passenger manifests to work out who was sitting where if the plane crashes. Makes identifying bodies less of a chore.) Funnily enough, G———'s stunt seems to have worked: I don't feel so bad about this act of appalling selfishness anymore. However since then a few other regrets I'd completely forgotten about resurfaced, and so I'm going to have to ask him to do it again. Then again one wonders whether he will find a big enough volcano. "Personally of course I regret everything. Not a word, not a deed, not a thought, not a need, not a grief, not a joy, not a girl, not a boy, not a doubt, not a trust, not a scorn, not a lust, not a hope, not a fear, not a smile, not a tear, not a name, not a face, no time, no place, that I do not regret, exceedingly. An ordure, from beginning to end." (Samuel Beckett, *Watt*, but he's not always that upbeat.)

I'm trying to think what the highlights were of 2018. I suppose getting slapped in the face by a woman has to be one. That hasn't happened to me nearly as often as you might expect. On the evening in question I could see it coming so braced myself but it turned out to be more of a gesture than an exercise in inflicting pain, so said "look, it's all in the follow-through. Imagine you're playing a forehand tennis stroke." We made up.

The two big highlights were, of course, finding somewhere to bed down for longer than a month. I got my heart broken in Oxfordshire but got it mended again courtesy of a woman from Wales. I got into a war of words with Rod Liddle, who then blocked me on social media, but then he's awfully sensitive so that's hardly a great achievement. At the time of writing someone is taking legal advice about something I've written but having looked at his email threatening it, and at the piece he objects to, I can't say I'm very worried. I saw some beavers swimming in the stream and took some inept and murky footage on them which has been seen on YouTube about seven times, although I don't remember what I called it (perhaps "murky and inept footage of beavers") and that number may have gone up. I remembered how to bowl a cricket ball and then lost the knack again. I got a tan in Scotland and then lost it again. That's what it's all been about, swings and roundabouts. And I have ended the year in the unusual position of being owed, literally, thousands of pounds, without having been paid any of them yet. I also owe thousands of pounds, mainly to HMRC, and their letters are piling up. The frequency of their arrival makes me wonder if that is where JK Rowling got the idea of thousands and thousands of letters cascading through the Dursleys' letterbox. I wonder if it would be a PR coup for the tax people to have their demands delivered by owls. Oh, and I'm about to sign a contract for a second volume of memoirs culled from these very columns. So that's good. After all, the first volume made me practically a household name.*

But the most extraordinary thing actually happened yesterday, when my friend S——— complained that her dysania was very bad that day. "Dysania?" Looked it up, and lo, it is a word for finding it very difficult to get out of bed in the morning. This made me reel. For one thing, English isn't even S———'s first language. (She has about four or five, "with Latin to hold it all together", but she's best at English and Turkish. She is awfully brainy.) I can hardly believe I have passed more than half a century suffering from this condition without having learned the name for it. To name a thing is often to tame it, or make it more real, and it's nice to know I can get a badge or a t-shirt made or something. I wonder what the condition is called for not being able to get out of bed in the afternoon.

I look out of the window and for the first time in ages I see buildings:

* And now? I can't walk a step to the shops without being *mobbed*.

the elegant Victorian terraces of Islington, beneath a crisp blue sky. Also, I am not freezing. That's new.

Actually, when I awake in the MacHovel I am not, strictly speaking, freezing, because I will have gone to bed under a heavy duvet fairly warmly dressed. It's only when I get out of bed that things get chilly.

Hands up all of you who don't have central heating. Hmm, not many of you. Now, hands up those of you who live *halfway up Scotland* and don't have central heating. Well, that's sorted the men from the boys, hasn't it?

Cold, I think, is something that only the homeless experience these days. To be without a system of radiators implies either misfortune, eccentricity, or malevolent human intention, such as – to pluck an example from the icy air – the previous inhabitants removing all the radiators from the home they had occupied.

Actually, I shouldn't exaggerate. I have three radiators that run off the wood-fired stove that heats the living room, although during a real cold snap I use the word "heats" only in its most relative term. When you have been feeding logs by the dozen into the stove's maw for six hours and your breath still steams, you wonder if there shouldn't be another word; one thinks of the almost total cold of outer space, that by some miracle, some leftover radiation from the universe's primal explosion, manages to hover just a fraction of a degree above Absolute Zero. The radiators that run off the stove are uselessly placed: one in the hall, one in the kitchen, which is so cold I put things in the fridge to stop them from freezing, and one in a little annexe of the kitchen which warms up nothing but the logs that are kept there. (There is also a window in this little box-room which doesn't shut, and that doesn't help matters much.) The interesting thing about these radiators is that the colder the ambient temperature, the longer they take to heat up; some evenings they don't heat up at all.

I like to think this is character-forming, as are the occasional power cuts. But what kind of character does it form? To revert to the nineteenth century or earlier may mean to embrace a more barbaric code, one that I have been immersing myself in, in between power cuts, thanks to a subscription to Amazon Prime. I've become obsessed by the TV series *Outlander*, in which Caitriona Balfe plays a nurse transported, via some spooky standing stones, from 1946 to mid-eighteenth-century Scotland. Well, these things happen.

I think I've mentioned before my curious predilection for immersing myself, in art, in the kind of landscape I can immerse myself in simply by going out the door. With *Outlander*, this is getting ridiculous. On the screen of my laptop, I see Highland landscapes, or feudal lairds with extravagant beards eating steaming haunches of venison in ancient castles. I can get that by walking three hundred yards down the lane. The only significant difference that I can see is that there's a lot more sex in *Outlander* than there is in my neck of the woods, not that I'm going to do a survey or anything. One goes by the evidence available. Also, there are fewer redcoats about, and if there is any anti-English sentiment I have yet to experience any. Also everyone's manners are better and women are treated with considerably more respect.

Otherwise, I might as well, for much of the time, have been transported back to a harsher, but perhaps more honest age. I get my fuel from Chris, the transplanted Devonian who does all the odd jobs here; I worked out that, until my landlady took pity on me, I was spending more money on wood than I was on wine. Yes, read that again. *On wine.*

So evenings are spent, basically, hauling logs from kitchen to stove and trying to keep the stove lit. (When it is running well, the flames lick its roof and the glass door in the most mesmerising way, almost as mesmerising as Caitriona Balfe's performance in *Outlander.*) Kindling is recovered from the floor of the woodshed, which is a large unconverted barn in which I have yet to see anything nasty apart from myself. I imagine the spectacle of a middle-aged man stooping to retrieve splinters of wood and putting them in an old grain sack could be quite affecting, in a Good-King-Wenceslasy kind of way.

It is all a long way from Islington, where I am currently lodging at my daughter's boyfriend's place. (It's her birthday, and I thought it would be nice to celebrate it.) It's cold here too, today, but everywhere there are organic supermarkets, weirdo art galleries and places selling 1974 Subbuteo sets in an ironic way. I had one of those once, and as I stared at it I felt like a victim of time's own irony itself.

And so back to Scotland, and the MacHovel. The train journey is punishing. I have not yet worked out how to book a seat on the homeward journey of an open return, so what I do is pile into the seat I can get nearest the buffet. There's no point trying for a seat in the Middle Class Coach - sorry, the Quiet Coach - as they get booked up early. Also, they're not that quiet. On the way down there was a couple a few years older than me who kept up a stream of conversation which was making me unable to complete the page of the book I was trying to read all the way from Leuchars to Newcastle. In the end I did what no British person has done ever, and asked them if they wouldn't mind being quiet, this being, you see, the Quiet Coach, not the Letting Everyone Know In Astonishing Detail What You're Having Or Not Having For Dinner Coach. (This had been their sole topic of conversation, and they were beginning to repeat themselves.) They were from Yorkshire, so they put up quite a fight, but I won in the end, and from Newcastle to York they glared at me, which made me feel like I was in one of Alan Bennett's nastier plays. And, as David Mitchell almost asked Robert Webb in their classic sketch as two SS officers: am I the baddy?

I suppose part of the problem is the expectation: when you assume that people will be quiet, the tiniest noise is an outrage. The Yorkshire couple hadn't been talking loudly - this was the burden of their counter-protest to me - but just as the drop of water landing on your head becomes intolerable after a few hours, so had the soft murmur of their talk about salads. (It wasn't even as if they were going to be having anything interesting for dinner. That was another part of the problem.)

When you get into the noisy coach, though, your expectations are different. You resign yourself to pandemonium. As I usually make the return journey in a state of extreme exhaustion due to stress-related insomnia, I'm not too fussed, and ever since that journey I wrote about where it was standing room only until Newcastle, and I got rained on even though the window was shut, I am simply grateful for a seat.

And lo, in the seat in front of me is a family of three small children and one mother, and wow, I have to admit the children really put their backs into it, especially the daughter, all the way from King's Cross to Dundee. Seriously, they were not silent for a period longer than three seconds, and although the mother tried to calm them down by saying "shh" every five minutes or so, she may as well have been saying "cat got your tongue?" every time instead.

This time, I couldn't say anything; I was in the Mad Max coach, after all, where normal rules of civilised society have broken down, and sometimes people who really should know better even put their shod feet on the seats opposite them. Also, being sole parent to three small children with strong opinions and a desire to express them without cease can't be easy, and wouldn't be made any easier by a middle-aged man asking them to shut up.

And oh, the train journey is *long*. This being the post-New Year scheduling, for some reason it takes seven hours rather than six. At one point the train pulls into Cambridge, which is normally not on the route, and we pause for a bit; I look up at the footbridge on which I would walk, the heels of my Loakes reverberating around the structure, and making it shake, on the way to, or from, the house of the woman once referred to in this column as the Woman I Love. The train seems to have stopped there deliberately, as if for my benefit. "Remember this? Eh? Eh?" it seems to be saying, and for a while the noise of the children in the next seats fades into the background. "Yes, I get it," I reply, and eventually the train, having made its point, although what that point is I am not entirely sure, starts again and moves on across the fens in the gathering night.

These journeys are killing me, I have to say. Seven hours on a train is no joke, and you can't even tilt your chair back a tiny bit, like in an airplane. An airplane! Just think how far you could go in seven hours in one of those! And the booze is, if you choose the right airline, free!

I wonder if there is a better way of getting to and from London. The route from the MacHovel takes me past Dundee airport, although "airport" suggests a scale far greater than the football pitch-sized airstrip I can see. For a while I fantasise about taking flying lessons and piloting myself down in a little Cessna. Then I remember I barely have enough cash to pay the taxi driver, and another dream dies. But I must go back to London again. I have compelling reasons, and miss my children.

※

The eldest child's birthday present is the Fuller's Brewery Tour. This involves going to the Fuller's Brewery in Chiswick, and being given a tour around it. But you probably worked that out.

Life often revolves around dyadic rivalries, and the choice one has to make. Canon v Nikon; Arsenal v Spurs (or Chelsea); League v Union; and, in London, if you like beer, Fullers v Youngs. Circumstances conspired to make me a Fullers drinker, which is fortunate, because Youngs is only ok, although their Porter, when they condescend to brew it, is pretty amazing, I'll grant them that; but Fullers ... I can still remember my first pint of London Pride, and staring into it as if I had discovered the Land of Oz, or Avalon. Here was something that was three-dimensional, alive. Could such nectar be? I asked myself. Until then my life in beer had been the wasteland of fizzy, bland keg stuff; in those days Real Ale, as it was called, had a samizdat, subterranean existence, and you had to either go miles out of your way or be lucky to experience it. Especially if you were under-age and looked it.

But beer underwent a revolution, thanks to the guerilla tactics of CAMRA, and now you can't move for artisanal brews, and I for one am not complaining. But the king of beers, the one I will always go back to, is a pint of Pride. And what is great is that my children, and especially my daughter, whose treat this is, seem to have skipped the alcopop phase and gone straight to discerning drinker phase. The sons went to school not far from the brewery, and once my eldest son said that one of his favourite smells was the heady, yeasty odour that drifted over Chiswick on brewing days, and, when the wind was right, could even be smelled in Shepherds Bush, a mile or two to the north.

We are ten in our group, seven of us being: me, my three children, their mother, her partner, my daughter's boyfriend, of whom I am most fond, and three other hapless individuals who spend much of the time wondering what the hell is going on. "Hang on. That man's holding that woman's hand. So why isn't that other man, who is clearly the father of at least two of those children, and that woman clearly the mother, thumping him?" Because we are awfully sophisticated and it is still the season of good will. And the days of my holding that woman's hand ended abruptly in 2007.

Our guide is a tall middle-aged man whom I will call John. He is like a 1950s educational film made flesh, and all the better for it. We are asked to don fluorescent tabards with the brewery logo stamped on the back. We can choose between two colours, and I decide not to go for the *gilet jaune*. The eldest son appraises his carefully.

"This could come in useful, I suppose," he says. "But how?" For the next hour, I can see the wheels turning in his brain as he ponders this.

We are shown round enormous mash tuns and things like that. I will spare you much of the technical detail. Every group, I imagine, has one person who aks irritating questions designed to show himself off. In this case, I am that person.

"So when you say the barley is converted to starch and sugar, what you're basically saying is it's sprouting?"

"Yes."

"When was London Pride first called that? Because it's a flower, isn't it, a perennial saxifragaceous one which grew on bombsites and became symbolic of London's survival."

"In 1959."

"Did you ever have a brewery cat, in order to keep the mice down?"

"Shut up or I'll throw you in the bloody river."

Actually, he doesn't say that at all. What he does say is that yes, there used to be at least one brewery cat, and, what was more, it was obliged to have a Union card.

"But we don't know how it voted in leadership elections."

The tour progresses. I have actually done it before, and know that when it is over, you hand back your tabards and they let you taste as much beer as you want, within reason. My daughter is almost frantic with desire to have some. Well, it is her birthday.

Finally, we are brought back to what is called the Hock Room, and we are given many half pints of various ales. I tell my children about the dark days of the 1970s and early 1980s, when the only beer you could find was piss brewed by Watneys. The tune for the Double Diamond advert floats into my head and refuses to budge.

And that's that. The party is over. I must return to Scotland in the morning, for London and I are over, London having spat me out. That's what I'm feeling. London Shame.

It has been a week of high drama up here. First, there was the lunar eclipse. Did you see it? I had a splendid view. The earth's shadow crept over its face, and the extraordinary thing is that the moon was darkening from the wrong side. When you live in the deep countryside and don't watch all that much telly you learn to follow the moon's behaviour without even trying. So watching something absolutely crazy happening to it can be almost unhinging. It was freezing cold outside but watching the moon darkening was like watching the minute hand of an enormous clock: you could see time. Also, this being something like four in the morning I was not exactly sober, and this often makes me think things like "you could see time, man".

This got me all excited and in the end I didn't go to bed until 6 in the morning. My old friend Nick, from whom I had not heard in ages, had sent me a bottle of Lagavulin which I had been intending to save for Burns Night but I'm afraid I put quite a bit of a dent in it. This meant Monday was a complete write-off, and I found that once again I had completely screwed up my body clock. (I gather that some goody-goodies went to bed early and set their alarms to get up for the eclipse; that's not really the way I operate.) And maybe other things: I found myself unable to drink more than a homeopathic amount of wine and spent pretty much 24 hours in bed. The thought of going down to a freezing living room and waiting three hours for it to warm up did not appeal. Also, at some point the curtain came down and I didn't fancy putting it up again. It would have involved standing on a chair, and I don't do that anymore.

I must say I recommend staying in bed for enormously long stretches. A reader of this column, a Mr Tom Birch, who is pretty much my ideal reader, said on a social medium that failing to read the rest of the magazine before the next issue came out was his very expensive way of finding out if I had got out of bed this week. Well, Mr Birch, after Sunday night/Monday morning's shenanigans, it was touch and go.

But in the end I had to. I needed food and tobacco and, unlike the good people of Dundee Majestic Wine Warehouse, no one was going to deliver them to me and also I had begun to weary of the empty bottles which were beginning to spread across the kitchen and out through the back door. That's two months of empties. Taken with a laissez-faire approach to cleaning and washing up, and the kitchen as a whole was beginning to look like a Tracy Emin installation.

(In my defence, I try to avoid the kitchen in the MacHovel, largely because it is as cold as Pluto.)

But somehow, I managed it. 64 empty bottles is quite a lot; I was worried the pick-up's rear axle would snap like a breadstick, and I had to clear a whole morning for the task. And the kitchen now looks as though a human uses it rather than a bear, and I even managed to wash the trousers which I'd been wearing when I fell over in the silage heap trying to get a phone signal. If you think that doesn't sound like much of an achievement, I should point out that doing the laundry in the MacHovel is no joke. First you have to get the extension lead because there isn't a socket in the utility room the washing machine is in. Then you have to find out the washing machine doesn't work. Then you have to plug the kettle into the extension lead to see if it is that, rather than the washing machine, which is at fault. Then you have to put your laundry in a bin liner and walk 300 yards to the Big House and ask if you can do your laundry there. Then you have to walk back, then, three hours later, by which time it is pitch black because the moon hasn't yet risen, walk there and back again with damp laundry which will take two days to dry, if it dries at all.

In fact, everything is no joke here. Using the bathroom is especially no joke. The only heating in it is a towel rail which consumes electricity but doesn't actually warm up. At least the radiators downstairs sometimes reach a temperature which, in a human, would not quite be high enough to get the day off work, but is at least something. To repeat my exercise from three weeks ago, hands up those of you who have unheated bathrooms. And who live thirty miles south of the town which regularly boasts of being the United Kingdom's coldest place. (Braemar, since you ask.) And whose windows face north. It occurred to me the other day that when I am having a crap I am probably the coldest person in the country who is also indoors, and I have discovered the freezing temperature of toothpaste. Well, as my mother always says, there are various ways of achieving distinction.

Regular readers will know that this column is a merry-go-round, in which the same horses come into view again and again: I'm broke, I'm bored, I'm not getting laid. Sometimes new horses appear, such as: I'm freezing my balls off, or that train journey was a pain in the backside. To bring back that last nag prematurely: there was a real doozy last week: a man got into the last remaining seat of the Quiet Coach at York and announced to the woman sitting next to him, but loudly enough for most of the carriage to hear, that he had intended to go to Doncaster but had got on the wrong train. He popped open a can of Stella and told us his life story, which included the details that this was not the first time he had made this mistake, and that he was from Hull, had voted for Brexit, and scorned the notion that people like him "didn't know what we were voting for." It struck me that the fate of the nation hangs on the opinion of someone who is, by his own admission, not competent enough to read a departure board, but I forebore to mention this. In fact I forebore to repeat my bravery of two weeks ago, when I asked a couple, also from Yorkshire as it happens, to bear in mind what the word "quiet" meant. I didn't interrupt this man because he was drinking a beer which in some circles is called "wife-beater", which could, by extension, become "passenger-beater". But that's enough about Quiet Coaches for a while, I hope.

Anyway, I was – am, until tomorrow morning – back down in London for a couple of reasons, not all of them pleasant, but one of which was to have dinner with my youngest son, his girlfriend, and two of their friends, who are off on a post-mocks trip to Paris. Now the youngest, like his siblings, has, over the years, told his friends stories about me, as a result of which I am considered an object of some fascination, and far removed from the experience of their own, or others', fathers. Their fathers do not get caught at Luton airport, embarking on a family holiday, with an accidentally-trousered half-ounce of excellent marijuana, and get away with it. Their fathers do not call a miserable, sub-Fawlty chip shop owner in Lynmouth "a miserable old c———" after exceptionally poor service (and food. N.B. This chip shop is NOT the Esplanade Fish Bar, which was, as Google Street View confirms, voted North Devon's favourite chip shop in 2010, and deservedly so). Their fathers do not live in a Hovel and play with air rifles with them. Their fathers do not . . . well, you get the idea.

The last time I was scheduled to meet the youngest one's friends I was unable to, and he was really cross with me. At first, I found this hard to believe, but the kids really do appear to have an affection for their old man, and relish his eccentricities (or "failings", as they are more commonly known. By an alarming coincidence, I've just received an email from a publicist whose headline is "Discover novel inspired by childhood trauma ahead of Children of Alcoholics Week").

So I found myself one evening in Shepherd's Bush, at the family table, with five youngsters (my daughter joined us; the other sibling is in Manchester), the mother of my children, and her beau. As I sat down to dinner I thought I'd better start embarrassing my son in front of his girlfriend, and said "I think it's about time we had The Talk."

Afterwards they dragged me off to the pub, and as we walked in we discovered it was quiz night.

"What kind of weapon," asked the quizmaster, "is a da-ringa?" A what? I asked myself, until I worked it out. I turned to him and said, summoning up all my dad powers of embarrassment, "I think you'll find it's pronounced /dɛrɪndʒər/." (Meaning, of course, the Derringer, or small pistol.) Were my children embarrassed? Not a bit of it, or if they were, they hid it well. It's funny, though, how one doesn't think of one's own children as young, but when they are in the company of their peers, you think to yourself, "my God, they're *twelve*." But they are not; they are still forming themselves, although the job is nearly done. A little soft round the edges, although the youngest's g.f. seems considerably more self-possessed than I was at her age. (Translation: she doesn't seem scared of me enough.)

The next day I got rather sweet text from the Estranged Wife, saying what a lovely evening it had been, and how pleased that "somehow we pulled a lot out of the wreckage". Thank you, I replied, for insisting on having children; I was worried that I would be a terrible father.

"You were!!!" she replied, "but they love you so that's all good."

Which is a double-edged thing to say, but at least I concentrate on the second half of it as I sit in the Quiet Coach tomorrow, listening to someone recite their autobiography for 500 miles. I wonder what county they'll be from.

※

Yesterday the Improbably Handsome Plumber (as opposed to the Other Plumber) came round and explained to me why my stove wasn't working.

"Your baffle's gone, the thermostat isn't working, and there's not enough air getting into it. Also . . ." My mind wandered. It wasn't as if I was going to be able to do anything about it myself. I picked up some details about how even he wasn't sure how old the stove was. The burden of his remarks was that I would be resigning myself to spending money on firewood which wasn't actually heating anything unless you actually sat on the thing. A friend suggested that I buy a load of remaindered copies of Piers Morgan's autobiography and burn those instead, an idea which has a certain appeal, but is probably not practical, and might gunk up the works. But what's the point? I reply. By the end of February everyone know that Scotland bursts into radiant, sub-tropical Spring weather.

And yet, I think to myself as I continue my reverie, there are still flies. Why are there flies? In my bedroom? After three months of solid Winter? Including record-breaking low temperatures? I was woken up by one the other day, flying around inside the paper lampshade.

Bop, bop, bop. I draw the curtain each morning and find a couple of them startled into wakefulness. I don't keep food in my bedroom so it isn't putrefaction that attracts them. Unless I'm putrefying. I don't think so. Perhaps it's quite the other, i.e. some natural personal aroma of delightful sweetness. I was having a bath that morning – the ambient temperature was above freezing, so I felt brave – and one of them just fell into it by my side. It was quite disconcerting. I was reading a fascinating article about Petrarch in the *London Review of Books* and next thing I know a fucking fly has fallen in the bath. It's not really what you want. Nor what you expect. Has that ever happened to you before? It's a new one on me. I tried to scoop it out and return to the *quattrocento*. Petrarch's Laura had eleven children and then died in 1348 so it's probable she got caught up in the Black Death, so I shouldn't grumble. This is assuming she existed at all. There is some debate on the matter, apparently. I am not sure where to stand on this. I do not want to impugn Petrach's veracity but I mean, come on, eleven children? And still fancying her?

The plumber finishes his litany of my stove's failures. What, as Lenin asked, is to be done? There's nothing much that can be done, he says, except get a new stove. I think of all the wood I've chucked into at, at some expense, and think of it all going up . . . well, going up in smoke. I feel cheated. I have missed out on a warm interior in Winter, a feeling which is strangely similar to being cheated out of a sunny Summer, either because the weather is rubbish or you're stuck in an office. I could have been so toasty. And it's not, I feel, as if I have all that many winters ahead of me.

I dig out the operating manual and hand it to the plumber, who is astonished that I have managed to keep and find it. Quietly, so am I. The quality of paper and typeface suggest that it dates from the 1760s, give or take a decade or so. He photographs a few pages and says he might be able to get parts for it, sounding a lot more optimistic than he was a few minutes before.

Later, I take the manual up for some bedtime reading. It is a Hunter Herald 14 CE V.II multifuel central-heating stove, which presumably means I could burn Piers Morgan's memoirs in it after all. (At first, I misread the "CE" part of its designation as "ICE".) I crank up the laptop and google the manufacturer and model. Gordon Bennett, they're still making them. Look, there's my very stove, on a webpage and everything. I read the blurb.

"As British winters become increasingly unpredictable, we put a high value on economy." I laugh hollowly. "The Herald 14 burns fuel with minimum waste and maximum output." Ha, I say to myself. "Don't want to get up shivering in your pyjamas? This super-efficient stove can be left to glow overnight, providing welcome warmth at dawn." My Aunt Fanny it can, I say to myself.

But I do not blame the Hunter Stoves Group, as they call themselves these days. Instead I will blame the previous tenants, whose neglect of the MacHovel is why I call it the MacHovel, and who also – for he was a plumber himself – managed to steal a boiler and a whole central heating system when he vacated the premises, which is, I have to admit, quite impressive.

"Come on," I ask the flies circling feebly in my room. "Tell me how he did it." But answer comes there none.

※

It's another quiet night in the MacHovel. (The days, by the way, are not quiet. I live in the middle of what must be the corvid equivalent of Rio de Janeiro, and the crows and jackdaws go on and on and on all day long. There is also a very noisy tractor that goes past my window every ten minutes.) I get a request on a social medium to be, you know, friends. Hell, why not? She has a nice face, and knows J——, who tends to have sound taste in people.

Up pops a private message from this person, whom I will call Cheryl.

"Hi", says Cheryl.

Naturally, the blood runs cold. The mistake, as Beckett said, is to speak to people.

Despite a certain terseness in my reply, "Cheryl" becomes garrulous, in a way that suggests she may not be all she claims to be, viz. a passionate, loving woman who loves life but is lonely because her husband died in a car crash a couple of years ago. She is also inquisitive. She asks me what I am up to. I send her a link to my last column. In fact, I send her a link to *all* my columns. This tends to sort out the dedicated from the faint of heart.

Cheryl, it seems, is a fast reader, for not long afterwards she asks me if I want to love and be loved.

"Nah," I reply. I ask her what she does, and this is where it gets a little strange. She is, she replies, "a sea worker". What the hell is that? Is it a typo for "sex worker"? And, if so, is that the kind of thing people admit to on first acquaintance? Anyway, she doesn't look like either a sea worker or a sex worker; she looks like a primary schoolteacher, or the proprietor of a slightly over-chintzy tea shop in Worthing.

"What exactly is a sea worker?" I ask.

"I am captain of a cargo ship in Panama," she replies.

This throws me a little. I can't say I was expecting that. However, something seems a little off, so I express my doubts to her, at which point she changes tack. (Thought I'd drop in a little nautical metaphor there.)

"Oh my god," she says. Her son, who is apparently called Kelvin, has been in an accident, and she needs $300. Can I send her $300?

"No," I reply.

She replies with a series of photographs of someone who has clearly been in a bad accident. On a stretcher, tubes and everything. Frankly, it looks like she's going to need a lot more than $300 to patch Kelvin up, although it seems as though the pictures are all of different people.

"I'll pass," I say. "Anyway, Kelvin had it coming. This will be a valuable lesson to him, stop him from hanging out with that bad crowd." After a while I get bored of this and block her.

I wonder how often these scams succeed. There was a time when a woman with a surprisingly conventional name like Mary would email me and say "Lezard! Are you in London?" The use of the surname wasn't very sexy, but it turned out she was furious with her cheating boyfriend and wanted to get back at him, but it was very important that instead of communicating by email, I should click on the link in the email in order to carry on speaking, as her boyfriend is very jealous and reads her emails. Also, if I click on the link I will see some lovely pictures of her. Blah blah blah. I am not so deluded that I imagine women all round the world are pausing in their sea work etc. in order to fill the void in their lives with me. Who falls for these scams? They're like incompetent versions of the Turing Test.

However, the best one came a few days ago, via the same social medium as "Cheryl". This time there were many more mutual friends. However, there was something familiar about her surname. I did a little Googling, then messaged her.

"Hang on," I wrote. "You're not Rod Liddle's wife, are you?"

It turns out that she is. Now, in case you've forgotten, or never knew, Roderick Liddle (his real name), the windbag who seems to attract accusations of racism more than is statistically probable, and I are no longer on speaking terms, ever since I drew his, and his editor's, attention to certain inaccuracies that had surfaced in one of his articles. I will spare you the details. The idea of being "friends" in that social media sense with his wife did, I must admit, have a certain appeal. It also seemed incredibly unlikely, and I wondered whether this was actually another scam, and that sooner or later she was going to ask me for £500 for a life-saving operation for her cockapoo.

But the next day, we were no longer friends. I hope it wasn't because her husband had had a word with her.

Note in 2025: Believe it or not, I'm not making any of this up.

⁂

In search of light reading, I go to the room in the Big House set aside for the holidaymakers who stay in the yurts, and pick out a John Grisham. You know where you are with a John Grisham. You're going to get chewing gum for the brain, pleasant but deliberately non-nutritious, something nicely plotted about lawyers written in a strictly utilitarian prose which will keep you turning the pages and two days later you will have forgotten absolutely everything about it. And there's nothing wrong with that, we can all do with this kind of thing from time to time.

However, it soon became clear that the book, published in 1998, was not one that I was going to forget in a hurry. Without going into too much detail about the plot, the novel, called *The Street Lawyer*, is about a young hot-shot who, for reasons that need not detain us here, resigns from his extremely swanky Washington, DC law firm and joins a tiny, perpetually broke firm which works in order to keep the homeless off the streets by enforcing their legal rights in the face of official and semi-official obstruction.

It's most implausible – our hero takes a massive pay cut, for a start – but one thing is clear: it was written in the white heat of rage at what the policies of politicians like Newt Gingrich and Rudy Giuliani (then mayor of New York City) were doing to those forced to sleep on the streets, or, rather, what they were doing to put them there in the first place. And even though it is set over twenty years ago, it is no less relevant today. It is about a Hostile Environment put into action.

Of course, the situation in DC in '98 is not the same as that in the UK in '19. For a start, the homeless in America then were overwhelmingly black; here, and now, we are much more equal-minded when it comes to putting people at the bottom of the heap.

And the reason this book freaked me out so much is – new readers start here – because in a couple of weeks, I have to move out of the home I've been living in since June last year. (Actually, I've been living in this particular house since December, but it is an annex of a larger estate. The principle's the same.) The problem is, I have nowhere to go. I'm not going to move back to my mother's;

I tried that, it didn't work. My Estranged Wife has helpfully told me that I could just move back into the house she ejected me from, but I'm not sure how her boyfriend would feel about that. Or, indeed, she.

To paraphrase an old joke of PG Wodehouse's: young people, starting out in life, often ask me how to set about becoming homeless. The answer is: you lose your job, or in my case my main job, the company which owns the place you live in decides it wants to make a lot more money out of it, and after that, you don't have to lift a finger. Circumstance does all the rest for you. The astonishing generosity of the people who've been putting me up lately has put a brake on the process, but I can't be a charity case forever. The only problem is finding somewhere else. I could, I suppose, move to Sunderland, where I don't know anyone and might not fit in, but at least rents are cheap, but a small, selfish part of me likes to think it would be nice to live in the same part of the world as my friends and family, like I used to.

I liked to fancy a similarity, more of mood than literal detail, between my circumstances and the chaos that this country is undergoing. (And, if you're a subscriber reading this on the day it's been delivered, I gather, at time of writing, today's The Day.) With this difference: my chaos isn't self-inflicted. And I can see the alternative to my situation staring me in the face wherever I go. It's not abstract, in the way a constitutional crisis is abstract. When I go on a train, much of the time it is spent going by houses. On my trips to London, I am surrounded by houses. Man, I say to myself, look at all those *houses*. All those windows behind which one can live, all inaccessible to me. I feel like an involuntary celibate looking at a beauty pageant. It taints every thought, every interaction. "That's all very well for you to say," I sometimes catch myself saying to myself, "you've got somewhere to live."

Grisham's novel made it very clear – and this is also a lesson that such charities as Shelter have tried to make clear – that one does not immediately jump from having a home to living on the streets.

It's a gradual process, one of whose key stages is sofa-surfing, and relying on the kindness of others. After a point, you realise, either their patience wears thin, or yours does: one gets sick of relying on other people. There is a desperate kind of pride involved. I'm getting to that point, and I haven't a clue what to do.

The last few days have all been very Bilbo Baggins's eleventy-first birthday party up here. A huge marquee went up on the lawn, and there was a huge sense of anticipation. The Laird and the Lady of the Manor were celebrating forty years of marriage. Forty years seems to be the proper amount of time for deep reflection. There's the play by Alan Bennett; it's the period of time that Colonel Clive Candy takes us back to as he plunges into the pool in *The Life and Death of Colonel Blimp*; and it's when, I was recently reminded, Joy Division were wrapping up their second and last album, and Ian Curtis was on the brink of suicide.

Maybe that's inauspicious. The Laird and Lady are clearly still very happy with each other, and suited to each other, although I can't help wondering whether the expense of a marquee, and the entertaining of 200 guests, will put a certain pressure on the Laird, who likes to keep his expenses to a minimum.

I find myself being dragooned into helping. They decide to put me in charge of the wine, which I concede does make a kind of sense, and involves putting what looks like not nearly enough sparkling and un-sparkling Vouvray into the refrigerated trailer, and opening what looks like not nearly enough Graves for the tables. I am also told to instruct Kelly, who has never done so before, how to open a champagne-style bottle. Matters are not helped when a co-worker shows her how to pop the cork so it flies right across the marquee.

"That," I say, "is exactly how *not* to do it." (Kelly turned out to be a natural.)

Meanwhile, I was nervous, thanks to an earlier conversation with the Lady of the House.

"I'd better warn you," she said, that "H—— is coming. With her boyfriend."

This was not exactly a punch in the stomach, but it wasn't exactly welcome news either. H—— was the Ex who had, when we were still an item, introduced me to this place before going off to get a job in Gothenburg for five years. She was not at all happy that I was here now and had recently told me, in a brief but powerful email, that she would not be visiting as long as I was here. I anticipated some Unpleasantness.

At least I was busy enough not to brood. I stood behind the fizz bar and poured and poured. I found I got pretty good at pouring the same amount of wine into the flutes, and was extremely pleased that - so far - I had not knocked the table over or broken a single glass. Also I found that there was often a little nip left in each bottle that I could pour out for myself, in order to ensure a steady hand. But people don't half ask some silly questions when they think you're staff.

"Can I take one of these?" (Pointing at four dozen unclaimed glasses of fizz.)

"No, they're for looking at only."

"Excuse me, are these all the same?" (Pointing at four dozen absolutely identical glasses of fizz.)

"No, some of them are poisoned." (I'm afraid I did say that.)

Meanwhile, I kept fretting about the amount of wine we had. Even if you discounted the Muslims (family by marriage) and children, and designated drivers, it seemed to me that there would be barely two glasses per punter. The bottles of red on the long tables, separated by yards, looked awfully lonely and beleaguered. There were six bottles underneath the table to be opened in an emergency.

Eventually, I sat down with Chris and Dick, the all-round handymen (Dick can do handbrake turns in the pick-up truck, and I kept asking him to teach me how), and Aileen, who more or less runs the place.

"We didn't know what to make of you at first," she said, "but now you're one of us."

And then there was the dancing. This is normally my cue to hide under the table or feign an ankle injury, but for some reason – well, that wine wasn't going to drink itself – I felt emboldened, and I even managed to dance a bit of a Scottish Reel with Kelly. A Scottish Reel, in case you don't know, lasts about half an hour and involves an insane combination of moves which are designed to baffle and humiliate the innocent Sassenach. Later on the DJ played "C'est la Vie" and Aileen and I did the John Travolta/Uma Thurman dance from Pulp Fiction, even doing that thing with passing your opened fingers across the eyes, probably because I'd opened the last six bottles of red and drunk most of them. The next morning I was invited to brunch with the family – and H——— and her boyfriend – but what with one thing and another I felt a little peaky the next morning, and, after receiving a bollocking for opening the emergency wine, although in truth it was all a bit of a blur, spent the next two days in bed. Which was probably the best thing to do under the circumstances.

※

My time in the MacHovel is drawing to a close, and it is time to make plans. To this end, I have decided to visit That London again, to do a bit of cat-sitting for a friend. Just as Spring is cautiously, hesitantly poking its nose around the corner of Scotland. (It is proving most hesitant indeed. As I write, hailstones the size of tic-tacs are bouncing off the window. I am glad to be indoors, and that the central heating is finally installed and up and running.) Not for the first time, I find myself astonished at how happy I am in the countryside, although it has to be said that I don't take as much advantage of its charms as I ought to. I should be taking long walks – let's face it, that's pretty much all there is to do in the countryside if you're not actually working – up and down the glens and whatnot but, just as when I lived in the middle of London and ignored more or less every civilised amenity it had to offer (apart from the Wallace Collection, which was free and five minutes walk away; and even then I eventually ignored it), I decide to save it up for later. Also, hailstones. I could, I suppose, go out and look at the stars a bit more, on clear nights, but even though they are amazing I kind of know they're there now, and I am happy to stay inside in front of the fire chatting with friends on the internet or watching Line of Duty.

One thing for which I have used my situation to good advantage is to practise the harmonica. I forget when I got it; but it seemed like the right thing for the travelling melancholic to play. However it is more about therapy than music, and I would not like to play it in front of anyone who was sober. There was a Jeeves and Wooster novel in which the latter repairs to the countryside in order to play the banjolele; I find myself in a similar situation. Sometimes the artistic soul blossoms only in solitude.

But oh, Scotland, am I going to miss you. It's not just the landscapes, it's the people: the high level of civility and courtesy, the general level of intelligence. It's nice to know that when you chat to anyone round here, the chances are they didn't vote for Brexit. I never got the whole golf thing but nobody's perfect.

It's an odd feeling, the thought that I might be coming back to London at a time when I am also seriously considering staying put in Scotland. I know a woman who gets sexually aroused by the words "Leicester Square" (long story) but the days when I considered London the only place in the world worth living in, with the possible exceptions of Paris and New York, are long gone. (Another possibility, for a few months at least, is Brighton, which I love. My friend B—— called me the other day and told me how he'd been clearing out his flat and had discovered two antique Colt revolvers hidden behind some pipes in a storage cupboard. When he went to drop them off at the local police station, he noted that the duty sergeant had green hair. "Typical Brighton," he said, although this anecdote is also typical of B———. Things like this happen to him more than is statistically probable.)

But the anxiety is that for the foreseeable future I am going to be once again at the mercy of the winds of fate. It's been nice having a place of one's own for almost a year; one gets used to little luxuries like one's own kettle, or a postal address, or a doctor's surgery. An incipient twinge at the back of the mouth the other day made me wonder whether it was time to register with a dentist up here, but now I wonder what the point would be. The twinge has gone, thank goodness, and touch wood it won't come back again, but the larger fear that I have is for my sanity. The political situation has apparently been driving everyone crazy with anxiety but when you add to this a radical uncertainty about where you are going to live and how long for, I begin to marvel that I am not falling to bits. Is the countryside soothing in itself? "I couldn't stand London, the pace of life is so fast there," I've heard quite a few times while I've been up here, but when I lived in London, right in its beating heart, I found I could quite easily potter along at 0 mph.

I suppose what I will miss most are the hens. There are three survivors of the Terrible Fox Assault of 2018, plus three newcomers. I hadn't seen them for a couple of months – it was too far, and too cold, for it to be worthwhile – but when I went down to see them the other day with some leftovers the three veterans ran to me with wild cries of delight. (The newcomers, on the other hand, huddled among themselves in a corner and looked at me warily.) As I dished out the grub, each one of them, by turn, came and gave me a single peck on the boot, as if to say "howdy". I almost burst into tears. How am I going to tell them I am leaving?

After a couple of weeks of suffering same, and thinking it would be best not to, I eventually decide to google "lower back pain". This may be have been something of a mistake. I know only one non-hypochondriacal googler of medical symptoms, and as she is an acute thinker she is good at picking out the relevant from the hair-raising.

I am worried about kidney disease, as this is what polished off my father, and two cats, and while I do not eat nearly as much dry cat food as I used to, my father's lifestyle was not a million miles away from my own, and let's not forget heredity.

I go to one website and read the following: "Over the age of 55, about one in twenty cases turns out to be a fracture, and one in a hundred is more ominous. The further you are from 55, the better your odds." I think they could have phrased that last sentence a bit better. I am exactly 55, for another month, so this means, if I'm following their reasoning correctly, that my odds are as bad as they can possibly be. I'm fairly sure they don't mean this but it makes me wonder if a large number of freak-outs by people checking their symptoms are down to wonky grammar. However, I know I can at least rule out pregnancy.

The problem is how unwell so many of my friends are, and almost all of them lead far healthier lives than I do. They're mostly about my age and it would appear that this is the kind of age when things start to unravel. One friend, though, many years younger than me and quite clean-living, has somehow contrived to get pneumonia. How I haven't ever caught it I don't quite understand. How I didn't catch it in Scotland, in an unheated house in wintertime is a complete mystery, but I'm not complaining.

Actually, I think I should stop complaining about my lower back pain. I have too many friends who are in actual hospital, or who are obliged to go there for regular visits, for me to start clogging up the NHS. I checked my pee and there has been no change recently so that can rule out kidney stones, which I gather are incredibly painful, and my pain is nothing more than a dull ache that sometimes goes away for a bit. I plan on fogging the mirror for a while yet. What I am suffering is nothing more than the usual wear and tear. A bit like my laptop, I suppose. The S key doesn't work half the time, and it has been joined in this sullen disobedience by its neighbours, the D and X keys, suggesting that there is a build-up of matter beneath the keyboard. The down arrow key has joined the choir invisible;[*] the DVD player doesn't work anymore but it still pops open without warning every so often, the battery lasts for about fifteen minutes, and the socket you plug the power jack into has a loose connection in there somewhere which means the jack has to be propped up with something – a penknife, a battery, a harmonica, that kind of thickness; and the whole keyboard is pitted with the scars of the embers from I dread to think how many roll-ups.

But the thing still works, damn it, and I refuse to abandon such a loyal machine. I wonder how long I've had it. Eight years? Nine? Something like that. It is a ThinkPad T410, and the thing about ThinkPads is that while they weigh a ton, they take an awful lot of punishment, and can often be fixed by whacking them. I know I've done it. They use them on the International Space Station, and used them on the Space Shuttle, even though the cost of putting them into orbit is enormous, compared to lighter machines. My great friend Toby, who realised early on that I needed a robust machine, said when he handed it on to me that whereas the ThinkPads going up on the Shuttle or hurtling around the planet have to worry about the possibility of a fiery immolation on take-off or a strike from a meteor or some space crap when in orbit, they have it easy compared to the ThinkPads I have had.

Well, at least this one won't have to worry about the journey to and from Scotland for much longer. Nexit, as I called it, in an effort to inject some humour into the situation, happens on May 2nd, and then the whole sorry business of trying to find somewhere to live starts again. This is a worry considerably more aggravating than mild lower back pain, especially considering my earnings, which

---

[*] Three laptops later, in 2025, as I compile this book, the down arrow key has gone again.

rule out living in London unless it is an act of charity or house- or cat-sitting. I was looking forward to staying in Shepherd's Bush for a bit, as my friend L—— was going on some travels, but she has recently broken her arm horribly and is no longer in a position to go on these travels (they were, I gather, the strenuous kind). She apparently tripped over her own front doorstep but as she is not a heavy drinker at all I don't see how this can have happened. Oh God, it's the same old story: the good suffer, and the wicked – i.e. me – thrive. If we use the word "thrive" in its loosest sense.

※

A slight change of plan has meant that I'm staying at the Castle for another couple of nights. Normally, when one announces to people that you're going to be there for 48 hours longer than originally advertised, this is the cause for lamentation, privately borne, yet usually discernible to the practised student of the human face.

This time it was different. "Joy unconfined" more or less sums it up, for some guests were arriving, and the Master and Mistress of the House were away, and someone plausible was needed to hold the fort.

I had to have it explained to me a couple of times. A Russian couple and their son were paying through the nose to be shown around the Castle and have dinner made for them. It was the son's thirtieth birthday and they wanted to give him the full Scottish Experience. This, I gathered, was the brainchild of M——, the Russian troublemaker, who would act as interpreter, and G——, her friend; they live in Edinburgh, and if you go out for a drink with them, make sure you have nothing planned the next day. My presence was welcome because I knew the ropes and can scrub up nicely; perhaps it was thought that I would add a certain tone. Well, I had been pretending I owned the place for a week, I suppose, but, I reflected, an occasion for which I was to be a major prop is an occasion with a serious design flaw.

There was another matter: these were Russians. Now, like Jeremy Corbyn, I am against all forms of racism, but, unlike Jeremy Corbyn, I do not – how best to put this? – tend to give Russians the benefit of the doubt when dirty work is afoot, and when I think about wealthy Russians, I do not immediately assume that their wealth was achieved through honest toil. And if you're going to effectively hire a castle for a night, you've got to be fairly minted. (There is also the small matter of my being half-Polish, in a way, and the two nations have never exactly got on. I was reminded of the joke in which a Polish army recruit is asked to imagine a situation where a Nazi soldier and a Red Army soldier are charging towards him, and he has only two bullets. Whom does he shoot first? The answer is the Nazi: "business before pleasure.")*

Still, I thought it best to give them the benefit of the doubt. My main preoccupation was how I was going to present myself. What, in short, would my cover story be? A refugee from justice, wanted for crimes unspecified by the police forces of two continents, hiding out in the wilds of Scotland until it all blows over, and certain matters . . . arranged? Or the laird's sleek and sinister factotum, for whom no task was too . . . unpleasant. I began to be alarmed at the direction my thoughts were taking. My wristwatch? Oh, that old thing? (It's a begrimed but still accurate 1960 Oris which I picked up for a song in Portobello Road, in the days when you could still pick up things for a song in the Portobello Road.) That was a present from my godfather. You may know him as John le Carré . . .

Meanwhile, fires were lit (I was worried about the place burning down) in the Morning Room and the Dining Room, rooms grand enough to deserve their capital letters; flowers had been arranged; a crisp white tablecloth and place settings (although I winced when

---

* *The New Statesman*, being cautious, asked me to remove this paragraph; in fact, to rewrite nearly the whole thing. No such circumspection here: so you are now the first people to read this apart from me, my editors, and their lawyers. I wonder what those Russians are up to these days.

I saw the positioning of the cutlery; I think we got away with it), the Dining Room itself lit solely by candlelight. I didn't even have to lift a finger to cook, serve, or even wash up; people had been hired for that.

"What, ye mean a glass for red AND a glass for white?" asked K——, and rolled her eyes.

Well, the Russians, as it turned out, were very nice, almost certainly not criminals, and very, very dull. G—— got a bit pissed and kept standing up proposing toasts to the Russian nation for saving our bacon during World War II. I murmured "Ribbentrop Pact" to myself, but not so loud that anyone could hear. The Russians themselves were charmed, and kept proposing toasts to their hosts; the impression that I was in some way the master of the house, or at least someone very important within it, was not one I was going to disabuse them of. ("Actually, I haven't got a pot to piss in, and until last week I was living in a freezing Hovel which only someone in the most wretched and impecunious of circumstances would accept.") When Russians make toasts, you have to stand up, so at least we got some exercise between shovelling down haggis and venison.

So, what, you may ask yourself, makes this evening a fit subject for a column called "Down and Out"? Well, I'm now back in London, writing this in my childhood bedroom, in my mother's house, in my underpants. I think that qualifies as Down and Out, don't you?

※

And now to Brighton. I stayed in London for a few days; rather fewer days than I thought I was going to, but the tale behind that is, like that of the Giant Rat of Sumatra in the Sherlock Holmes stories, is one for which the world is not yet prepared. (It's a good one, though.)* The change of plan obliged me to beg for shelter at

---

* I've forgotten it. I think a woman was involved.

L———'s place, and because she is one of the kindest of souls, she obliged.

The only problem with L———'s place, it turned out, was that it was in Shepherd's Bush, normally an area I not only have no problem with, but actually am fond of, especially when my children are staying at their mother's. But they are far-flung now (although the youngest is not too far from Brighton at the moment, which is great news), and the peril that lurks in the bosom of the Bush was one that I had forgotten. That peril goes by the name of Stupid P———.

His name was originally "Nicholas", which, as you might imagine, I consider to be a perfectly good name. It is useful for, among other things, gauging people's characters: if they start calling you "Nick" without invitation or precedent, then you can draw some pleasingly suspect conclusions about them.

Anyway, this is by far not the worst thing about Stupid P———. (He got the nickname after sitting next to my friend T——— at an *intime* New year's dinner. "Who was that stupid person?" he asked, and the name has stuck, including with my children.) We got to know him because of the NCT, that supremely middle-class institution which assumes that all middle-class people who have children at the same time are going to have similar interests and life goals. At first, I gave Stupid P——— the benefit of the doubt, because he seemed original, smoked a bit of weed, and had dreadlocks, even though he was white. For some people, that is grounds for dismissal, but I have met a few who are not bell-ends, and their politics tend to be at an end of the spectrum I am happy with.

Not so, I soon learned, with Stupid P———. I worked this out when I saw the copies of the *Telegraph* at his house (I had to go there often, to pick up the children, for his and mine were of the same number, genders, and ages. His children, incidentally, are wonderful, or were, last time I saw them). I also had to endure his rants, in which I learned that he was not wholly satisfied with the way World War II panned out; he went, despite living in one of the most urban areas you can think of, on the Countryside Alliance March of the late 90s, and as far as I know its sticker is still on his front door. He rails against the welfare state but, having given up his job under the delusion that he was a writer, happily accepts benefits himself; and a clause in his *alma mater*'s charter has allowed him, I have been told, to have his children educated there for free. His house, I was also told, was bought for him by one of his wealthy schoolfriends; I can hardly believe this, because it is a whopping great house. He once held a dinner party where all the other guests were in close orbit to David Cameron's circle – this was around the time DC became leader of the Tories – and never have I been in such disgusting, entitled company. As I listened to their brays, I thought to myself: Until now, mine has been a sheltered life.

So I ran into him while waiting for a bus on the Uxbridge Road, still be-dreadlocked, still arrogant, and – a new development, this – smelling like he hadn't bathed in a fortnight. My Estranged Wife has sometimes accused me of not bothering to conceal my contempt when faced by a bore or a cretin; in this instance, I didn't want to conceal my contempt; I wanted to radiate it. But, because he is Stupid, he didn't pick up on it.

So, it turned out, the *magnum opus* he has now devoted twenty years of his life to has not yet been published; I suspect not because it is a work of ground-breaking genius, but because it's shit. (He's not a reader. I mean, *really* not. I think he might have read a Sven Hassel or two.)

Oh, I was polite enough. I didn't tell him to give up even trying to pretend he was a writer; I didn't even ask when he was going to get the hot water fixed at his house. I have a horrible feeling that he went away thinking we are great chums, which distresses me beyond words, and is probably why I am venting here at such length.

Well, here I am in Brighton, and there are more white men with dreadlocks here than you can shake a stick at. But this is a risk one accepts when one stays in Brighton for any length of time; and good luck to it. And for one thing, I don't think there are many of them who think that the Nazis got a raw deal at the end of the War.

I was sitting in L———'s drawing room with her and D———, who used to be my agent. We were talking about my circumstances, the fact that I was on the move again.

"I can't quite understand how you're coping with this so well," she said.

"It's being so cheerful," I reply mournfully, "as keeps me going."

This gets a laugh, but sometimes it's only when someone tells you how well you're doing that you pause, and suddenly find the burden unbearable.

"I'll leave you to it," I say. "Packing to do."

And there are worse places to be packing for, I reflected at the time. I may be Fate's football these days, but right now it feels as though I have been subjected to a sweetly-executed pass just outside the box. If that pass were 500 miles long, that is. As I mentioned lat week, I am in Brighton, for the first time in about a year and a half, and it is sunny, and the whole town reeks of weed and incense, like a teenager's bedroom, and I love it. I may miss Scotland keenly, but, really, there are worse places to end up.

Once again this is thanks to the kindness of Laurie Penny, who is currently being a Success in America, which pleases me greatly. I may only be here for a couple of weeks longer, but I intend to make the most of it. Yesterday I passed the time in the Battle of Trafalgar, a very nice pub about two minutes' walk from my front door, which I had hitherto scorned, on the grounds that any pub so near a train station can't be any good. Oh reader, how wrong I was. There are very few pubs in Brighton which are not any good.

I'm listening to my friend B——— tell us the latest instalment of his never-ending battle against cold-callers and scammers. His reasoning is that the longer he keeps these people on the phone, the fewer people they can con. This time someone had unwisely called him asking for details about the car accident he had been in which was not his fault. B———'s speciality is in constructing long, mad yet strangely plausible fables on the spur of the moment. ("You gotta have a backstory," he says.)

"Can you describe the circumstances of the accident?"

"Glad you asked me that. Okay, so ever since 1992 when I came out as gay and left my wife and three kids I've been going out with this bloke called Gareth Large, who is known on the scene as Glam Boy Gal. Proper catch. Anyway, yeah, last year, we moved in together and initially things were fine. Cos, you know, love 'n' shit."

"Sir? Sir? Can we talk about the car accident?"

The weather is glorious. I had spent the day walking around town, soaking up the sun, reading on the beach. I am determined to get myself fit; Brighton has a quite unnecessary number of hills, many of them ridiculously steep – steeper than anything I encountered in Scotland, which seems bizarre – and I am bracing myself for the climb back home. The Battle of Trafalgar is about a third of the way up a *ridiculously* steep hill, but I think another pint of Harvey's will take much of the edge off it

"So me and Glam Boy Gal move into together and we agree on the whole décor thing. Grey, yellow and green, yeah? But then it comes to the floors, and he's like 'We have to go with Carrara marble, Benjy'. And I'm like, 'No way, cos I am not going down on my hands and knees to polish that stuff'. And he's like, 'But it's so sexy'."

"Sir?? The accident???"

Yesterday I sat on a wall in the Churchill shopping centre eating a Bratwurst hot dog, and listening to the conversation beside me. An English language teacher was chatting to three of her pupils; one German, one Chinese, one French (I think). It occurred to me that I might be able to set up as a teacher here. You can't throw a brick here without hitting an English Language School and not all of them are going to be that fussy about qualifications. I suppose you have to do a course of some kind for the prissier kind of establishment but surely all you need is a Longman's textbook and a plausible air. This teacher had been sending her pupils off to ask people about their gambling habits. The young German had come back puzzled, because one of the people he'd interviewed had said that all the horses he'd ever backed had been dead. "How can this be?" he asked, in honest puzzlement.

B———'s story, which gets ruder and ruder, far too rude to be included in a family magazine like this one, reaches its conclusion ("... and he goes completely garrity, and rams his Range Rover into Dave's Audi TT ..."), and everyone, including people we do not know but who happen to be in earshot, is in hysterics. I think I am getting a tan.

It was my birthday last week, and so the clock hand judders forward another year closer to my eternal rest. And yet I find myself in strangely chipper mood, despite being vagrant and broke as ever. I might be out of Brighton in a week; or it might be a matter of months. Who cares? Medulla oblongata, as they sing in *The Lion King*. I have three recurring dreams: in one, I am returning to university, but this time they are going to make me work, and I have only one term in which to do it; the other has me visiting the Estranged Wife in the family home, which has since been mightily enlarged, with about four extra bedrooms, a vastly expanded study area, and, in one particularly harrowing version, with an amusement park in the back garden; and in the third, my mother is doing something to enrage me. I've had these three dreams lately, with these differences: that the university authorities are quite happy for me to loaf around the place as long as I like, without doing a stroke; that the family home is exactly the size it ought to be; and my mother behaved in a perfectly civilised manner. That one was particularly weird, and I woke up wondering whether I was coming down with a fever.

But no: I am for some mysterious reason in good spirits. Maybe it is the weather. But I went down to London to see a friend and my daughter, and her Sort Of Boyfriend; my friend and I had a craving for truffles, but the restaurant that she'd booked online looked ghastly, and the menus looked laminated, and the matter was settled for us when a middle-aged couple, who looked like they'd come specially to London for their dinner, told us, as we were peering at the menu in an unconvinced fashion, that the food wasn't very good at all, the service was indifferent, and the prices – oh, the prices. So then I rang up John-Paul, manager of the Casa Becci, my favourite restaurant on earth, and I asked him if he did a pasta dish with truffles in it and he said of course he did, there'll be a table for you at half nine. (I have mentioned the Casa Becci before. It is on Paddington Street, W1, and is an unpretentious family-run restaurant which has several good signature dishes, one of which, I can now confidently report, is linguine with sliced black truffles.)* So the four of us went there, and we sat in the smoking area until midnight chewing the fat, and daughter and Sort of B. Departed, and when I went to pay the bill it turned out that my Sort of Son-in-Law had already paid it.

I suppose maybe my mood has something to do with staying close to my children, or seeing more of them than I did when in Scotland. (And having a whopping restaurant bill delivered from one's hands.) I went to The Battle of Trafalgar again, to see my youngest son, his girlfriend, and their best pal, Barney. I apparently fall into that very tiny demographic, Fathers Whose Children Are Not Ashamed to be Seen With. The youngest has been telling his university chums my stories, and even gone so far as to show them some of these columns, and they have found themselves deeply impressed. (By the way, can I jut say how nice it is to have a local again. Scotland does many things very well indeed, but not the pub. With very few exceptions, and those mostly in the big cities, the Scottish pub, usually signposted with a brutalist T (for Tennants) outside, makes, from the outside, the kind of architectural statement which goes "fighting catered for inside"; it is some way away from the

---

* This restaurant no longer exists; Covid killed it.

cosy, wisteria-bedecked honey-coloured pub you get in the English countryside. Also, I don't have to walk three and a half miles to find a pub these days.)

I was also in a good mood because my eldest son has made another short film as part of his university course, and I watched it, and it was hilarious. I think his tutors want him to make Bergman-esque investigations into the futility of life and the darkness of the human soul, but I think there is something in the Lezard make-up which demands to see the funny side, even if it means being marked down in one's Finals.

Anyway, there I was in corner of the Trafalgar. My youngest son had just floored me with the revelation that in the days when I smoked a pipe - long story - he thought that my doing so was really cool. At first I didn't believe him, and looked searchingly into his eyes for traces of sarcasm, but he swore he meant it. I asked his friends what their favourite story of mine was, and they agreed it was the one about being caught with a huge bag of weed at Luton Airport at the start of a family holiday. And then my phone went: it was Maggie from the Mascara Bar, who had asked me if I could think of anyone to do a gig there under the aegis of the Stoke Newington Literary Festival. I had an inspiration and said: "how about me?" So that's settled, and if you're in Stamford Hill on the 8th of June at 8 p.m., drop in. I don't think I'll tell the weed story, though. That's for family only.

Seeing a friend off at a pub near the station, I notice on the bar a pile of small leaflets which depict on their front cover, underneath a Fuller's brewery logo, a mock-up of a pub sign which says "MY DAD'S PUB." This is, it turn out, a Father's Day promotion: the idea is that children nominate their fathers and thereby enter a draw in which the prizes include the renaming of his favourite Fuller's pub for the day, and his very own pub sign to keep.

Well, it's all partly in aid of Prostate Cancer UK, which can't be a bad sign, but I have to say my face darkens when I think about Fuller's these days. I once went on a tour, with my children, of the Fuller's brewery in Chiswick for the eldest one's birthday; we had a great time, got dewy-eyed at the video stressing what a great old family firm it was, each worker personally tucked up in bed by Mr Fuller himself etc., and then toasted the company with pints of London Pride. I wrote about it. And then, the week after that piece was published (and @Fullers followed me on Twitter), the company announced "a new chapter in [its] history" and you don't have to be fluent in Corporate Bullshit to know that new chapters in companies' histories usually mean something pretty bad, and in this case what it meant was that the company was flogging its entire production off to Asahi, a Japanese company that makes beer which is not very good. No more the family business; no more twinkly-eyed old Mr Fuller reading *Goodnight Moon* to his Assistant Head Brewer. My daughter and I howled across the internet to each other; it seemed almost like a personal betrayal.

Worse was to come: last week, a friend alerted me to a petition which asks its signatories to pressure Fullers, who own the freehold, to renew the current landlord's lease of the Coach and Horses in Soho. If Fullers get their way, we are warned, the Coach will turn into a soulless chain pub; its interior will be ripped out and replaced with the echoing, dismal open-plan space which seems to be the norm these days (I hold that the more and smaller rooms a pub has, the better it is. Every bar should be a snug bar). I've signed – along with, at time of writing, 11,000 others – but I fear it may be too little, too late. The Coach, I should point out, is one of this column's spiritual homes; it may not be a place I visit very much anymore, for the ghosts press against me too much there, but it was the haunt of my occasional drinking partner Jeffrey Bernard, whose "Low Life" column, not a million miles away from this one in tone and subject matter, started, as not many people know, in this very magazine.

There is a part of me, though, that wonders whether I do not open too much of my heart to the past. I bemoaned, in this column a couple of weeks ago, the loss of the watchmakers in Goldhawk Road; do I want to become one of those people whose conversational topics are gradually whittled away, leaving only "things used to be much better when I was younger"? Doubtless there is some brave contrarian at *Spiked* online, the magazine for ghastly attention-seekers, writing a piece whose subheading is "why keeping pubs the way they are is the true betrayal of the working class", etc. I must be brave and look to the future.

Actually, balls to the future. Right now it is beginning to look as though the future holds the prospect of Alexander de Pfeffel Johnson (enough of this "Boris" malarkey) as Prime Minister, followed by a rapid economic collapse, Nigel Farage's fugly face EVERYWHERE, and, further down the line, complete climatic breakdown, and Lord knows what kind of fun and games in between.

I stop my reverie and look back at the Fullers Father's day leaflet. On the back are some perhaps made-up testimonials from sons. "He has made me the man I am today. A great father, Granddad and top bloke." Aw, that seems nice. "Dad's a grumpy old git but he loves us all really." It would appear they are not setting the bar too high, then. This is encouraging. "My father is the kindest man. He would best describe a pub as the jewel of Socialism." You know what? I really like that one, once I've had a think about it. Although perhaps it doesn't bear too much scrutiny. Most of the boozers at the bar of the Coach and Horses were alarmingly right-wing, and old frog-face himself likes nothing better than to be photographed in a pub, holding up a foaming pint and looking like a cunt.

Later on I chat on the phone to my friend S—— about the Father's day promotion.

"I wonder what I would say about my father in order to win the competition," she says. "I suppose it would be something along the lines of 'lots of people think my father murdered Olof Palme, but he didn't, which makes him sad.'" Which just goes to show that there's always someone with a better story than you.

Bip

When I first stayed in this place, about a year and a half ago, it had only recently been bought, and so was lacking certain amenities. I knew I wasn't going to be a permanent resident, so I couldn't go around buying any major household goods, but I reasoned that at least I could buy a toaster for the place, which I did from the local hardware store.

Bip

Of course, being somewhat low on funds, for a change, I couldn't get a really good toaster. And I thought to myself: in the final analysis, just how superior can one toaster be to another? They are, after all, composed of essentially the same elements. A slot for the bread to go in, a handle to push it down, wires which glow red-hot when current flows through them, and a timing device which stops the toast from getting burnt. (Don't get me started on Dualit toasters, by the way.)

Bip

Anyway, this toaster turned out to be quite appreciably substandard, in that it set the toast on fire and, thereby, almost the whole flat. The electricity shorted and I spent the next few hours in darkness because I couldn't find the fusebox, and the next day I spent £100 in cash getting an electrician to point to it, above the door, which, he told me, is often where fuse boxes are these days. To this day I'm still surprised I had £100 to spare for such fripperies.

Bip

Since then, a smoke detector has been installed. I'm pretty sure there wasn't one during the Great Toaster Crisis of 2017, because I'd have remembered it. About ten days ago, it went off, when I was doing nothing more flammable than goofing out on Netflix and eating Doritos dunked into hummus. (Why is that such a good combination? I mean, they come from practically the opposite sides of the globe.) It made a noise like the Last Coming, which nearly killed me, for I am a man of sensitive disposition, and unhappy with loud, sudden noises which I have not requested.

Bip

When I'd checked that nothing was on fire, or even smoking, I composed myself, and continued to spoon hummus into my face with a trembling hand. I wondered what on earth had caused the smoke detector to have a nervous breakdown like that, and soon it became clear: it was its way of telling me its battery had run down. But this puzzled me, for when I checked it, it appeared to be connected to the mains, so therefore there should be no battery to run down. And yet, shortly after it cried its pain to an uncaring world, it carried on making a little *"bip"* noise every few minutes.

Bip

As I say, this has been going on for some time now. It once happened to me in the Hovel, with the novelty that the smoke detector was not only hidden beneath an enormous pile of clothes and rubbish in the wardrobe, it was also a smoke detector whose existence I had hitherto been unaware of. I also didn't even know then that smoke detectors whose batteries are plucking at their coverlets and gathering their families around them go *"bip"* every so often. The noise is also very hard to track down – it seems to come from everywhere, and nowhere, and indeed, for about a month in the Hovel, I was driven to the brink of insanity. (Some might have said that I was driven right over it.)

Bip

Anyway, a you might have guessed by now, I have not yet solved the problem of the dying battery. I glare at the wire that quite clearly goes from the detector to something electrical in the wall. Sometimes I stand underneath it just to make sure that this is indeed the smoke detector that is making the noise, and that there isn't another one hidden on top of a shelf somewhere, but it is a curious feature of this safety device that if you actually get close to it, it stops going *bip* entirely, and only starts going *bip* again when you give up and go back to doing something that takes a certain degree of concentration;

such as, oh I don't know, writing a column for *The New Statesman*.
Bip

Anyway, there it is, my new companion. I've become quite used to it; almost fond, in a way. It's like the pulse on a heartbeat monitor: it reassures me that everything is ticking over. The strange thing is that it has become internalised; I could swear I heard it when I walked along the seafront the other day.

Anyway, I have just heard the excellent news that my stay here is going to be extended to the end of the year. I will have to start paying a bit towards the upkeep and all that, but that's fine. Of course, one shadow hangs over me: will I, by the end of the year, have managed to stop this noise, or will I have gone absolutely stark, staring mad?
Bip

※

"Oi!" A cross text from my daughter begins. "Why didn't you invite me to whatever it was you were doing on stage in London yesterday?"

"Because," I reply, "I had a hunch I'd be shit."

You might recall that I ended a column a couple of weeks ago with the news that I'd be doing a gig at the Mascara Bar as part of the Stoke Newington Literary Festival. Maggie, the Mascara's splendid owner, had called me asking if I knew anyone who'd like to read some of their stuff out to a crowd in exchange for money. I couldn't think of anyone until I had the bright idea of suggesting myself. Maggie was delighted with the idea, and so was I.

However, as the date approached, I began to be overcome by misgivings. The Mascara is a splendid place, one of my favourite watering holes on earth, and it would be lovely to see Maggie again, but as I went through my columns, deciding which ones to read out, I kept thinking "is this really the right material for this kind of venue?" Every joke I looked at fell flat on the page; in my mind's eye, I saw the faces of dozens of people in an audience, not knowing where to look.

My public appearances are few, and far between, largely because I rarely get asked to do them, and the reason that's the case is that I like it that way. Occasionally I hear multi-millionaire raconteur David Sedaris on the radio and ask myself, with some pique, why I'm not a multi-millionaire raconteur.

"I could do that," I say to the radio, while his audience of thousands has hysterics. But I know, in my heart, I couldn't.

Long ago I worked out that I was at my best when taking questions from the audience. My best gig ever was in Norwich, when I decided to read for fifteen minutes and answer queries for forty-five. In the front row was a woman of stern mien, dressed like a Dick Emery character from the 1970s, all fox-fur and those glasses that sweep up to a point at the sides. And not that Dick Emery character who shoves men in the chest and says "you are awful . . . but I like you", but another one, the kind who would make a withering remark as powerful as a wallop with her handbag. She sat in the middle of the front row, about ten feet away from me, glaring at me with raw hatred before I'd even opened my mouth. She asked the first question, in tones as acid as the Xenomorph's blood, "and what does your wife think of all this?" By the end of the evening I felt I was speaking only to her, almost as if I was in love, and when I showed the audience – well, her, really – the little circular band-aid I had in the crook of my elbow following a test at the STD clinic, she turned ninety degrees in her chair, to face the wall, and never looked at me again. It was *glorious*.

The worst gig was at an art gallery, talking about Beckett's funny side to a roomful of unsmiling artists and art students, nervous sweat dripping off the end of my nose so fast it was as if a tap had been turned on. Never again, I thought to myself, and also: artists can go screw themselves.

Anyway, Saturday evening saw me at the Mascara Bar in good time; Maggie poured me several glasses of Maker's Mark, which was very kind of her but didn't do much to soothe my nerves. The last one I had, to take with me to the stage, I asked to be quite dilute; I had a fancy that I could use it as a prop, both raffish and charming, in much the way that that sublime comic, David Allen, used his glass of whiskey. (Which was probably cold tea anyway, if I recall correctly.)

Well, David Sedaris I was not. David Allen I was not. The Mascara Bar is only open at one end; its performance area is separated from the main bar by a curtain. The air was still and warm, and there were about - ? - people in the audience, in little chairs. I say there were ? people there because I couldn't bear to look at them. Twenty? Thirty? Quorate, anyway. By which I mean enough people to humiliate me. Even my brother and my sister-in-law were there. Someone I had been particularly hoping to impress was running late, thank God.

And so I started reading, and as my jokes fluttered feebly into the air before falling to the ground, occasionally helped by polite but faint semi-laughter from the audience, the sweat started pouring off me, and I began to fluff my lines, even though they were right in front of me. I glanced at my watch. Time seemed to be going backwards, if it was moving at all. A very nice young man who works on the Londoners' Diary of the *Evening Standard* asked me a question; my answer made it into the paper the next Monday. Well, that's showbiz. Never again, until the next time.

Would I, I am asked by his mother, like to drive the youngest back from university. That would be a pleasure, I reply. He is studying at Sussex University, which is just, according to the internet, a fifteen-minute drive from my place in Brighton. However, nothing in life is simple, and when I realise that I can't find my driving licence, and that renting a car will be more expensive than a day return to London and borrowing the Estranged Wife's car, I find myself yo-yo-ing back and forth to and from Brighton four times, when I could have just done it twice. However, having long become inured to six-hour train journeys, the hour it takes to get to London seems almost poignantly fleeting, like the life of a mayfly, or a romantic poet.

I manage to get to the campus site without using any maps at all. My phone doesn't do the internet anymore, and the road map is in the boot, but I think it's important to make life difficult for yourself from time to time. It builds character. This I the kind of thing fathers say.

"You shouldn't rely on satnavs so much," I tell my children. "You do realise that civilisation's going to collapse within the next ten to fifteen years, don't you?"

"We'll learn to read a map when we have to," they say, "and not before."

However, on the drive back, I ask the Youngest what his phone's map has to say about the state of the M25. The journey down had taken rather a long time, and only for one brief period had I exceeded 50mph. As I like to drive fast – really quite fast – this was somewhat irksome, and when I'd arrived at the campus I'd refused to help carry any of his clobber down. (He did have two friends with him, though.) He told me that if I wanted to avoid traffic, then the M25 was going to be a no-no. He recommended a much straighter route, but one which would take us through parts of South London with which I am unfamiliar. I would have to swallow my pride and use him, or rather his phone, as a navigator.

There was still traffic. We spent much time stationary. Luckily, conversation flows well between us. Up to a point. I found myself getting increasingly rattled by our snail-like progress. It was around this point that I decided that I really like driving, but only for about twenty minutes. And then only if we're moving.

"I spy," I say, "with my little eye, something beginning with L."

"Oh God," he says.

We are on the A23, and the thing, or things, beginning with L are all around us.

"Life?" he asks.

"Well, in a sense," I say. "But I am after something more specific."

I wonder why I've started this game. I can't stand it, either. I suppose it is to remind him that however grown up he considers himself, he will always be my little [infant nickname redacted. I'm not a complete monster].

In the end he gives up. He is squirming in his seat.

"Leaves," I say, for the trees on either side of the road are burgeoning with them. He cries out, as if in pain.

"I spy," he says, "with my little eye, something beginning with E."

Reader, I'll spare you. (It was the exhausts, as in exhaust pipes, on the cars in front of us. I don't think that's fair.)

Later on, as we crawl through somewhere called Norbiton, I ask him to teach me young person's slang. "Blem", apparently, is a cigarette. "Chip" is tobacco. "Butters" and "clapped" mean ugly. "Leng" means attractive. A "zoot" is a cigarette which has been augmented, by the addition of a certain herb, to something that is illegal in most parts of the country, but not, for some reason, in Brighton or Bristol. I start to wonder if he's making these up as he goes along, just to make sport with me. What's he going to say next? "'Nong' means 'water in the washing-up bowl that's gone unpleasantly cold'". "'Chonky' is weirdly specific. It means that feeling you have when there's a stone in your shoe but it's not quite big or uncomfortable enough for you to take it off."

Well, we arrive safely, although I am so sick of driving I am thinking of bailing out of the next university challenge, which means a trip to *Manchester* and back.

A few days later I am sitting on Brighton beach with Will Self, who has heard I am here and wishes to buy me lunch. We discuss the current shitstorm of politics, and the rise of Trump, Farage, and Johnson.

"These are just epiphenomena," he says, "based on people's inability to grasp the fact that thanks to climate change, civilisation is going to be ending soon. I give it ten to fifteen years."

Bingo, I think to myself.

So today I am bracing myself for the drive to Manchester in order to pick up the eldest son. I'm not looking forward to it, although his company for the return will be most welcome. On the way up there, though, all I will be doing is brooding. I am delighted to report that he has graduated with First-class Honours; a boast whose force is somewhat reduced when placed against the achievement of his father. "A chip off the old block," a friend wrote. No, not really. If he'd really been a chip off the old block, he would have got himself a solid, gentlemanly Upper Second.

How he got this I'm not entirely sure, although I'll probably find out during the drive. As far as I know, he didn't take any exams. The degree is in film-making, and he has written and directed at least two brief films that I know of, both of them, I am proud to say, small masterpieces of comic timing. I know he also had to produce at least one long essay – I think it was about 10,000 words, and listening to him talk about the prospect of writing it was one of the very few times I have heard real fear in his voice. Well, he can't have cocked that up. Still, he's the only person I know who managed to do even less work at university than I did.

How does one do it? Take exams in the summer, that is. What kind of arbitrary sadism is it that builds the academic year around the fact that students of almost all ages are, throughout the land, revising or sweating while the blossom is out, the trees in full leaf, the birds and the bees doing their things? My birthday's in mid-May, and the number of times I had to sit exams on it is beyond count. It struck me as a deep injustice. I always thought you didn't even have to *go to school* on your birthday, let alone take an exam. I remember once, in the hall used for exams at my school, watching a small lake of piss expanding beneath a contemporary's chair; he had been too terrified to raise his hand and ask for permission to leave. I took no delight in his shame; everyone felt it too, and thought, "there but for the grace," etc.

I remember how my own university days went, in the first year. I managed, somehow, to produce three baffled essays in my first term. The first one was on Sir Philip Sidney, and all I remember of it was that I never wanted to read a word of his ever again, and that I was strongly advised not to use the word "hermeneutic" until I was very certain what it meant. (Up until then, I have a feeling that the only critical writing I had ever read had been published in the *New Musical Express*. Well, it was awfully good in those days.) The next term, I decided that three essays was overdoing it a bit, and so instead of the mandated four, which was hardly a stretch, I wrote two. By the time summer rolled round, though, I was so exhausted that I could only manage one essay, an absolute stinker on Henry IV Parts one and two, written in a caffeinated haze over a single night, and completely failing to mention Part two, on the grounds that I hadn't found the time to read it. I recall advancing the theory, with barefaced hypocrisy, that Falstaff was actually a tiresome boor, and it was quite right that he should be shunned by . . . by . . . whoever it was who shunned him. At this point the university authorities clamped down on me, and I was told that if I didn't shape up they'd throw me out for good. I remember looking out of the window during my telling-off, and thinking: look at all that sunshine. Look at all those young women, in their summer dresses. Look at all those pubs, with their beer gardens basking in the light. Hmm, sorry, Mr Senior Tutor? You were saying?

It is not, perhaps, a healthy attitude. I produced a more respectable amount of work later on, but worked out fairly quickly that the only way I was going to get a First would be if there was some kind of mix-up at the marking stage. The night before my Finals began, I realised that it was really too late to do anything about it, so my revision the night before consisted solely of my rereading all the Narnia novels.

And so I have, in a way, escaped the awful syzygy of summertime and exam time, largely because I thought of exams as things to be brushed aside as brusquely a possible, in order that the easy living that was waiting for me in the world outside could be enjoyed. As I might have mentioned before, the very verb *lézarder* means, in French, to make like a lizard: that is, to bask. I couldn't have had a more nominally determinative surname, unless it had been "Shiraz". (Or, in those days, "Greene-King-IPA".) Anyway, it's off to That London now, and then That Manchester, and some stern words for my son. "You're making the rest of us look bad."

The trip to and from Manchester was a success, I suppose, in that we survived it, my eldest son and I; on the way up, I'd spent a merry few miles going the wrong way on the M56, phone on my lap, listening to directions on speakerphone. "Is the sun in your eyes?" "Yes." "Then turn around." "Shit." This was better than the last time I'd driven to Manchester, last year, when poor signage – yes, I repeat, looking you firmly in the eye, poor signage – took me almost to the borders of Scotland. (On the way back, with the son navigating me around a tailback on the M6, we suddenly found ourselves staring at an impossible, surreal beauty: among the trees, a vast saucer cradled in scaffolding as gleaming and white as a film-star's teeth. "Jodrell Bank!" I exclaimed, although I'd never seen it before. I think my son was rather impressed. We didn't see it this time round, though.)

I played with his housemates and stayed the night. Student houses are always a special kind of disgusting, but the students themselves are always divine. There was the added bonus of a pool table in one of the bedrooms, which we were invited to use. It would appear that my son has been putting his time at university to good use after all: he is now, and I hate to admit this, better than me at pool. Or at least he knows the curves and bends of the table. I remember my father, playing snooker with me in the bar of Hampstead Cricket Club, saying "you're rather good at this; have you thought of becoming a snooker hustler?" For context, I should point out that he had, at the time, switched to playing left-handed in order to give me a chance;

and I'd been stinking up the family home for an unemployed year after graduating. I searched his face for sarcasm and found none. It was the only career advice he ever gave me.

On the way back, before hitting the motorway, we found an impressively decrepit petrol station and topped the car up; I had to borrow the money from my son. This on top of the £100 I'd had to borrow from his younger brother, without which I wouldn't have been able to get from Brighton to London in the first place. It's always a rite of passage, isn't it, when you first borrow money from your children. (The rite is for both of you.) The first time you do it, you can't believe you've sunk so low. The second time it's not so bad, and by the third time the awkwardness has evaporated, if not entirely.

Meanwhile, back to the car journey. The son had slept on sofa cushions on the floor; he'd given me his bed, on the grounds that the driver should be the one who was well-rested. The son had managed, by his estimation, about two hours of fitful slumber, and on the way back he spent almost the whole journey asleep. "Thank God we're nearly home," I said, as he woke up around the time we were crossing the M25. "Your incessant rabbiting on has been driving me round the twist."

Anyway, he now faces the challenges of adulthood. These were bad enough when I were a lad, sending doomed applications to publications – any publications at all, as long as they were advertising in the Media Jobs section of the *Guardian* (I swear I sent my miserable CV off to something with a title like *Pig Farming Monthly*; hey, I thought, it's a foot in the door) – but now it must be even worse, and with a whacking great loan to pay off on top of it all. How do you cope with that? What's the psychic cost? What's the *actual* cost? I earn a bit less than the national average wage these days but this puts me ahead of an awful lot of people whose main or sole source of income is writing. If I had a five-figure loan as well the temptation would be to find a caravan in the woods somewhere and go completely off-grid. In a sense, I am; there is a long and devious chain of forwarding addresses before a letter or parcel sent to the Hovel ends up going through my letterbox. I think of my children looking at their father and thinking to themselves that this represents rock bottom, a situation that they should aspire to avoid; anything would be better than that.

We're nearly home now. The M40 has become the A40, and we pass the Hoover Building. When we were a viable family, that is, with all five of us, including their mother, in the car, we would all pretend that the Hoover Building was actually a giant Hoover, and we would make sucking noises and tilt ourselves in its direction. I'm about to do this but there comes on the radio a special report on death squads in, if I recall correctly, El Salvador.

"That reminds me," says the son. "I'm going to go backpacking in South America with my friends in January." Ah, Jesus, I think to myself. Can't he just stay somewhere safe, at home, and perfect his game of pool? He could become a hustler.

※

I've just been appointed a temporary theatre critic for another magazine, which is nice. It's only for a month, which means I only have to go to the theatre four times, which is about all I can handle. I can't remember the last time I went to the theatre. I have a feeling it was Fiona Shaw's 2007 production of *Happy Days* at the National, and the PA system played the theme tune from the TV show "Happy Days" as we filed out to the bar in the interval. If I hadn't been with my mother I wouldn't have gone back for the second act, so outraged was I by this crassness. Oh wait, there was that time a couple of years ago Radio 4's Front Row made me watch a play and I said "I've never been, dramatically speaking, so insulted in my life" on air, and they've never asked me back.

My first gig will be *Peer Gynt*, or rather, *Peter Gynt*, which according to the National's website is "by David Hare after Henrik Ibsen". Here's Martin Amis on David Hare: "Whenever I run into my contemporary Sir David Hare, he amuses me so much that I can't think why he isn't more amused by being called Sir David Hare – a ridiculous appellation, like Sir Johnny Rotten or Lord Vicious." Amis considers theatre "handily inferior" to the novel and poem, and says "I agree that it is very funny that Shakespeare was a playwright. I scream with laughter about it all the time. This is one of God's best jokes."

Anyway, Peer Gynt or Peter Gynt, it doesn't much matter, as I don't have either of my copies of the play – one the Penguin Classic, the other Geoffrey Hill's translation – to hand, as they are in a box in East Finchley, along with almost all my other possessions, apart from those books and LPs which have been allowed to stay in the family home in Shepherd's Bush.

Yes, twelve years on from my ejection and it's still the books I miss the most. A week doesn't go by without my dreaming about them; I dreamt about them last night, as it happens. Nothing much happens in this dream, except that the collection has expanded to include all sorts of rare and fascinating codices and incunabula, great lost works (Byron's memoirs, etc.) and books I have been asking for for years but with the pleas falling on deaf ears (Empson's *Essays on Renaissance Literature*, etc.). I suppose last night's dream was set off by the discovery, yesterday, of a second-hand bookshop just inside the covered market in Brighton: although small in terms of footprint, the shelves were tall and full and labyrinthine; I got the feeling I could have spent a lot longer in there than I actually did. (The books I bought: *The Ballad of Peckham Rye* and *The Adventures of Augie March*. I nearly bought a copy of the Oxford Classics edition of *Ulysses*, which would have been my fifth copy. The others are scattered from East Finchley to Scotland. I don't feel comfortable without being near a copy of *Ulysses*, but I think five copies of the same edition is a bit much, even for me.)

Well, this is the kind of thing that happens when you don't have a permanent home. It's doable, the whole living out of a suitcase thing (here is what you need in terms of clothes: six shirts, six pairs of boxer shorts, three pairs of trousers, a dozen or so socks, all black, so you don't have to worry about mismatches, and a smart jacket and a rough-weather jacket, one pair smart shoes, one pair rainproof/all-terrain. And that's it), but it is psychically exhausting. I do not have the book collection, the tasteful knick-knacks, the carefully ordered disarray, the four dimensions (the three usual ones, plus time), with which I can show off my character; I have to rely on my wits alone. I marvel that I can cope without tears of envy when I visit someone else in his or her own home. "Look at all these *things*," I say to myself. "They're all *theirs*." But it could be worse: there are people who live their whole lives without love, or in pain, and there are people I know who have been doing this for much longer than me. "To turn a key in the first place you've considered home in 20 years is quite something," began a post I saw this morning on a social medium, and I have to say that made me think a bit. I've been doing this for nearly two years; eighteen more will see me well into my seventies, and I'm not sure this is an old man's game.

Meanwhile, I browse the second-hand shops of Brighton simply to satisfy, or at least appease, my appetite for clutter. I particularly recommend the Snooper's Paradise in Brighton's Kensington Gardens: room after room of wonderful *junk*. So much flotsam, waiting for a home. And without one myself, all I can buy there are presents for others. I got Laurie Penny a charming tea tray. One day I hope to have one I can call my very own, although I use tea trays about as often as I voluntarily go to the theatre. It's the principle.

A busy week, spent travelling up and down from Brighton to London, to Cambridge, and back down to Brighton. Thanks to Thameslink, there is now a train that goes direct from Brighton to Cambridge. It's not terribly fast and on the day I used it was more of a zoo on wheels than a train, but I was ill and exhausted and was grateful to have somewhere to sit down for two and a half hours without having to get up. Although the woman who kept talking all the way from Royston to Saint Pancras was beginning to drive me a bit crazy.

"It's the safest form of transportation," she was saying to her companions. "The train is. It's the safest. It's safer than aeroplanes. It's safer than cars. It's safer than bicycles. It's safer than motorcycles. It's safer than . . ." and she went on to list every single mode of transportation that had ever been invented. "It's safer than cruise liners. It's safer than yachts. It's safer than coaches. It's safer than . . ." Well, it's not that safe if someone throws you off it, is it? But I was so tired that I found it all rather soothing in the end, and I dropped off to sleep.

First up had been a book launch given by my great friend, the Moose. It is not just friendship alone that compels me to give his book *Greta and the Labrador* (go to www.hhousebooks.com) a plug; it's the quality of the work itself, ostensibly about a dog devoted to Greta Garbo, but actually a lot deeper than that. The party itself was one of the best I have been to, largely because of the people there, and the venue, on the towpath at King's Cross, next to a barge which serves as a second-hand bookshop.

Well, not all the people. A woman came up to me and introduced herself. The name was vaguely familiar; we were connected on a social medium. She then went on to tell me that she was a member of the Conservative Party, was going to vote for Boris Johnson as leader, and had voted for the Brexit Party in the European elections. All this told with a certain defiant pride. I held my peace even though I hadn't asked for any of this information, apart from the question of whether she'd voted for Farage and his gang of runts, as I suspected she had (I know a few Tories, and they all voted for Farage's gang of runts). Her husband, she said, had had a job to do with tax in Brussels, and the way she said this seemed to indicate that this meant her opinion was considerably better-informed than mine. So I asked her my second question, the one I often use on Brexiters: "can you give me one – just one – European law or regulation that has irked or inconvenienced you in any way at all? Just one." Normally this makes them go away, because they never have an answer. This woman's reply had an interesting twist to it, though.

"I know this sounds bad," she said, "but I'll have to get back to my husband on that."

Yes, madam, it does look bad.

The trip to Cambridge was somewhat more melancholy: a memorial service for the late Doctor Eric Griffiths, who had done his best to teach me about English Literature when I was there. A stroke had robbed him of his (considerable: I once saw him make the late Norman Stone burst into tears) powers of speech, and he spent the next ten years trying to die; last year, he succeeded. He was not universally loved, and the Moose, who knew him well, and lives in a nearby village, didn't want to go to the service, but he did want to see those of his friends who were going, so a few of us slipped away from the revels and joined him at the Eagle for a bottle or two.

The Moose was in fine form, grateful for the conversation: his parents, particularly his mother, were no longer *compos mentis*, and the caring staff, while all absolutely wonderful and dedicated, did not have English as a first or in some cases even a second language. Still, he said, everything was better than writing. I started quoting Oliver Goldsmith's line at him ("no turn-spit-dog gets up into his wheel with more reluctance than I sit down to write"), and he brushed it aside with a "yes, yes", as if it was inadequate to express his disdain for his own profession.

"Let me put it like this," he said. "I had to wipe my father's arse the other day, and even *that* was better than writing."

And yet this is what we have to do to put bread on the table and wine in our bellies – "to keep body and soul apart", I once said, thinking I was being witty and original; but I discovered the other day that the phrase is Dorothy Parker's. The Moose, however, is a more original thinker than I am, and once said, while in the grip of a bad hangover, "but I know that my liver redeemeth." Now that's pretty good, you have to admit. Hang in there, Moose.

Regular readers of this column might have heard me mention my new local a couple of times: the Battle of Trafalgar, which lives a third of the way up the steep hill that's on your right as you leave the station.

When I first lived in these parts – about a year and a half ago – I didn't go out much, and the pub, as I passed it, didn't look particularly welcoming. But that was foolish of me (and almost certainly due to the depression that had settled in my bones; I didn't think *anywhere* looked inviting). However, a year in rural Scotland certainly changes your notions of what a welcoming pub looks like. Scottish country pubs are generally not encouraging either on the outside or the inside. I did go to one in Braemar which was in a fine building; inside the place had been redecorated to look like something halfway between a Sealink ferry and a conference centre. I had never seen so many TV screens in one place at the same time; they were all showing some dismal football match, and the staff outnumbered the customers. We drank up quickly and left.

So, I didn't feel I was missing out too much when I lived three and a half miles from the nearest pub, but the day after I moved to Brighton in May I thought it would be a good idea to check the Trafalgar out.

I found, inside, something that was not quite the pub of my dreams – the pub of my dreams is a bit more higgledy-piggledy, has an inglenook fireplace and an old fart smoking a pipe in the corner – but wasn't too far off it. A decent choice of beers (but Harvey's, the local brewery, beats the rest hands down); a nicely unconventional layout that somehow manages to supply a seat even when the place is packed with football fans (who are civil to each other on match days even when supporting rival teams); no television, no music, and a large beer garden that gets the sun in those dangerously tempting hours between three and six in the afternoon.

I've brought several friends here, treating it as, in effect, my living room; but it's the kind of place where you don't feel like a weirdo if you just want to sit with a book. (It's also dog-friendly, which is on the whole great, apart from the time that the excellent Greek journalist Yiannis Baboulias's dog tried to have sex with me. But that's another story for another day.) There was always a gentle hum of conversation between the staff and the regulars at the bar; and the staff themselves are friendly and good at their job. This was a pub that minded its own business and got on with the job. There is, in short, nothing wrong with it.

Well, according to Enterprise Inns, this is where I'm wrong. What's wrong with the Battle of Trafalgar, according to the company that owns the lease, is that there aren't nearly enough TV screens in it, and it isn't a sports bar. They had a team of about a dozen "consultants" down to look at the place the other day, and as one of the regulars said, "you don't have a dozen people round to look at the place if you're just going to give it a lick and a flick." Someone is planning to do some serious work here, and assurances that there will only be one telly and no changes to the internal layout are being treated with a certain degree of scepticism.

The whole situation is a bit complex, I've now learned: in the world of drinks companies, things are, well, fluid, and Enterprise Inns are being bought by the Bermondsey Pub Group (the first word on whose website is "Pubbiness", and I would dearly love to know who signed off that one), or the Stonegate Group, and the whole thing is going to the Monopolies and Mergers Commission, on the grounds that the conglomerate will own more pubs than anyone has ever owned in the history of Great Britain, and it might be all a bit unfair.

I have to say that although 2019 hasn't sucked hind tit in the ways that 2016, 2017, and half of 2018 did, there have been moments when it could have done better. First Yiannis Baboulias's randy dog, then Boris Johnson becomes Prime Minister, and now just when I've found a boozer that's five minutes' walk away and suits me (and many other people) right down to the ground, up comes a lease for renewal and a bunch of pointy-heads decide that what this world needs more of is pubs showing football matches on nine-foot screens and bouncers outside the door. There's an online petition which you can find pretty easily, which has racked up, at time of writing, about 4,000 signatures; a paper one has a thousand more. I've checked out what EI, Bermondsey and Stonegate are capable of doing to a pub, and I can tell you that it's not catering for the likes of me.*

⁂

To London, to have lunch with the children and catch up with some old friends I haven't seen for about a year. I travel to London a lot more these days, and the Network Railcard paid for itself pretty quickly. The day is warm, and I am thirsty, and I have time to buy a bottle of Coke. (A parenthesis: while there is a perfectly good independent shop about ten seconds' walk from the station, some kind of force-field prevents me from leaving the precincts, and I go to WH Smith and pay £2.19 for a drink that generally retails at £1.10 or so. Why is this? And, more to the point, how are WH Smith actually allowed to do this?)

The train fills up a bit at Hayward's Heath; opposite me sits a man, about 30 I'd say, with ginger hair and a beard; not a hipster beard, just a, you know, beard. Pinstripe shirt, suit trousers, jacket over his arm, rucksack. He looks mildly harassed, as if he has been slightly over-promoted in middle management. I think little of him; I sip my drink, I read my book. After a while the motion of the train and the sunshine through the leaves induce a mild sleepiness, and I take a little nap. From which I am awoken not too long afterwards

---

* As of 2025, the pub still survives, thanks entirely to this article, largely unchanged, but there is a telly now. And as I write these words, I shall be meeting my good friend Dr Rosy Carrick there early this evening.

by a "pschht" sound, as of that made by a one-third-drunk bottle of Coke being opened by someone sitting in a train seat diagonally opposite. I open my eyes, and there is Mr Ginger Beard, drinking from my bottle of Coke.

As I have said before, while I am genetically only a quarter-English, I was raised among the English, and have absorbed their best characteristics into the very fibre of my identity. I drink tea; I like a bit of self-deprecating humour; I love cricket. And I have absolutely no idea what to do when faced with a situation such as this. Douglas Adams tells the story of how a complete stranger at a train station café opened, and started eating from, his packet of biscuits. "Now this, I have to say, is the sort of thing the British are very bad at dealing with," he says. "There's nothing in our background, upbringing, or education that teaches you how to deal with someone who in broad daylight has just stolen your biscuits." (For the whole story, which I won't spoil for you here, just google "train biscuits" and it comes up. You don't even have to type in Adams's name, so I suppose it's pretty well-known by now.)

I found myself in a similar situation. On the one hand, the inclination is to do nothing. On the other hand, there is the sense of burning injustice. Inside me, something stirred; some ember of Pole, Frenchman or Jew flared back into brief life (I must get that DNA test done) and asked me whether I was a man or a mouse. Mouse, generally, but then this was clearly the worst outrage that had been perpetrated against me since that little shit Douglas Green "accidentally" pulled my shorts *and* undercrackers down in front of the whole school in 1971. So when Ginger Beard Man put the bottle down after his swig, I put my finger on top the cap, looked meaningfully at him over the rim of my glasses and said "erm . . ."

He looked about him in something of a panic, said "oh my God, I'm so sorry," then looked to his own rucksack, and pulled, from an exterior pocket, a bottle of Coke Zero. "Never mind," I said, a gentle smile masking my anguish. Is he going to offer me his bottle in exchange? I wouldn't want it, as I prefer the full-fat version, but he started drinking from it himself. And then after a while he made a phone call. He was wearing Bluetooth headphones and was speaking hands-free, which means an even louder conversation than normal, so I got to hear ten minutes or so of a conversation about a water softener he was thinking of buying. It was as gripping as these conversations usually are, with the amazing twist in the tale, worthy of Roald Dahl himself, that he decided not to buy the water softener. So in other words, a conversation that in the end proved utterly unnecessary.

I started wondering whether there might be some retribution in store for this man. Had we been travelling to Brighton, I could have called upon divine justice to make a seagull shit on his head, but there aren't so many seagulls in London, so instead I settled on the mental image of him falling down an open manhole. This of course rarely happens, so I entertained the possibility more in hope than expectation; but it helped pass the last ten minutes of the journey.

And then when he got up at Victoria I noticed that he had left his jacket on the seat. Wow, I thought, karma really works fast sometimes. That is seriously going to screw up his day. And then I thought: maybe he's distracted because of bad news; maybe he is congenitally absent-minded. And maybe he is himself an instrument of Heaven, placed here to test my virtue. Also, do I really want to be that mean?

So I tapped him on the shoulder, and said "erm . . ."

I look out of the window. It is the middle of August, and the first day's play at Lord's has been rained off, and outside, in Brighton, the vapours weep their burthen to the ground. Two days before that I got caught in my shirtsleeves in the second-most violent rainstorm I have ever encountered; the most violent one I was caught in was in London a couple of days before that. The rain it raineth every day.

Those I love most are in the warm South, languishing by pools; I am anguishing by puddles.

So in between getting soaked, I have been staying in bed an awful lot, even more than usual. I can't take my laptop to bed anymore; if it moves, it dies, and it becomes more difficult each time to make it start up again. So I read, mostly, and then nap for a bit. Napping has become much easier these days since I bought curtains. The most exciting thing I have ever done in my life was have sex in a thicket in St James's Park in daylight on a summer Sunday, but that was a long, long time ago; buying a pair of curtains from Debenham's in Brighton runs it a close second. Okay, it doesn't really, but for the first few months the only barrier between the bedroom and the light had been a pair of net curtains, which really don't do the job. But these curtains are thick and dark, and by some miracle I picked a pair which fit the window space neatly, and even though I have had them for a couple of weeks I still admire the way they work so well. Look, they close! And look! They open! Hours can be spent doing this.

The shrewd observer with experience of freelance ways will have worked out the reason behind this time-wasting: there is a looming deadline. And this observer would indeed be on the nail, for I am meant to be sending off to the publishers the typescript for the second selection of this very column. (The first is called *Bitter Experience Has Taught Me*, and is available from all good landfill sites.) I've gone through the typescript, all 300 pages of it, with a biro in hand, crossing out some of the more obscure topical references, and most of the feebler jokes; adding footnotes to let the reader know of subsequent developments. And now I have to transfer all these amendments to the electronic file. Do I really have to do this? It will take me *ages*. It is all hugely dispiriting.

But it has to be done. During those crazy dreams one has during the second nap of the day I found that it had become a surprise best-seller, and that I had become famous; people stopped me in the street; the young men at the check-out at the Co-Op would look at me shyly as they packed my bag at the till and ask "excuse me, are you . . .", and I would, with a becoming smile, sign their proffered slips of paper, pose gamely for their selfies. Ok, this is more of a waking reverie than an actual dream, I must admit, but it helps pass the time and certainly beats working.

And then a strange thing happened: I got a text from my oldest friend, Stephen, the one who packed me off to a house in the mountains outside Los Angeles for five days so that I could write a film script based on *Bitter Experience* . . ., and I did, but when he read through the script and asked me "but what does Nick *learn?*" and I answered him with a look that said "what a stupid question", he said, "ok, maybe it'll work better as a sitcom." So he sent me off with instructions to write a couple of episodes and page of character descriptions, three years ago, three years during which I have, for reasons of my own, chiefly idleness, done nothing. After a couple of years he asked me if I'd mind if he wrote the damn thing instead, which I suppose was what I'd been wanting him to do all along.

But his text: he says there has been a development which he wants to discuss ASAP. I wonder what it could be. I must admit, it sounds encouraging. I had more or less given up all hope. When in Los Angeles, questions like "who do you think should play you?" assume greater force and reality than they do in idle conversation in the pub; there is a chance that this could happen, you realise. These people *know* the people who can make this happen. It makes one feel quite giddy.

Hopelessness isn't such a bad place to be: you can't be tormented by visions. I think maybe this is where Dante got it slightly wrong when he wrote "abandon hope" above the gates of Hell; you go, "all right, do your worst, then, see if I care." Although I really don't want to find out if this is actually the case when you do go to Hell, when, after a life in which you have squandered your talent with little or nothing to show for it, it's . . . well, Curtains.

I've been here nearly four months, and the asthma medication is running low, so it's off to the doctor's to register. I look for the nearest GP surgery. There's one which gets two stars from its patients, and another, a little further away, which gets four and a half. First, I wonder that you can actually review GP surgeries. Second: that's some difference. I wonder how a GP surgery manages to get a bad review. Have the seats in the waiting room given someone herpes? Is one of the doctors called Crippen? I start dwelling on it and decide that this is not a good idea. Does Dr Phil Whitaker know about this? A friend of mine who's a teacher told me that pupils can now leave reviews of their teachers on the school website, which adds a whole new terror to the job. I am shown a couple of examples. Bloody hell. They didn't really think it through when they invented the internet, did they?

It's a sunny day, but the wind is racing all the way up the hill from the sea. One rarely sees the immaculately coiffed in Brighton, I realise. At the moment the largest demographic out and about are grandparents and their grandchildren. I am aware that if I were to father another child, everyone would assume I had grandfathered it instead. Meanwhile, I notice that the grandparents have different skin tones to their grandchildren. One grandfather, who looks like he has come straight out of central casting for a Werthers ad, has two coffee-coloured children in tow, which I find immensely cheering. He shepherds them, with great care, over a zebra crossing. But boy, does he look old. Will I make it to that age?

None of my children look like they're going to be reproducing any time soon. This is fine by me, but at my back I always hear time's wingèd chariot hurrying near, and the fact that I'm walking to the doctor's doesn't help these feelings of mortality go away. Let's say the eldest decides to have a child when she's 30, in six years' time. Her mother didn't want children until we were six or seven years into our relationship. She said at first she didn't want children; and after a certain point she didn't want anything else. I remember agonising about this to a certain novelist I knew well and he told me to get on with it: if I didn't, I'd be missing out on an essential aspect of the human condition, and, besides, it was all good copy. He was right.

I do the maths. So, let's say the eldest reproduces in seven years. I'll be well into my sixties by then. It'll be another five years before I start registering with them. That puts me at 68. I am getting slightly out of puff walking up the hill. Am I going to make it to the Montpelier Surgery on Victoria Road, let alone the age of 68? Christ.

I make it there, and am handed the usual 78-page form. Who doesn't love filling in a good, long form? Of course, my favourite bit is the "how much do you drink?" section. As I have said in this column before, it is my policy to answer honestly on these occasions. Doctors have a difficult and demanding job, and it is important to offer them some light relief from time to time. Any doctor doubling my intake, as they are said automatically to do with all such declarations, would be pursing his or her lips in admiration. I can't help doing it myself. At least a bottle of wine, or the equivalent, a day since the age of about 24, and the years between 16 and then weren't exactly dry, either.

The hand holding the biro pauses over the page. You know what? Maybe this level of intake isn't that healthy after all. Maybe I should be cutting down, and drastically. Get healthy, go to the gym or something. My friend Ben has been trying to get me to go along with him to the gym from the moment I moved to Brighton. And if not the gym, then boxing. I giggled like a young girl when he suggested that. Me, with my epicene features, my large and fragile hooter? You're having a laugh.

"No seriously mate, you'd be a natural. Anyway, it's important knowing how to punch someone properly."

"Ben, you're a qualified bouncer. You *have* to know how to punch people properly. I'm just a writer. If someone pisses me off, I'll write a really nasty review of their book. One that will make them *cry*." Ben runs up the sixteen floors to his flat every time, instead of taking the lift. Even the thought of it makes me gasp for breath.

I hand in the form, whose worst moment involved my having to recount the circumstances of my father's death. (Kidney failure, aged 83.) Back outside, the wind is still blowing fiercely, but this time it is at my back. But is that the wind? Or is it a wingèd chariot, hurrying near? I don't want to look round and find out.*

It's half past three in the afternoon as I write these words. That means, with only brief intervals, I've been in bed for thirteen and a half hours. Yes, our old friend hypersomnia is back, the very sensible reaction of the human body to external and internal pressures, that feeling that one is not good company, even to oneself. Remember: any fool can stay in bed all day. But it takes real dedication to spend the large portion of that time asleep.

So, you ask, how does one achieve this state of grace? Well, the usual method is heartbreak, or, in my case, a condition of extreme anxiety about a personal matter I am not at liberty to go into in any detail whatsoever. But for the real, the copper-bottomed "I am only getting out of bed to go to the bog" deal, what you want is not just this but the knowledge that your country is in the hands of an unprincipled maniac, supported by a gang of toadying maniacs just as unprincipled as he is.

I always knew this would happen. According to Lyall Watson in his superb *Heaven's Breath: a Natural History of the Wind*, the seafarers of the Santa Cruz islands of Melanesia can tell, from the swells of the ocean their boats ride on, exactly where they are and what course they are taking. Some navigators lie on their backs in

---

* I am still fogging the mirror, and still registered at the Montpelier Surgery, who are beyond reproach. One of the doctors even has a shelf of *Wisden* almanacks in his office. When I said "I'm writing for next year's edition" he might have thought I was having an episode of dementia; but I was, and I did. I wonder if he saw the piece.

their canoes to feel this swell; but most stand up, with their legs lightly apart, "plumbing the swell, feeling its effect in subtle shifts from the vertical, detected largely by the pendulum swing of their own testicles."

And the patterns of history can feel, at times, like the movement of the sea: you can feel it in your balls. (This pretty analogy or metaphor breaks down, of course, if you don't have balls, but let's not worry about that right now.)

In the current political climate you don't need to be that much of an expert in historical currents to be aware of a sense of impending doom; and I don't think there are many readers of this magazine who are not in despair right now. I'm writing this a week before publication. If a miracle has happened, and Boris Johnson has been flattened by a meteor, or (for some reason I like the sound of this one) a rogue elephant, then let this column stand as a historical curio, while all around it, a nation rejoices.

But I'm not getting my hopes up. I can't think, offhand, of any occasion when a lying charlatan in high office has been hit, let alone killed, by space debris or crazed pachyderms, so I'm not going to put my shirt on it. I'm just going to have to assume that on the 5th of September, he will still be there, still stinking up the place and still driving the country to ruin.

Meanwhile, and this is rather pleasing as it continues our nautical theme, I get a nice card from a Ms Catriona Illegible from Edinburgh. It's an answer to the question I posed a Brexiter a few weeks ago, viz. can you name a single EU law or regulation that has inconvenienced you in any way? Ms Illegible begin by saying some very nice things about my writing indeed, and I graciously accept her compliments. She then goes on to point out that she has been inconvenienced by EU maritime laws. "Briefly," she writes, "the same rules apply to the subsidy (if required) of inter-island ferries in Greece in the non-tidal Med as applied to the ocean-going ferries providing the lifeline service to the Shetland Isles. I know, I was one of the civil servants tasked with delivering the lifeline ferry service and steering a course through the maritime state aids rules.

"Will this do?"

Yes, this will do, up to a point, and I can just picture a concerned civil servant tearing her hair out at the injustice of it all, and having to wade through all the red tape to boot, but it is not quite the kind of thing I was looking for, but as this is the first proper answer I've had to my question for three years it will have to suffice. And her card did send me off on a reverie, in which I was the skipper of a sturdy vessel crashing through the gales of the North Sea, busy delivering Marmite to the noble people of Shetland. A reverie that crashes once I realise that unless Boris Johnson is stopped, there will be no Marmite, no oil to power the ferry, and Shetland and everywhere north of the Tweed will be independent anyway.

So it's back to bed for me. The more one sleeps during the day, the more crazed the dreams become, and the more muddy and disoriented the thoughts on waking. Which means you just go back to sleep again. Which is fine, because right now, from where I'm sitting, absolutely anything is better than being awake.

※

A visit from two of the children – the eldest and the youngest – to Brighton. The youngest is going to be staying here, as he's in his second year at Sussex University. He's studying maths; every so often the Lezard genes pop out someone good at the subject. The eldest drove him down. I wait until they've unloaded the car before going to the nearest pub, where we play a game of pool, and I keep an eye on the Arsenal-Spurs derby. (I don't really care much about football, unless Arsenal or England are playing. Cricket, though – I'll watch a game of beach cricket being played by complete strangers. But that's another matter.)

The pub is the kind of pub which the developers are trying to turn my local into: that is, one with several television screens, all showing the same thing. However, there is place for everything, and the pub is awfully near, and the landlady is lovely, and no one beats anyone up for either being, or being related to, a student. In fact, students get a discount. It is, though – how shall I put this? – the kind of pub in which you will find someone at the bar, who is not necessarily Mexican, wearing a sombrero. Well, why not? It's a Sunday.

As always, it is a great pleasure to see my children, although it would have been even nicer if they'd all been there. They'd all gone on holiday with their mother and the man who I suppose is *de facto* their stepfather, and although I am happy everyone gets on together, I cannot pretend that I was unmoved by jealousy when they sent me photos and videos of them all enjoying themselves, and just because you recognise your own jealousy as ugly and profitless, it doesn't inoculate you against it. Then I remember that when I'm asked how old they are, I have to stop and think for a bit, in a way that I do not have to do when recalling, say, the release dates of Beatles LPs. (I had to rebuke a friend the other day for reminding me of a programme which was going to be celebrating the 50th anniversary of the release of the White Album. Tsk, I had to say to her, you mean *Abbey Road*.) With two of them I can remember the dates but not the years, and with the other I can remember the year but have to double-check on the date. So maybe I am not the ideal father. Well, the ideal father would be *there*.

And yet they are there, in my head: I dream about them regularly, although, curiously, they only ever appear as they were when they were very young, when they could still ride on my shoulders and steer me by holding on to my ears. I take this for an act of kindness on the part of my subconscious, for it is a re-enactment of the last time I actually experienced domestic happiness. I was reading a collection of Eve Babitz's journalism the other day and one of her interviewees brought me up short with this somewhat banal observation: "All we're looking for is to wake up in the morning with someone who makes you happy, who makes you laugh and with whom you have great sex." (You'll never guess who said that. Give up? It was Jackie

Collins.) It's been a long time since I have had that joy on anything like a regular basis: six years, I think. That's a long time. Is it that much to ask? Apparently, it is.

I do not hold out much hope. You do not get to my age without recognising patterns, and just as the mariners of Santa Cruz islands of Melanesia are said to be able to recognise and navigate the ocean swells by the swinging of their testicles, there are times when I fancy I can feel the future as fundamentally, and unless something miraculous happens, well, that's it. It's not as if I'm getting any younger, or handsomer, and the end of the road is a hell of a lot nearer than the beginning.

However, there are still the children. I may be vague about their birthdays but I am not vague in my affection for them. When we part, I give the youngest boy a hug. He's in front of friends, so is a little awkward about it, which itself breeds a certain awkwardness on my part, and we are teased by his sister. "You guys."

But I think a certain amount of awkwardness is becoming in a paternal hug. It shows that a reluctance has been overcome by the force of emotion. (I think my own father would have died before hugging me; in fact, he did just that, but that was his generation.)

That evening, I lean out of the window after closing time, smoking pensively. A couple of young men, possibly also students, are walking past my front door. One of them looks at me and says, "fuck me, that's my *grandad*." So I scramble out of the window and chase him all the way down the hill, calling him an insolent whippersnapper, and brandishing my walking stick. Oh, the look on their faces.

According to the system I use when writing this column, this is the 500th "Down and Out" I have written for this magazine. I hesitate to mention this in case my sainted editor says "well, that's a nice round number to end on". Round numbers scare me, especially since I was ejected from the Hovel ten years to the day from when I moved in, and if this column goes then I really am screwed, in a way which will have made the previous years look like a soothing back rub. I am now more worried that I will be sacked than I was when I had emailed "I'm sorry, I'm too poorly to file today, cough cough", and then bumped into the Editor-in-Chief of The New Statesman, Jason Cowley, at the Test match. That was some years ago, and since then I have tried to walk the strait and narrow.

Then again, because my system says this is column number 500, then that means it is almost certainly *not* number 500, for there have been times when I have miscounted, when files have gone missing, and so on and so on. It's a bit like the fact that 1AD is almost certainly not the year of the birth of Our Lord; it's just that an accounting error slipped in very early on and it would be too much bother to change things.

Still, 500 of these things, give or take. That's a hell of a lot of grumbling. Even the word count has gone up over the years. It started out at 830 words of mawkish self-pity every week, and then for some reason a year or two ago I was told that I was 60 words short. No one knows why. It's not like the typeface has changed, or the size of the pages. Still, no skin off my nose, I have a job to do.

As it is, and by an amusing coincidence, illness and cricket again coincide this week. A trip to Lord's was floated by the team I occasionally - *very* occasionally - play for, the Rain Men, to watch a day of an end-of-season four-day country championship match between Middlesex and Durham. The idea was basically to sit around gossiping and getting vaguely sozzled, and I would show people round the Pavilion. I also invited my friends John and Marie round; Marie, his partner, has recently become obsessed by cricket in a way which gratifies both of us immensely, and I had a feeling she would get a real kick out of being shown round the sacred edifice. Also, it was her birthday. And furthermore, I liked the thought of John's being there, as I had a strong suspicion that he'd be the only person in the ground who had played for the Jesus and Mary Chain.

However, on the day I was due to go it was quite clear that I wasn't well. It's sometimes a fine line between my own despairing lassitude and actual illness, but this time there was no doubt about it: I was poorly. Sweats, shivers, incessant cough. But duty is duty and friendship is friendship and sometimes the two coincide. You don't go around promising someone a really good birthday present and then bale out at the last minute.

So it was a dank, miserable day, punctuated by rain, and Durham scored 10 runs in the first 10 overs, Finn pounding in from the Pavilion end and although bowling well, you knew he wasn't going to be taking any wickets in a hurry (I gather this was why he was dropped by England); but Marie's face lit up pretty much all of NW8. I don't think I've ever seen anyone so pleased. The Pavilion is stuffed with oil paintings of the game's grandees and while I never bother with these – although there are many kitsch delights, the only one I really have time for, in terms of both technique and subject matter, is Brendan Kelly's massive, brooding portrait in oils of Sir Viv Richards – Marie, who is an artist herself, oohed and aahed at pretty much all of them.* Her enthusiasm was, I hope, more infectious than whatever it is I was suffering from.

As it is, I am still suffering from it. And it was bad. The kitchens in the Pavilion were serving up roast pork baps, and there was an enormous bowl of crackling to one side, which no one seemed to be eating from. I think I could live on crackling; but this time I could barely struggle a piece down. For tea there were scones with jam and cream, which I also think I could live on, for £1.60 each. £1.60! Even I can afford that. But I couldn't even eat one. Not a crumb. So I left John and Marie and my fellow Rain Men there and took an early train back to Brighton, and since then I have been coughing, wheezing and shivering beneath the duvet for eighteen

---

* I have since discovered a few Lowries in the reading room opposite the Long Room, and they're delightful.

out of the last twenty-four hours, and when I've finished writing this I'm going right back there again.

Anyway, let's say this is the 501st column. It has a Brian Lara ring to it. And he, don't forget, was not out when he made it.

I had a hot date and my hair was going a bit mad, in a Doc Brown kind of way, so I thought I'd better get a haircut. The problem was I didn't have much time and so I realised I wouldn't be able to go to the barber's I'd discovered in Kemp Town a few months ago. I'd been strolling through this wonderfully louche area in June sunshine and saw what looked like a pleasing establishment, and went in. Just like that. Sometimes I am almost shockingly spontaneous like that.

The surprise, as I went to sit down, was that my barber was to be a woman. It's been a long time since I've had my hair cut by a woman. When I was young, and haircuts were arranged by my mother, this meant humiliating trips to the so-called Unisex salon on the Aylmer Parade in East Finchley. "Unisex" meant "for women, and male children who have not yet achieved independence from their mothers." One ended up, as one began, with a hairstyle that looked like that of a 1970s footballer, partly for the very good reason that this was during the 1970s. When I was much younger, my father would take me to Trumpers in Saint James, because that was Where One Went, which involved an absolutely terrifying encounter with a ceiling-mounted rotary brush, like something out of Heath Robinson, and by "like" I mean "exactly like". Readers who know their *Tintin* well may remember a similar machine invented by Professor Calculus in *The Secret of the Unicorn* which is designed to brush clothes, but which ends up shredding them, while their owners (in this case, Captain Haddock) are wearing them. Also involved were cut-throat razors, talcum powder, hand-operated clippers that pulled the hair out rather than clipped it, and an agony, that seemed to last for weeks afterwards, of itchy bristles lodged around the back of the neck. So going to the gentler hands of the Aylmer Parade Unisex salon was, for a while, a welcome relief.

But after a while I got fed up with the place. There was something humiliating about it. When Punk Rock happened and I decided that my flowing locks needed to be properly shorn, they flat-out refused. "We can't go above the neckline," I was told, so basically, I carried on looking like a a beardless Bee Gee until I went up to university and could take matters into my own, or a sympathetic man's, hands.

This wasn't much better. For one thing, I was reluctant to have my ears exposed – they stuck out like the turning signals on a vintage car when I was a child – and for another, the electric clippers reminded me of the instrument of torture at Trumpers. The barber in All Saints Passage in Cambridge in the early 80s was famous for his exchanges with male undergraduates, most of whom were, of course, not getting laid, unless they owned a car, or Leicestershire. Leering: "Anything for the weekend, sir?" "No thanks." "Sure? Nothing for the weekend?" Another ghastly leer. "No." "Really? NOTHING for the weekend?" "NO!" Pause; then in a tone of 50% disappointment and 50% contempt: "Well, have a nice weekend anyway."

And then, a few years later, I discovered the Trendy Hairdressers in Notting Hill Gate. This cost a bit, but I was earning money in those days, and, moreover, most of the staff were beautiful women, and I discovered the joy of having my hair washed by them. It wasn't sexual, but it was very soothing. My favoured *artiste* was called Pam. One day I rang up to make an appointment with her.

"Pam's left," they said. "But Steve's free."

"No, not Steve."

"Well, there's Robert."

"Mmm, not Robert." I was trying to give them a hint, but mainly hoping they'd work it out for themselves.

"How about Alan?"

I sighed, and replaced the receiver. (It was that long ago.)

Since then, it's been old-fashioned male barbers, but cheap ones.

In Shepherds Bush, this meant years of enduring a steady stream of racist comment, but at least I wasn't paying through the nose for it.

And then I found Claudia, the wonderful barber in Kemp Town, who actually delivered the best haircut I have ever had. When I went there the other day she wasn't working. And I couldn't ask when she'd be back, because it would have made me look like some kind of creepy stalker. So in the end I went to somewhere much more local, in Seven Dials (which has, literally, more hairdressers than food shops), and got my hair cut in silence by a man my age. And the hot date never materialised.

※

Ting-a-ling! Ting-a-ling! What is that sound, as of fairy bells, from the room next door? Why, it is Diogenes, the budgerigar. Tweet! Chirrup! Ting-a-ling!

Let me rewind. This must be a bit confusing for you, my jumping in at the deep end like this. The story begins over two years ago, when I receive a slim volume of poems by one Bethany Pope, called *Silage*. It is extraordinarily good, and, because in those days I have a weekly column for a well-known newspaper called "Nicholas Lezard's Choice" (the column, not the paper) in which I can write about any book I please, as long as it has been recently published and in paperback, I decided to review it. (The newspaper in question asked me not to, on the grounds of the book's obscurity, but I referred them to the title of my column.)

Afterwards, coincidentally or not, Ms Pope's life changed, and she could finally give up her soul-destroying job as a cinema attendant in Swindon, and became instead a teacher of English in China.

I became a friend of hers on a social medium before her job changed, and learned that she had a budgie called Diogenes. By all accounts, this was a bird of character and distinction. However, the paperwork involved in bringing a budgie to China is fearsome, and Diogenes was obliged to stay with another lady poet, our mutual friend Katy, who lives in the delightful if somewhat sleepy Kentish town of Faversham.

And then it came to pass that Katy, who is American, had to go to a family reunion in Virginia, and the cry went out: who will look after Diogenes the budgerigar? And a small, still voice piped up: "I'll do it." To my astonishment, and possibly everyone else's, that voice was mine.

And so here I am now, in a garret flat in a 16th-century building in Faversham. Don't get too excited: pretty much every building in Faversham is 16th-century, unless it's earlier. And I am *in loco parentis* to a yellow-plumed *Melopsittacus undulatus*, Tweety Pie to my Sylvester, if you will. Not that I harbour any evil designs on the bird. It's just that there's a certain physical resemblance between us both. Or rather, us four. If you see what I mean. Me, Sylvester. Diogenes, Tweety Pie. That makes four.

"Remember," said Katy, as I saw her off at the station, "Diogenes likes Chet Baker and Ella Fitzgerald. You'll know he's enjoying himself because he gets very vocal."

"Well in that case," I replied, "Diogenes is bang out of luck, for while I respect Chet Baker and Ella Fitzgerald as artists, I don't like the noises they make enough for them ever to have featured on my playlists. What does he think of the Beatles?"

"I don't know. I've never played them to him."

Good God.

When I got back, I started singing The Kinks' "Victoria" to Diogenes, but replacing the word "Victoria" with "Diogenes". It works. I then asked the bird if he'd prefer it if I sang The Fall's version of "Victoria", replacing the word "Victoria" etc., instead. Diogenes did that brilliant thing, which is sort of like moonwalking for *Melopsittacus undulatus*, of shifting along his perch without seeming to move his feet. I am going to assume this signifies assent. Too much jazz that bird's been having: time for some overlooked classics from the 1960s, and their reinterpretations by the alternative music scene of the 80s.

Meanwhile, I am petrified by responsibility. The last time I had to look after an animal it was a cat called Tybalt and he was pretty much capable of looking after himself. (Yes, I know, I know. Their names. These pets, and their owners, are fully-fledged, and in Diogenes' case I use the word "fledged" advisedly, members of the Remoaniac Liberal Elite. Deal with it.) Now I have to deal with seeds and cuttlefish bones and feathers and whatnot. There is also the whole matter of a caged animal. I had mentioned to my friend S―――― that I was going to be looking after a budgie, and she went full-on A Robin Redbreast In a Cage Puts All Heaven In a Rage, and I didn't know where to look. What I didn't know then was that according to Katy's testimony, based on experience, is that Diogenes actually *prefers* to stay in his cage. This is fine by me, as I foresee only disaster if I let him out of it.

Then again, what's so bad about a cage? It's just like a home, or a good marriage, and there's nothing axiomatically wrong about either of those things. Once again, I find myself in another cage, albeit a temporary one, and one with an excellent library; but I wonder when I will find myself in a cage I can call my own. Diogenes seems happy enough; I've just checked. Meanwhile, the bells of hell go ting-a-ling-a-ling.

Faversham has the feel of a film set. At first, as I lean out of the window and see the large triangular front of the Sun Inn, I think I'm in A *Canterbury Tale*, and half expect to see a wagon piled with hay, a small boy riding on top of it, going past the window. There are hops all over the place; there was a festival a month and a half ago. It's actually called the Faversham Hop Festival. There are even some, appropriated or rescued by the person whose flat I'm staying in, strung along one of the beams in the bedroom. If I blow a puff of air at them they quiver a couple of seconds later. It passes the time.

Then I thought it would be fun to imagine that the town's prettiness concealed a dark secret, and that I was on the set of *Hot Fuzz*. So I imagine hooded figures, sauciness behind the scenes at the Amateur Dramatic Society. After a while that doesn't feel right either, so I settle on deciding that I am Patrick McGoohan as Number Six in *The Prisoner*. I have been sent here because I am a retired book reviewer Who Knows Too Much.

A Londoner is always going to look at small market towns with skewed and suspicious vision. (I may not have lived in London for nearly two years now, but it's hard to get out of the bloodstream.) We don't go here. When or if we go on holiday we go to the seaside or the mountains or somewhere abroad. We don't really go to quaint market towns with a population around the 20,000 mark. We go to places either smaller than that or bigger than that. Faversham is just the right size to make Londoners feel they have wandered into somewhere unreal.

I keep trying to get London friends to come down here, but they are strangely reluctant.

"It's beautiful," I say. "And the pubs are great."

No dice.

"There's a stonemason and sign-painter down the road. He works in the window, and the other day I found out who'd won this year's mixed doubles at Whitstable Tennis Club. Whitstable itself is only eight minutes away by train. Whiststable! Think of all those oysters!" Still, no one bites. I send pictures of the market square, whose central building is so ridiculously venerable that if it was used as an advertisement by the English Tourist Board, the place would be overrun by Americans in a week.

"I saw someone sweeping beneath its arches the other day! It is a scene that has been replayed in that very spot for several hundred years!" Even my friend M——, who is an architectural historian, says she can't make it.

"Everything shuts at 4! Even when they say they'll be open until 5!" Actually, I don't say that bit.

The Estranged Wife, sensing I am going slightly loopy with solitude, suggests I go to a local meet-up.

"A what?"

"It's where locals welcome new residents. You can meet like-minded people."

I try to do the thought experiment of meeting people with minds like mine in Faversham but it doesn't really work. Besides, do I really want to meet anyone as mentally appalling as me? Jesus. I mean, imagine. (There is H———, of course, the award-winning wine journalist I ran into, but I can't see him every day, he has a wife and young kid. But he does say he's going to pour buckets of free Port down my throat tomorrow, which I'm rather looking forward to.)

Meanwhile, there is Diogenes the Budgie to look after. I'm too scared to let him out of his cage in case he decides never to go back inside it again. He seems happy enough. I put my hand in through the door and he sits on it and nibbles my knuckles. It took me a while to summon the courage to do this because when I put my fingers against the cage, he jumps at them, shockingly quickly, almost instantaneously, and pecks at them, hard. His beak is sharp. What possessed me to put my hand inside the cage I do not know. Wine, and sympathy. His tender reaction surprised me but it is something I do every evening now.

Looking after him is pretty easy. Every day, a bit of fresh fruit. Every other day, more birdseed, fresh water, clean out the bottom of his cage. The only problem is remembering the alternate days. Time, as you might have begun to suspect, works differently here. At the moment I am dating things from Sunday, when S——— was going to come down here but didn't. I'd got Diogenes and his cage all spruced up for the visit. Which – guess what? – never transpired.

So Diogenes looks at me and I look at Diogenes, and each of us wonders who's the more imprisoned.

Another health scare, and now is not the time. I've been reading Alan Bennett's *Writing Home* – another one of those books that Everyone Has – and came across this entry for 9 July 1984: "After four days feeling under sentence of death, having found a small lump on my foot, I go to the doctor." It turns out to be nothing much, a thrombosed vein. The doctor reassures him that his anxiety is normal.

"'It's quite natural. Most people are the same, particularly when they get to . . .' and he looks down at my notes.

"'My age?' I supply.

"'Yes. No way of saying that in a complimentary way, is there?'"

Alan Bennett was fifty years and two months old when he wrote those words; that is, over six years younger than I am now. The insolent pup. My worries are a bit more serious than that: I can't breathe. I have torn through my asthma medication and it is running out, and the Brighton pharmacy's fax machine is broken so they can't fax over a prescription, which causes further anxiety, which makes the asthma-like symptoms even worse, and . . . well, you get the picture.

But the real reason this is not the time is because last week Deborah Orr died, of cancer that had spread more or less everywhere (although septicaemia may have been the final cause of death). She was a friend as well as, for a while, my editor, and she was only a year older than me. I didn't see her that often; the last time I did in a social setting was at a Saturday lunch party a couple of years ago, shortly before London spat me out and stopped me from seeing all but my very closest friends and relations. We were in the garden, and she was smoking both cigarettes and a vape. I tried the vape and I nearly coughed my lungs out.

I visited her in hospital a couple of months ago; she was going to move down to Brighton, where she'd bought a house following the terrible end of her marriage. I was glad she was going to be my neighbour, and volunteered to help her with anything she needed, and she gratefully accepted. I was glad, because she didn't accept favours unless she needed them. One visitor brought her some apple and turmeric juice, and she was scathing on Twitter about the assumption behind the gift (i.e. that turmeric somehow cures cancer. It was a bit late for that). My favourite story about her, which I heard only the other day, was about her relationship with the editor of a certain daily newspaper, who had earlier, and for no apparent reason, sacked her – and moreover had, it is said, used her assistant to sack her. When this editor sent her a text to her not-quite deathbed expressing sympathy, Deborah's reply was succinct: "go fuck yourself."

The cancer ward at Guy's wasn't quite her deathbed because she was moved to Brighton, but she was too ill to move into her home, so she was in a nearby hospital. That's ok, I thought, I'll be able to pop in. And then I volunteered to look after this budgerigar in Faversham. It's ok, I thought, it'll only be a month, she'll last that long. But she didn't.

So now here I am, wheezing and coughing drily; on bad days I work up a sweat just walking along the flat. I find myself sleeping most of the day, even more than I did in Brighton, and with an almost total loss of appetite. The breathlessness is the worst part of it; after walking up the two flights of stairs I thought I was going to pass out. (I am smoking much less these days; one or two a day; sometimes none. But then, like a bottle of apple and turmeric juice, it may be too little, too late.) I wonder if I will actually die the next time I have sex, but as I am not sure if I am ever going to have sex again this is not the first of my worries. The first of my worries is dying. The second of them is whether I will ever have sex again. The third is taxes. The fourth is whether I will die during sex. Maybe not even fourth. I mean, I should be so lucky. There are worse ways to go, although it can't be fun for the other party. I heard a story that Patrick Troughton, the actor, died on the job, on top of a fan at a Doctor Who convention who had insisted on his wearing the costume. Can this be true?

So I now go around wondering how much longer I have. I have

only a week left before I discharge my responsibilities to Diogenes the budgie; I should be able to hang on for that. And then I read a reference to "bird-fancier's lung" in the latest *Viz*. No sniggering at the back. I look it up: "Initial symptoms include shortness of breath (dyspnea), especially after sudden exertion . . . anorexia, weight loss, extreme fatigue . . ." So that's it. I'm going to be killed by a fucking budgerigar.

※

So, I seem to have upset at least one resident of Faversham, if the letters page of two weeks ago is anything to go by; although I do wish that people would read a little more attentively. I said "not as Brexity as you might think" while our correspondent says I have maligned the place as a "provincial Brexitville". Ah well. That said, I did overhear a splendid conspiracy theory at the Sun Inn while I was nursing a pint by the fire: "the reason Corbyn wants the election on the 12th is so the students can vote twice, you see, once in their university town and then again in their home town." What does one say? That you're not allowed to vote twice in General Elections, or that for various reasons, Corbyn is not as popular with students as he was? I let it go, because it is too cosy by the fire and there is no point in getting into an argument. This country is having enough arguments.

Anyway, this will be my final night in the town, and in the care of Diogenes the budgie. Our relationship is very good these days: he's stopped pecking at me and does a lot of chirping, in a manner which suggests articulate thought, although what can he be thinking about? He listens to the news with me so perhaps he has his own theories on the wisdom or otherwise of holding an election on the 12th of December.

Meanwhile, I reflect on my time here. One of my favourite radio shows is *Mark Steel's in Town*, in which the comedian researches and fossicks around a town, and then gets up in front of an audience and then takes the mickey out of their birthplace/place of residence in a manner which both sails very close to the wind and yet is somehow endearing. He always manages to leave the town with its residents' cheers ringing in his ears.

I am not sure this will be the case with me. Never mind Mr Tim Jennings, who gave me a piece of his mind in the letters pages; it's difficult to make new friends in a certain place or at a certain time of life, and with only a month to do so. The newsagent who stocks *The New Statesman* is a nice chap but we're never going to be sending each other Christmas cards; ditto the barman at the Sun who lets me put logs on the fire. (The Sun Inn is a venerable old pub, with a very comfy armchair by the fire; if Heaven does not have a very similar arrangement, then I'm not sure I'll be interested.)

The second-hand bookseller beneath me might miss my custom, but not my company, which has been furtive and slightly shameful, in that following the advice of a couple of friends I have discovered Lee Child's Jack Reacher novels. For those who do not know him, Jack Reacher is a tough-as-nails ex-Military Policemen (US Army) who keeps getting himself into scrapes despite wishing for a quiet life. To judge the books by their covers one would suspect the typical reader to be an inadequate male of a certain age with an unhealthy interest in reading violent scenes (you don't want to get into a fight with Jack Reacher, even if you're outnumbering him eight to one; he always wins) making a deep inner insecurity, like Mark Francois. But open the inside flap and you see laudatory quotes from the likes of Lucy Mangan, Patricia Cornwell, and Philip Pullman. I gather that Margaret Drabble is also a fan. One does not expect Margaret Drabble to be a fan of books where so many people get elbowed in the face or kicked in the nuts but there you go.

But the thing that really makes me like these novels is that Reacher's major character trait is that he is a drifter, rarely staying in one place for more than one night. His only luggage is a toothbrush. He buys cheap clothes when the old ones are too used and leaves them in the bin. As you can see, there is a certain similarity to my lifestyle, at a superficial level. I do not get involved in violent scenes, although the other night I was walking back from the chip shop and a boy, aged about twelve perhaps, screeched to a halt on his bike and asked me for my saveloy. I wondered what Reacher would have done. Probably a punch to the solar plexus followed by an elbow to the face. Nothing too hard. Just hard enough to make the kid think twice about asking for people's saveloys in the future.

However, I am a peaceable chap and decided that in the end the best thing to do was to say "nice try". It is not a situation I have experienced before, in all my fifty-six years on the planet, and I have led a rich and varied life, so I didn't have a better quip to hand.

The boy looked at me again, but in a different way this time. His brow furrowed.

"Are you famous?"

I thought of my readers, both friendly and unfriendly, and the impression I had made in town.

"Round here," I said, "I think the right word is 'notorious'."

It's been an unusual week, in that I have actually spent it seeing people, instead of just staying in bed all day and reading. (I'm having a break from Jack Reacher novels, and am currently on The Pickwick Papers. I haven't read this for ages, and it's much funnier than I remember. Also, everyone in it is pissed almost all the time.) The first trip was to London for a party given by the Folio Society to celebrate a new translation of *Dr Zhivago*. The FS were my first employers, and they paid me so pitifully at the time – I think it was something like £5,000 a year, which wasn't a lot even in 1985 – that I feel honour-bound to eat and drink as much as humanly possible on the rare occasions they invite me to one of their beanos.

As the theme was Russian, the food was tiny blinis with lumpfish caviar and sour cream; the drinks were both proper champagne, and shot glasses of chilled vodka. I got into pleasant conversation with

Craig Raine – who has featured in this column before* – and we drained quite few vodkas. It was important, I thought, to get into the spirit of things.

I looked around. The only other person I knew there was C——, who was the one who had invited me; I'd known her from her first days at the publisher; she's now a director, but authority has not gone to her head, and she is as delightful company as ever. Knowing only two people at a book launch is fairly unusual for me, but then the FS is an unusual publisher, in that it's subscription-based, so it exists at right-angles to the conventional model of publishing.

Just how unconventional it was I soon realised while scanning the room, for there, among the intimate gathering, was the former Chancellor of the Exchequer, George Osborne.

This was something of a shock. I spent his entire term of office, from 2010 to 2016, entertaining dark fantasies about what I would do were I to run into him. The only person I entertained darker and more frequent thoughts about was, of course, his boss, but when I saw that photograph of him, you know, the one where he's doing that thing with his *legs*, something snapped and he went to the top of the shit-list. (Not forgetting Alexander de Pfeffel Johnson, whom I once almost literally bumped into in one of the inner courtyards of the Palace of Westminster. I was so taken off my guard that I didn't take the opportunity of punching him in the stomach, or calling him a Bad Word.)

But here was the funny thing. Such are the desperate and depraved times we live in, I could no longer summon up any hatred for the architect, or enabler, of Austerity, despite the countless thousands of lives it has ruined, and continues to ruin. (Not to mention the cruel idiocy of the policy itself.) My first thought was: good for him for being here, instead of [redacted] with [redacted], which legend has it he used to be fond of doing, in his wild youth (and, to be

---

* For full hilarious anecdote, see *It Gets Worse*.

fair, sounds kind of fun).* My second thought was: hang on, he's giving me a rather funny look. Surely he can't fancy me? I didn't think I was his type. I thought he preferred [redacted]. The third thought, which to tell you the truth followed hard on the heels of the sixth vodka and the fifth glass of champagne, was "I'll go and say hello to him. For he is, after all, when I write a book review for the *Evening Standard*, my editor."

That thought was probably prompted by the miniature version of me, red-coloured, with bat's wings, a goatee beard and trident standing on my left shoulder, with an evil grin. On my right shoulder, a miniature version of me in white robes, much nicer feathery wings and carrying a harp, said "for Heavens' sake, don't do anything of the kind."

In the end, the evil version of me won the day, but with a compromise: I didn't say anything stupid or malicious. Instead, I just congratulated him on the books pages of the *Standard*. I didn't slur my words, or burp, or throw up over him; it all passed off in a very civilised fashion. Of course I should have said nothing to him at all, but then how often does one get the chance to do something like that? ("And," I thought to myself, "I can get a column out of this." Sometimes I wonder whether the only reason I do anything at all is to get a column out of it.)

Later on, I thought about my change of heart vis-á-vis the former Chancellor. He has gone from someone who was my Private Enemy Number One to ... well, I mean, look at the current bunch. Amoral, lying, wicked shysters the lot of them. Osborne may have immiserated thousands, if not millions, but he was a Remainer; he was regularly horrible to and about Theresa May when she was PM, and he's at least pretending to be interested in Pasternak.

---

* If you think I was going to say "snorting cocaine off prostitutes", you would be wrong, very wrong indeed. That is very definitely NOT what he would have been doing, or has ever done. I want to make this perfectly clear.

The solitude almost assumes physical form after 11 o'clock at night. Everyone else goes up the wooden hill to Bedfordshire; I imagine them all, in their nightgowns and their tasselled nightcaps, yawning, and holding a candle to light their way. Meanwhile, I brood darkly on loneliness. I come across this passage in The Pickwick Papers, advice given by Mr Weller Senior to his son, Sam:

"So I've only this here one little bit of adwice to give you. If ever you gets to up'ards o' fifty, and feels disposed to go a-marryin' anybody – no matter who – jist you shut yourself up in your own room, if you've got one, and pison yourself off hand. Hangin's wulgar, so don't you have nothin' to say to that. Pison yourself, Samivel, my boy, pison yourself, and you'll be glad on it arterwards.'"

It's comforting advice, in its way, especially to someone who's starting to think about going on a dating site or something. The concern should also be for the other person. I've had my heart broken how many times in the last twelve years? I think it's about four. But how many hearts have I broken? Probably about the same number. There is no democracy in love relationships, as the philosopher Gillian Rose once said, only mercy.

Anyway, it's half past eleven at night, and I have run out of poison. I thought I had another bottle in reserve but I don't. Luckily Brighton is a place which has 24-hour shops within walking distance who will sell the thirsty night-owl a bottle of Casillero del Diablo for a small mark-up. As I leave the flat I see a young couple sitting on the front steps of the house next door; the man says "all right?" to me in a way which sounds pleasant, i.e. not mad or threatening, which is welcome at that time of night. On the way down the hill to the shop I think, crazily, that I should have asked them if they wanted anything.

When I get back, they're still there.

"Excuse me for asking," says the man, "and this might sound like a weird question . . . but do you write for *The New Statesman*?"

Well, there's no denying it; I do. So I say "um . . . yes."

"Are you by any chance Nicholas Lezard?"

This is a question that can, of course, go two ways. I have said "no" to this on two occasions which I will probably never forget: once to a tax inspector, and once to a bailiff. The tax inspector just rolled his eyes and said, in a tone of heavy sarcasm, "well, when he gets back, could you hand him this card and tell him to call the number on it?" The bailiff just laughed and said, "well, you certainly look a lot like him," and showed me a photograph of me. I didn't even know they were allowed to do that.

Anyway, this young man doesn't *look* like a bailiff. And I don't think they operate in pairs, or at this time of night. So I say "you have me at a disadvantage, sir."

"I told you!" says the man to the woman I presume is his partner.

And off we go. I suggest he gets some glasses, and I pour the wine out, and we start chatting in the cold night air. For about an hour and a half. That's a long time to stand around nattering. But it is delightful. I feel as if it is I, and not the wine, that has been uncorked; out comes a bubbling stream of anecdote and conversation. I learn that he is a video editor, and she is - have I got this right? - an Arts Project manager, or something like that. (Forgive me for my vagueness on this point. I am reminded of my friend Sally, who has a high-flying job and whenever I ask her what it is, she says "I'm not sure really, but I do go to a lot of meetings.") They have a two-year-old asleep upstairs, the flat close enough for them to hear if he awakes.

It is remarkable how much one can say after long silence. There are some things deep and personal that you either tell people immediately or only after many years of friendship; this pair get the works. I'm conscious of monopolising the conversation, but they don't seem to mind. It must take some nerve to ask someone if they are so-and-so, and if so-and-so doesn't say "piss off" but instead hands out wine and chats to them, I imagine that must be fairly pleasant. Even when I offer some extremely impertinent parenting advice ("well, you've kind of screwed up already by having a male child as the first one", etc.) they don't seem to mind. After about half an hour, I have an idea. "Wait there," I say, and go back to the flat to give them a copy of my new book, which I then sign for them. And that is how I got to sneak a plug for my new book into this column.

※

No place for false modesty here; I used to be a good cook. No, dammit – I still am a good cook. I just don't do it anymore. What's the point, when you're on your own? After a point you say to yourself: "why make a fuss about what you eat?" And a short while after that, you ask yourself: "why eat?" The common answer is "to stay alive", but after a certain point of getting fed up with things, the comment "ask a stupid question, get a stupid answer" crosses your mind.

However, something happened the other day: There was a knock at the door – one of those nice, tentative, friendly knocks. It was one of my neighbours – not the ones I wrote about who recognised me, but the ones who are in the next flat to me. Or, specifically, the female half of the couple in the next flat to me. She was holding a plate with what looked very much like a home-made pizza on it. It turned out that her husband, who is actually a cook, had made too many pizzas, and would I like one?

It happened to be one of those evenings when I was beginning to get hungry but had not yet formulated any plan as to what I was going to eat, or even if I was going to. But if there is one thing I know, it is that ninety-nine times out of a hundred, a home-made pizza will beat a shop-bought pizza, and the one time it doesn't is when something has gone terribly wrong with the cooking process. (It will also be better than most restaurant pizzas – all right, *pizze* – unless you are going to quite a high-end pizza restaurant. Pizza Express restaurants are exempt from the usual criteria because there is something wonderfully democratic about them, and I wish them luck during their current troubles, both financial and in terms of unwelcome and implausible customers. You know who I mean.)*

The pizza was, as it looked it would be, delicious. There were no anchovies on it but my tears of gratitude were salty enough to do the job. And then a few days later she brought round a daal he'd made.

"We don't want you wasting away," she said.

How do people get to be so kind? It's wonderful. And the thing is, it worked the other way round. Not that I've been kind to them, or not yet, but I have started cooking and eating again properly, or like I once did. Couscous! Curry! Proper sausages and mash! I have been getting up earlier, drinking less, smoking less, working harder. Well, I was until a few days ago, when once again there was a dental emergency underneath the right-hand lower molar. Something is very wrong with the tooth, and beneath it there are strange and painful things happening. It's not toothache, but very painful indeed; I suspect there will be pus involved. (Why is "pus" such a wonderfully horrible word, though? We used to say "flux" which is also horrible, but that's because of the reality it describes, not the word. But there is something about that single "s" at the end. But I digress.)

So now I can only eat on one side of my mouth again, and I have just discovered I have been struck off my dentist's NHS list because I have not been for a year and a half. Fair enough, I suppose, even with the mitigating factor that I have been homeless for much of that time, or in Scotland. Eating with only one side of the mouth is a bit like flying a twin-jet airliner on only one engine; you can do it, but if the other one goes, then you're in deep trouble.

And it's not even as if eating on one side of the mouth is itself pain-free. If anything even gets close to the right-hand side of my mouth, I howl. It is down to the Co-op for soup; so much for my new-found joy of cooking. And it is off to the nearest dentist, who

---

* In case you have forgotten, I mean Prince Andrew, who used the Woking branch as an alibi once. Woking!

is very close, which is good, but who is not taking on any NHS patients, which is bad, so in an hour's time I am going to have to pay £65 to be told (I presume) that I have an infection, and if I want the tooth pulled on the NHS I will have to go to a hospital.

Everything once again is falling apart. About five weeks ago, in Faversham, in front of my daughter, which for some reason made it worse, the right arm of my glasses fell off. I did a temporary repair job with superglue which amazingly is still holding up but ever since then my glasses have been canted at a twenty degree angle to the horizontal, and they're just going to have to stay like that as I don't have the money for a new pair, or not if I want to get the kids anything for Christmas.

I wonder if they can fix teeth with superglue.

What to say, on the registration form at the new dentist's, when they ask you how many units of alcohol do you drink a week? I like to tell the truth. It is a good way of finding out your dentist's mettle. My old dentist never made comment. What has one's alcohol intake got to do with one's fangs, anyway? (I anticipate a flood of correspondence.) I wrote "50", but I am prepared to admit it may be more than that. For my previous dentist, whom I had been seeing for twenty-five years before he even got round to asking this question, I wrote "lots".

I am led into the dentist's surgery by a nurse whom I immediately want to marry. Standing by the equipment is a small boy, aged about 12, wearing a dentist's scrubs. He is also wearing a pair of thick black round glasses and a straggly beard, which makes it all the more adorable.

"Hello, sonny," I say, ruffling his hair. "Where's the dentist?"

OK, I don't really say these things. The point is, though, that I could have.

He is, of course, the dentist. I explain what the matter is: a cracked tooth, as useless as Boris Johnson's moral compass, and beneath it a surging sea of pain. He pokes it; nothing. He pokes it again, a few millimetres along, and I scream.

"That tooth's got to come out," he says.

"Ho hit, Herlock" I say, my mouth still open.

"And you have an infection." He looks at his notes. "It says here you drink fifty units of alcohol a week." As he does not look old enough to drink, I imagine that to him this seems like an awful lot. He prescribes me a week-long course of Amoxicillin; in fact, he gives me a packet. But before he hands it over he says: "you must not drink while taking these."

"Orrock," I say, which is my attempt to pronounce the word "bollocks". I have taken Amoxycillin before – the last time was three months ago, for a chest infection, and I didn't lay off the sauce, and it was fine.

"The alcohol will block the effect of the drug, and the extraction will be more painful."

Ah. Which am I more scared of – not drinking for a week, or a more-than-necessarily-painful extraction? It's at times like these that one discovers what one is made of.

So, halfway through my course as I write, and I am on my fourth day of not drinking. Because NHS dentists for new patients now only exist in fairy tales, I am going to have to pay £85 for the extraction. If I don't go to the pub and don't drink wine for a week, the cost will be covered by my abstention. I will also see if not drinking has a beneficial effect on my middle-aged gut. And I am curious to see if I can do it without having some kind of seizure.

Meanwhile the pain continues unabated; and thus begin the Days of Soup. I have also started having porridge for breakfast. (Being sober, I am awake in time for breakfast. This morning, as for the previous few mornings, I got up at 7am, and have found myself asking, with a deep existential bewilderment, the question posed by Richard Scarry's famous book for children: what do people do all day? It's half past ten in the morning and I'm so bored I'm writing my column almost a day early. After this I am going to go for *a walk*.) Because I can now eat only mush, hence the porridge breakfast. I spent a year turning my nose up at the stuff in Scotland and here I am at the opposite end of the landmass eating the stuff like it is going out of style. OK, I exaggerate: like it is tentatively coming into style. Afterwards, it is soup. The thing about soup is that it has to be really good, because each spoonful is going to be exactly like the others.

I am surprised, though, how I am not consumed by cravings for drink in the evenings. The only bad time is when I walk past the Prince Albert on a cold winter evening, for it does a delicious Porter and has a proper open fire. (My apologies to the Battle of Trafalgar, but you don't have a fire. I will be back, promise.)

So what? You may say. Not drinking for a week? You think that's a hardship? Millions of people either don't drink at all or save it up for the weekend. Ah, I reply, but you don't understand: this is *me*. I am having to reconfigure a significant part of my identity. Yesterday I developed crippling stomach pains, and a friend asked if this was more about not drinking than a reaction to the antibiotics. "Do you use alcohol as a relaxant?" she asked. (She doesn't know me very well.) "Relaxant, muse, social lubricant," I replied. It suddenly occurs to me that the main reason I'm doing this is to show my baby dentist that I'm not the alcoholic he clearly thinks I am.

A seagull crapped on my head in Brighton, and I thought, "that's it, I'm outta here." My friend D—— had invited me to stay with her in New York, a possibility that had struck me as an unrealisable fantasy until she said that she'd pay for my plane ticket and put me up for free. I felt the seagull shit running down the back of my head – even when you wash your hair, the sensation never really leaves you – and said "yes". Also, I was getting very sick of seeing Boris Johnson's ugly gurning mug all over the place.

I haven't been to New York for – oh, I don't know, five or six years. The last time I'd gone I had managed to wangle a free ticket by accompanying my mother and helping her with her luggage. She would then stay with her friend in her fancy apartment in Riverside Drive and I would go to Chelsea and stay with Razors. We plucked the gowans fine and heard the chimes at 4 a.m. as I pounded on the doors of a bar, shouting, "you can't be shut! This is meant to be the city that never sleeps!" I don't think I'd have got away with that kind of behaviour if I'd been staying with my mother.

Nowadays I am much more restrained and instead find myself loafing round in bed until all hours. My host is most accommodating and brings me gin and tonics at 3 in the afternoon. Well, my liver thinks it's 8 o'clock in the evening, so why not? And there is a cat to play with.

Ah, New York, how do I love thee? Let me count the ways. Let's start with the Oyster Bar at Grand Central Station. Actually, let's not, because it was shut – *at lunchtime on a Sunday* – when we went there. So, we'll start with Grand Central itself, with its ceiling celestial and old-timey ticket booths. We were going upstate and had to use one of these as the ticket machines were acting up – well, to be strictly accurate, I insisted we used the ticket booths so I could pretend to be Cary Grant pretending to be Roger Thornhill pretending not to be George Kaplan in *North by Northwest*. Who knows? I might get to meet Eve Marie Saint on the train to Peak-skill, NY. And when we got on the train the conductor had a fine white beard and one of those also old-timey US conductor's hats. I could hardly believe my eyes: he was perfect, straight out of central casting. I nearly swooned with pleasure.

I suppose that's the thing about New York, and much of America: its small-c conservatism. For all that it presents itself as modern and dynamic, you can't get away from the fact that there is something eternal and unchanging about the place. I first came here in 1966 when I was three and I can still remember the impression it made on me: and the view of the river of traffic at the bottom of the skyscrapers' canyons, the gentle music of car horns (used, as ever, continuously, but without anger, more as an extension of the turn signal) drifting upwards is the same music as it has been for decades. The design of the infrastructure remains the same, or is remarkably consistent with its predecessors; the exterior of the Metro North train to Peakskill may have looked modern, but inside, the seats, the laminate wood-effect panelling and the very spaces between the carriages look as though they have been beamed from the 1950s. In the apartment building where I'm staying – in Queens, my first time in this neck of the woods (I've been fortunate, or spoiled, to have only stayed in Manhattan all the previous times I've been here) – the lift-call button panel looks like it's from the 1920s, the steam pipes still hiss, and you still put your trash in a chute, although I gather it doesn't go down to a furnace anymore. (The idea that each building in the city was somehow powered by its own rubbish was one I used to find immensely appealing.)

As for New York City itself, there are some strange survivals. I had never been to McSorley's before, having considered that if I'd heard of it, it must be something of a tourist trap. But D— insisted we went. There are two choices of drink there: porter or ale. I suppose you could get a glass of water if you asked nicely but eyebrows would be raised. We were shoved onto a table already occupied by a group from upstate and we made four new friends, just like that. Anyone who says that New York is an unfriendly city is either being silly or has been extremely unfortunate in their encounters.

Meanwhile, for those of you wondering what the hell a column called "Down and Out" is doing in New York City, let me assure you that I have just checked my bank balance, and unless I have some kind of New Year Miracle, my time here is going to be spent sitting on the sofa, not going anywhere, and surviving on Cheetos dipped in cat food.

I'm reaching the end of my stay in New York. Whenever I travel anywhere, I entertain the possibility of living there. For a long time these were no more than fantasies, for I was tied to London with children. These were dreams of escape, of an unreachable alternative life. Also, I was highly selective in my fantasies. Paris, New York, Los Angeles, Florence . . . I even thought of haunting the canals of Venice like some shade, as the city sank around me. I never thought of living in, say, Bristol. (For some reason Brighton always felt viable, which is just as well, seeing as I've ended up there, for the time being.)

But New York . . . New York is the one. I first came here in 1966, when I was three, and it kick-started my memory process, so vivid an impression did the place make on me. I visited in 1980, when the city was a wreck, and the cabs were checker cabs driven by Travis Bickles, but I felt like Snake Plissken, in a good way (even though *Escape From New York* had yet to be released), and bought a Joy Division single ("Atmosphere") from Bleecker Bob's without even knowing that Bleecker Bob's was *the* hip record store in Manhattan. (Actually, now I come to think of it, I looked more like Bickle than Plissken, what with affecting an army surplus jacket at the time, and not having a beard or an eyepatch.) Periodic visits since have not dimmed my love of the city.

Well, it's dimmed a bit now, because oh, the *prices*. Twenty bucks for a Maker's Mark on the rocks? Jesus, what's going on here? Am I buying a drink, or an out-of-world experience? Is there manna in the ice cubes? And the rents, God, the rents. If you want to listen to a pair of New Yorkers talk for about an hour without stopping, ask them about the rents, or whether there is anywhere affordable left in the city. Long story short: the Bronx is your best bet, and also, unless you're pulling in 60 grand a year, fuhgeddaboudit, and even 60 grand is going to leave you skimping on trips to the bars, cinemas, diners, well, everything, really. A smoked salmon beigel - oh, I don't know how to spell it - costs, I am told, $20 in Russ and Daughters deli in Houston Street. I could pop round to the White Horse for a large bourbon and hole my bank balance below the waterline. In

WH Smith's in Brighton I bought a copy of the *New Yorker* as part of the preparation for my visit, and marvelled at the price – eight quid or something like that – but when I bought a copy in New York, it was nine bucks, and that isn't really a whole lot cheaper. That said, as I type the words "WH Smith" I am overcome by an overwhelmingly powerful sense of British *dreariness*, and the thought that in a few days I will be back in the land of WH Smith instead of PJ Clarkes makes me feel as though all the air had been let of me.

For it is hard to have a lousy time in New York, if one has a nice place to stay and friends in the city. I have been very blessed in both regards: my host has refused to let me pay for a thing here (although I have to say that one day, she said she didn't feel like taking the subway into town, and spent $45 on an Uber instead, an extravagance that made me feel a little queasy; that she and the driver complained about rents all the way from Queens to Greenwich Village struck me as mildly ironic, to say the least), and has given me use of the bed while she stays on the sofa; and every couple of days I've suddenly remembered another friend who lives here. Last night I saw my old friend N———, now a professor whom I first met in 1980 (not long after that trip to New York, now I come to think of it), who lives in splendour near Union Square, and has a beautiful and clever wife, a car space in a heated garage, and a house in Long Island. I have a dim memory of offering to look after the place when they weren't there. As I look at that list of ingredients of the good life, I think of the Talking Heads song, and I ask myself: how did I not get there?

But it's back to Blighty soon, and it will seem colourless in comparison. I am trying to make myself feel better by thinking of all the things I won't miss. That dish made with Velveeta and Rotel (Velveeta: a kind of cheese, I suppose; Rotel: chopped tomatoes and jalapenos from a can) into which you dip specially-shaped tortilla chips; Frito Pie, in which thick corn chips, sour cream and god knows what else are cooked, and presented to you, *in the bag the chips came in*; even the corn dogs tasted wholesome next to this mind-bending dish. (My host has a weakness for American junk food.) Actually, after last night's excesses, thinking about these things isn't making me feel better *at all*.*

※

It's twenty to eight in the morning and I've given up on trying to sleep. I've been awake for six hours now and have read about six hundred pages of various books, including an entire Jack Reacher novel, half of *Tinker, Tailor, Soldier, Spy*, and a third of Iris Murdoch's *The Bell*. I list these books not to boast about the breadth of my reading – well, ok, a bit – but to show how a mind can toss and turn as sleeplessly as a body. I wonder if it's jetlag. Since coming back from New York my body has been acting very strangely indeed. But I don't normally get jetlag. When I flew out I just told my body what time it was and it knuckled under. My trick is to get hammered on the flight as quickly as possible and then sleep. This is also my trick for flights back across the Atlantic.

I am beginning to revise my strategy for flights eastward across five time zones. I have a natural tendency to stay awake far later than I ought – unless, as I mentioned in this column a few weeks ago, I am not drinking, in which case my eyelids start dropping at 9.30. Put a glass in my hand and keep filling it up and I can stay awake and surprisingly lucid until the dawn. Can anyone explain this? Anyway, right now, my internal clock has absolutely no idea what time it is apart from Deadline Time. Which admittedly is not for three hours yet but in three hours I hope to be asleep, even if it means I have become exactly twelve hours out of step with the civilised world.

---

* D——— and I spent a lot of time feeling crap and not moving from bed or sofa; and since then we have reached the conclusion that we were early adopters of the trendy new pathogen, Covid-19; which means I'm responsible for bringing it back to the UK. Sorry, everyone.

Part of it has to be anxiety, of course. I am resolved to fill in a tax form by the end of the month, i.e. on time, for the first time in my life, but the thought of how I am going to be able to afford to pay that tax fills me with, to put it very mildly, a certain degree of anxiety. A very closely related question, this time involving rent, is also bothering me. Come the end of January my income will be reduced by £400 a month and how I will make it up I do not know. These are not the greatest times to be someone whose only income is writing. Everyone else I know who is in a similar boat to me has got some sideline teaching something to do with writing at a University somewhere but I'm not sure I have the patience to do that. How would my lessons go? "Oh, just keep plugging away and try not to begin consecutive sentences with the same words. Now piss off and leave me alone." As a plan I am not sure this would impress many institutions of higher learning. And the idea that I could impart wisdom . . . well, come on, let's not be *ridiculous*.

I suppose I am also deflated at being back in the UK. I've been back for few days and people have been talking about nothing but Meghan and Harry, with only brief interludes in which people snigger about Gwyneth Paltrow's vagina-scented candles. The strongest smell I can pick up from these discussions is misogyny, and I'm not going to contribute to *that* toxic atmosphere. (Imagine how Paltrow would be being treated if she had a black parent. The mind boggles.)

I think of uprooting to the US. I have dual nationality, after all. And D——, whom I stayed with, said I was the perfect guest, happy to loaf about the place, instead of demanding to be *shown things*. Well, I have seen plenty of them before on previous trips. But I had not seen the new Wall Street subway station, which is the only man-made structure which has given me vertigo while I have been standing on the ground floor - I think of the old Romantic notion of the Sublime which actually means "the heebie-jeebies, but in a kind of good way". Nor had I seen Jimmy's Corner, a dive bar off Times Square full of boxing memorabilia, but which also serves the cheapest drinks in Manhattan.

"You should have seen the look on your face when the barman said the bill came to $7.50," said D———. The only unpleasant thing about the place was the presence of another Englishman at the bar. And I bet he thought the same thing about me. Englishmen in dive bars in New York, I suddenly realised, are like cats in New York apartments: while you might think the idea of having more than one in the same place is cute, they really won't appreciate it. Especially when some wag says, "hey, I think you've found your new best friend." As these words were uttered, the other Limey and I glared at each other, united only in suspicion and loathing, and it was only lunchtime.

So here I am again, disillusioned as ever, if not more so. What are those splendid lines of Uncle Monty in *Withnail and I*? "We live in a kingdom of rains, where royalty comes in gangs." I feel I have come back from holiday by mistake.

❧

"Would you like to keep your answers?" asks the quizmaster, handing me over the sheet of paper.

"No," I snarl. I have no wish to be reminded of this latest humiliation.

Yes, I have succumbed to the unholy allure of the pub quiz again. This one is held on Mondays at the Battle of Trafalgar. Eight rounds in which to expose one's ignorance to the world, or rather oneself and everyone else in the pub.

It all started innocently enough. My friend J——— and I had gone to the pub one Monday evening, without knowing it was Quiz Night. We missed the start, but were early enough to overhear a good many of the questions. As is invariably the case when one has no skin in the game, the questions are laughably easy. We reel off the answers. "India." "Stanley Baldwin." "Lithium." The same thing happens when I watch University Challenge. When I'm on my own, I get about half the questions right, even some of the science ones. If I watch it in company with anyone else, I am reduced to impotent, embarrassed silence. It is the neatest demonstration of the quantum observer effect that I can think of.

So why don't I learn? I suppose part of it is the companionship. J—— is a fellow hack and wears a fedora, pin-striped suits and has black nail varnish, so he fits into Brighton like a hand into a glove, even if – or perhaps because – he's from the West Country and calls people "my lovely".

The worst one was the pre-Christmas quiz we went to in another pub, in which one of the questions – and here the word "question" has to take an awful lot of ontological strain – involved each team being given a lump of plasticine and being asked to make a representation of Father Christmas and the Baby Jesus "being friends". I thought of making a run for it.

"I refuse to participate in this tomfoolery," I said, pinching one of my daughter's lines, although in the end I helped by making the manger, in the most rudimentary fashion possible. We got a point for sheer ineptitude, but I was, I must admit, impressed by one team's effort, which showed Father Christmas doing something to the Baby Jesus which I would prefer to draw a veil over.

That quiz, presided over by some twelve-year-old who thought he was funny, was so traumatic that I don't think I'll ever be able to go back to that pub again whether it's hosting a quiz or not.

But back to the Battle. J—— and I were handicapped by being only two people. We had two other team members but one broke her arm and the other left the country in order to avoid the grisly business. As for me, I might as well not have turned up. But come on, how on earth am I meant to know, let alone remember, who wrote *Jonathan Creek*? (Actually, I think J—— got that one.)

But now I'm beginning to wish that I had kept that answer sheet. Not only would it help me to write this column but I could frame it and put it on the wall as a reminder that I am not, as I would like to think I am, one of the sharper knives in the drawer. I have a dim memory, which I try to repress, of becoming horribly unglued about African geography.

"At least we didn't have a Tabasco Moment," said J——— at the end. This is a reference to the previous week's quiz, in which we both failed to work out which Mexican state was also the name of a spicy sauce. People have committed suicide over lesser humiliations. But then a string of small Moments like that add up, and take their toll on the soul.

I mentioned this to my daughter recently and she told me of a particularly brutal quiz she went to in which her team came a very distant last place. One round asked contestants to name all the eight varieties of grape that can be used to make champagne. *Eight?* Can that be right? Even Wikipedia says that only seven are allowed.

But it is an extraordinary institution, the pub quiz. Is this a purely British thing? The thought that every evening, pub across the land are filled with people trying to remember which month the Cheltenham Gold Cup is held in, or who was the first child to be born to a reigning monarch in the twentieth century. I took a wild punt at Elizabeth, the Queen Mother, which is wrong for more than one reason. The answer, we learned, is Prince Andrew, and I am now even more of an anti-royalist than I was before.

Well, as it turns out, my finances are now so rocky that I can't even afford to go to the pub anymore. So every cloud has a silver lining, I suppose.

※

It's been a pleasant enough week. (Or at least it was until the money started running out, but that's a subject we shall return to later. But maybe not this week. I don't want to spoil the mood.) It started with a bit of a panic: I had a looming deadline in which I had unwisely involved myself by persuading the editor of an online music publication that I could write a thousand+ words on why Wire, a post-punk band which has been going for over forty years, were the new Beatles. At some point one has to actually write the damn thing, but the only way I could recapture the state in which I had had the initial inspiration would render me unfit to spell, let alone write, anything. (Let us just say that I had the idea at the end of a long, long evening.) The only common ground I could think of at first is that they were a band with two guitarists, a bassist and a drummer, had some nice tunes and were from England.

But I'm a pro, and after two snivelling pleas to extend the deadline, I handed in the piece and thought: "well, if they publish that in its original form I will be most surprised," but the editor said it was a nice "jigsaw piece", which sounded faintly insulting but meant he couldn't be bothered to ask me to rewrite it. Then I heard that the band – or its lead singer and songwriter – had read the piece and said that as far as he was concerned, my tentative speculations about the influence of the Beatles on the band were "exactly as the article describes."

Reader: this *never* happens. No musician, in the history of musical criticism (which begins with Plato saying, in *The Laws*, that it was a pity Orpheus didn't stay in Hades because that was the best place for his derivative rubbish) has ever read an article on their work and said "you know what? This writer's bang on the money." Until now. This was a considerable fillip to the system and it was made all the better as my friend J——, he of the fedora and the black nail varnish, had a spare ticket to see the band in Brighton a few days later. It was the first gig I'd been to for years, when I dropped into the Prince Albert in Brighton after hearing an appealing racket coming from the first floor and heard a Very Angry Woman screaming, in front of three cowed male musicians, about how terrible men both in general and in particular were. I was the oldest person there by a matter of decades, and, for reasons too complex to explain, I am pretty confident I was the only person there carrying a teapot. The band had the c-word in their name so weren't that interested in chart success, but they were pretty good, and I chatted to the lead singer after the set and she was – for some reason this came as no surprise – charming. We even corresponded for a while afterwards.

At the Wire gig, though, I was by no means the oldest person there and for a while I was dazzled by the glare of spotlights off the shaven heads of the many middle-aged men in the audience who had taken an aggressive approach to male pattern baldness. Afterwards I blushingly introduced myself to the bassist and simpered like a teenybopper in front of Paul McCartney. So that's another thing they have in common with the Beatles.

That was one kind of highlight, but the others were visits from the two eldest children. The youngest is studying here so I see him for a pint fairly regularly. The daughter is off to Paris for the foreseeable future (I suppose this means while Britons are still allowed to live and work in the EU) and so we had much to chat about, staying up until 4.30 in the morning. The boy turned up a few days later but he does not have her stamina and only made it until 2.30. He even left a glass of wine only half-finished, I discovered the next day. We went to a local café because I didn't feel like cooking, or washing up from dinner either, and I had just enough money in the account to buy us breakfast. (There was a sign saying "Eggs Benedict £8" which I thought seemed ok. It was not. This is Brighton, so a classic dish was ruined by not only a woefully substandard hollandaise, but between the ham and the bread was an inch-thick layer of something called "beetroot hummus", which, I realised soon afterwards by glancing at the food prep area, went into *everything* – even, if you asked, your coffee. The moral of the story is this: look at the menu carefully before ordering.)

I toyed with my coffee and chatted with the eldest son. I told him about the whole business with the article and the gig and wondered aloud what on earth my editor had meant by "jigsaw piece". He replied: "it's because the readers have to put it together themselves." I pecked at my inedible Eggs Benedict and thought about this. "Yes," I said after a while. "I suppose that's exactly what he meant."

As I write, it seems as though Storm Ciara* has finally blown herself out. This will be old news to you, for I write this column a week before publication, but for me the howling and whistling of the wind is still ringing in my ears. When I was up in Scotland, living at first in a castle and then in an exposed and dilapidated Hovel you kind of expect the wind to make a noise like something from a corny horror film. Not so much in the basement flat of a 19th Century house in Seven Dials, Brighton. But, once the feeling of being cosily warm, dry and protected wore off, it started driving me crazy.

Winds do this: there's the *föhn*, the Alpine wind; the Mediterranean *sirocco*, the American *chinook*, and the Toulousian *autan*, all of which can unhinge people with their persistence. I have slightly more reason than most people, though, to be made anxious by high winds, for they always make me think of my death, or how close I came to it once.

I was in the living room of a mansion block apartment in Earl's Court. I had a narrow sofa to sleep on but it was very comfortable, I was having a lot of sex on it, and the rent was £30 a week; the owner of the flat was kind and stunningly beautiful (she had been a model), there was a healthy and fascinating Bohemian culture among her friends, a handsome and friendly cat called Stanley, and so what had been a temporary, three-month arrangement turned into three years. But after a while, we realised that it was time to move on. Well, she realised. As I might have mentioned, I am not the world's tidiest person, and even though Jenny, for that was her name, had the patience of a saint, even saints can say Enough Already, especially if their son is coming back from boarding school for good and will

---

* From Wikipedia: "Storm Ciara was a powerful and long-lived extratropical cyclone that was the first of a pair of European windstorms to affect the United Kingdom and Ireland at peak intensity less than a week apart in early February 2020, followed by Storm Dennis a week later. Ciara caused widespread wind and flooding damage across Europe, and at least 13 fatalities."

be taking up a third of the available space on a permanent basis.

So after three happy years I packed my stuff up and took it, trying not to cry, to my parents' house, and I installed myself in my childhood bedroom. I felt like a failure. To be 24 and reduced to living with one's folks again! My then-girlfriend shared a tiny flat in Clapham; not enough room for me, and besides, the relationship was going to end; I had met and fallen in love, without yet telling anyone, with the woman I was to marry and have children with.

I went to the Old White Lion by East Finchley station and drank myself silly in order to still my thoughts. When I got back to the family home I noticed that it was a bit windier than normal. The weather, I remember thinking at the time, was doing a good job of impersonating my mental turbulence. The trees, too, were swaying almost as much as I was.

"Bollocks to everything," I thought, and went to bed.

The next day, I got a call at work. (Yes, it was so long ago, it was when I had a *job*.) It was Jenny, sounding a little freaked out. It turned out that at some point during the storm, part of the 4th floor of the mansion block had decided to move into the 3rd floor, and the sofa on which I had spent most of the previous 1,001 nights sleeping was now underneath a heap of late-Victorian masonry. In other words, if I'd stayed one more night in that flat, I'd have died.

The thought of this close shave gives me goose-bumps to this day. (This was, of course, the Great Storm of 1987.) The general take on this, by me and my friends, is that this is an example of Providence at work, or some Higher Power, and that I have been Spared for Some Great Purpose. As I journey towards the autumn of my life without anything particularly Great even on the horizon, this theory begins to look a little threadbare. I mean I haven't even been on Top of the Pops, unlike my fellow-columnist, Tracey Thorne.

The concept of a guardian angel is one that has not survived in this part of the world, at least. It does not bear too much rational scrutiny, and even though I know three priests well enough to ask what the official church position is on them, I would feel a little silly asking. What happened to the guardian angels who were meant to be looking after all the people who were flattened by rubble, or trees, or powerlines, during that or any other storm? Why am I so special? I'm nothing. I don't *deserve* saving. Or has everything that's happened since that night been my extended death reverie? (I promise I am not writing this while stoned.)

I can't say. Luck is dumb, but it can't be that dumb, surely? Unless the clue lies in the words "the woman I was to marry and have children with". For now I think about it, it wasn't me who was being spared, it was my children's very existence. So perhaps from now on I can be a little more nonchalant when crossing roads, walking through storms, or, um, smoking cigarettes. My work is done.

The other day, Southern Rail casually announced that, as of my birthday, it would be ceasing all off-peak trains between Brighton and London. They didn't say "as of Nicholas Lezard's birthday" in their press release, they just named the date, but I know when my birthday is, and I know when a railway franchise is out to get me. This is, they said, because of platform-lengthening works at Gatwick. The disruption to the timetable, they said, would last at least two years.

Two long years. This, I realised, was going to create huge problems for me. Over the last couple of years, since ejection from anything that might have looked like or pretended to be a permanent home, I've taken an awful lot of trains. Enough to justify buying a Network Railcard – but then you don't have to take that many trains before the Railcard starts paying for itself. Brighton to London: fourteen quid day return during the week, twelve quid on weekends. This is all, of course, off-peak. Those of you who have to take the train at rush hour – you have my bottomless pity. To have to pay through the nose *and* stand up for the whole journey seems an injustice that cries to heaven, a cruelty that calls for revolution.

However, travelling at off-peak has its drawbacks too. The main problem with it is that one is promised a journey of ease and comfort – one gets in the train ten minutes before departure and looks at all the empty seats – only to have the ease and comfort cruelly snatched away. This will be because a Business Person will get on the train and start a conversation about spreadsheets that you know, from the pace and tone, will go on for the entire journey. There are a few tunnels beneath the South Downs where the signal cuts out, but you know that once the train has burst out of them, the conversation will resume.

Then there will be the Person Eating Crisps. On one recent journey, which Southern Rail had, on a whim, decided to lengthen by an extra hour by going round the houses to Worthing and back, I saw, and heard, a trendy man in his early thirties go through an entire family-sized bag of Kettle Chips, which as everyone knows are the noisiest crisps on earth, one by one. The rustle of the bag as the hand enters it. The blind rummage for the crisp. And then the mastication. Trendy Crisp Man might look on the young side but he was clearly brought up in an old school way and told to chew his crisps five hundred times before swallowing. He managed to make the bag last all the way to Clapham Junction, i.e. five minutes or so from our final destination, by which time I was ready to commit murder. Crisps are great. I love crisps. But there should be rules. As there should be with hot food. The other day a woman started eating a pastie, and it wasn't one of those artisanal pasties supplied by the Cornish Pastie Company, it was one of those pasties filled with dog food.

Then there are the kids. Schoolboys aren't so bad, and they tend to only stay on for a stop or two. But half term can be brutal. The other day I saw someone who was ineffectually saying "shush" to what sounded like four children having hysterics. Poor guy, I thought, but when he got off the train at Gatwick I saw that he had only been accompanied by one child all the time.

"Get noise-cancelling headphones," a friend advises me. I don't know. When you're on a budget of ten pounds a day the idea of spending anything between £40 and – Jesus, I've just looked this up – £314.99 for a pair of headphones *which don't actually play anything* seems unjustifiable.

"Earplugs, then," said the friend when I objected, but really, what kind of a knob puts earplugs in when going on a train journey? (By the way, I should point out that if a passenger is attractive enough, she can be eating crisps, talking with her mouth full on the phone and texting with sound-on keyboard all at the same time and it will be fine by me. This is awful of me, don't think I don't know it.) Also, I keep forgetting to buy them. The chemist isn't on the way to the station.

Anyway, as of my birthday, all this will become academic. Our MP, Caroline Lucas, claims to have extracted a guarantee from Southern Rail that people will be able to use the Gatwick Express at the same price as a Southern Rail ticket, but I'll believe that when I see it. The real reason Southern Rail are doing this, I suspect, is because they don't make all that much money from off-peak trains and so are quite happy to do away with them altogether. And this is how the country as a whole is going to be run from now on. If it doesn't make money for the directors and shareholders, screw it, and screw you. Send not to ask for whom the train service is cancelled: it is cancelled for thee.

※

I am getting a little sick of hearing about the Coronavirus.* Of course, I write this a week before you read it, and by the first week of March the country may be full of the dying. But somehow I doubt it. The statistics so far show that not many people get it, and not many people who get it die from it. As someone with an existing

---

* This column has not aged well at all. Which is why I have included it: to show just how wrong and silly I can be.

respiratory condition, I am on the at-risk list, so I'm allowed to be cavalier. It'll get me before it gets you. And Brighton can be proud to have had one of the first super-spreaders in the country, if not the first.

It's funny, though, seeing people wearing face masks. I saw a couple walking up the hill in a near-gale; far, I would have thought, from the kind of humid enclosed spaces that viruses thrive on. I saw a young person in the Co-Op with a very serious-looking mask, and also, as if for added protection, the hood of her parka pulled as far over her face as it could go. I could only make a guess at her gender, but I'm going with "her" because her eyes looked to be lightly rimmed with kohl. The Imp of Perversity entered my soul as we squeezed past each other in the cold meats aisle, and I considered faking a full-blown coughing fit; but then I thought the better of it. Although when I found myself behind her in the queue, I couldn't resist just doing two little coughs, coughettes, nothing that couldn't be heard in any Co-Op queue at any day of the week, at any time of year, and she turned round slowly to look at me. Then looked away. Then looked at me again. This happened three times; I've never been looked at like that before. But because I could only see the eyes, her expression was unreadable. I feel a bit bad about this now.

But I am insouciant. I have been to London; I have been to the pub. I even went upstairs, to the unventilated and packed room where bands perform, to check out who was playing (they weren't very good, and were wearing cowboy hats). In London I went to the British Library, where always, but especially in winter, you can hear a steady *continuo* of coughs, sneezes and sniffles. I travelled there on the tube, and that really is Infection City. I plan to be going there next Tuesday as well, and the Moose is coming on Thursday to Brighton where he swill buy me lunch at *a Chinese restaurant*. (I have just read in the *Guardian* that "a multi-academy trust has closed its three schools in Wolverhampton, Stoke Poges and London 'because our schools have some students of Italian origin'".)

Actually, last week I *was* poorly, but it was one of those poorlinesses that leaves one all dizzy and confused, and makes you wonder how much of it is actually illness and how much is despair. The last two weeks have been spent under conditions of the strictest austerity; what with people not paying me, and with the bank account going further and further into the red even though you haven't been spending any money, and Vodaphone turning a £40 bill into a £175 bill, I've been on a budget of a tenner a day, which is pretty tough to maintain when you have to either meet your son at the pub, or take the train to London, or drink at least a bottle and a half of wine before you feel anything. Here is my tip: get a bottle of The Signal Post Shiraz, which is absolutely disgusting, but is on offer at only a fiver a bottle at the Co-Op. You will only be able to drink half a bottle at a sitting.

The other tip is to just stay in bed, reading. This is something I do quite well, if I say so myself. With no prospect in sight of anyone actually sharing it, the bed itself becomes a library, and there are about a dozen books in various stages of having been read, or, in some cases reread. One of them I'm even being paid to read, which means that I will need a pencil to makes notes in it. Luckily, I bought a pencil from the British Library for this very purpose. BL pencils tend to come with some rubbishy inspirational quote about how great books are from someone you've never heard of. This pencil is no exception.

"Today a reader – tomorrow a leader", it says, attributing the quote to one Margaret Fuller, of whom I had not heard. According to Wikipedia, she was the first ever female book reviewer, so I salute her from across the centuries, but that quote ... well, it's not her fault, I suppose. How was she to know? I entertain a brief and bitter reverie in which the world is actually run like that. I am President of the United States of America, and Donald Trump is sitting in a basement flat in Brighton, wondering where it all went wrong. And, now I come to think of it, feeling a ticklish feeling in the lungs and wondering if he was right to laugh at people wearing face masks. Cough, cough.

Single in the time of Coronavirus: I pinch this shamelessly from my friend and fellow hack Y——, who has been dumped. I can't think why: he's very funny, half my age and has a head of thick, dark hair. (I find myself, during conversations, staring at young men's hair. "Look at all that . . . hair", I say to myself. Not in any homoerotic way: I just wonder if they appreciate it, and know that it won't always be like that.)

Anyway, this whole self-isolation thing: I've really got that locked down. I have seen a steady trickle of ha-ha-I'm-a-freelance-writer-here-are-some-tips-about-working-in-your-jim-jams pieces (the best and most amusing of these, so far, by the superb Rhiannon Lucy Cosslett in Tuesday 10 March's *Guardian*. "There's a way of answering the phone that sounds as though you weren't just asleep," it begins. Brava!). But I think I have the expert's eye on this one. Plenty of books, plenty of booze, plenty of whatever else takes your fancy, don't get out of bed until the afternoon is well advanced, and there you are.

It is important to have several books on the go at once. Nothing contemporary if you can help it. I'm on an Iris Murdoch/Graham Greene jag at the moment. Sometimes something will leap out at you. From *The Honorary Consul*: "I used to pray in the police station. I prayed I would have a girl in bed with me again. You are not going to tell me that was not a real prayer." No, Antonio, I'm not.

But sometimes you can pick up something that might not be contemporary but has contemporary resonance. A couple of years ago, when I was living here last, I bought, for no reason that I could think of at the time, a copy of Camus's *The Plague*. I can't find my copy here; I must have left it in Scotland. But I do remember making lots of pencilled notes on the inside cover, and I'm kicking myself now, because I could have used these notes to say something superficially clever about the current situation. Right now I'm racking my brains to remember (a) what happened in the book and (b) what

I said about it. Of course the plague that the town of Oran suffers is a metaphorical one – everyone is pretty much agreed it's about fascism, but it isn't an act of hopeless literalism to see the book as being about an actual plague, too.

The odd thing about the current situation is that – for the time being at least – there seems to be a reaction out of proportion to the number of cases and the seriousness of the disease. Plagues tend to involve buboes and horrible, inevitable deaths; here we are talking about something that kills only a fraction of the number of the people who are killed by 'flu.

But I'm no epidemiologist, and so cannot say whether everyone has gone mad or whether the precautions that are being taken are sensible ones. I suppose, by definition, a precaution is sensible, and also a useful rule in life is generally to do whatever the opposite is of whatever Donald Trump tells you to do, so if he says everything is fine (his latest position on the subject) then perhaps a little panic might not be a bad thing.

As it happens, as of today, I *do* have a dry cough (if no other symptoms, unless extreme lassitude is a symptom rather than a state of mind) so I am glad I did all my stocking up yesterday. I spent £21, which is the most I have spent on any shopping which didn't have alcohol in it. I have been so affected by the national mood that I even bought a cauliflower. I am trying to remember the last time I bought a cauliflower. I think I bought one in Scotland but I can't be sure.

But, as I said, if anyone's prepared for self-isolation, it's me. When you're on a budget of £10 a day then even going to the pub becomes an unrealisable fantasy, and the main thing to do is, as I have always said, and keep saying, to spend as much time in bed as possible. The afternoon, did I say above? No: the thing to do is wait until *the evening*. I went stir-crazy some months ago but that was because I was acutely conscious of the sway that everyone else was living a normal, sociable life. If the rest of the country is in lockdown – and how the Italians are coping I can't even begin to imagine ("it's like living in a Ballard story," says my friend D——— from Milan when I ask him, and presumably not one of those happy-go-lucky, finish-with-a-smile-on-your-face Ballard stories, but one of the grimmer ones in which people end up eating their dogs). The other day I thought to myself: I know what, I'll pretend I'm in prison, and use the time to write a novel. I'll let you know how that goes.

Meanwhile, Y——— writes to me asking if he can stay for a couple of days. That, I assure him, would be a delight. And we can pretend we're rewriting the Decameron, and tell each other dirty stories while civilisation collapses around us.

ACKNOWLEDGMENTS

MANY, MANY PEOPLE have helped me over the years, and in the years covered in this book; I cannot name them all, for reasons of space and memory. But the greatest debt is owed to the then-editor of the *New Statesman*, Jason Cowley, who asked me to write the column in the first place; it looks like his successor, Tom McTague, is keeping me on, fingers crossed, so thanks to him too. The editors to whom I have submitted my copy every week have always been a delight to work with: take a bow, Kate Mossman and Michael Prodger. You have saved me from countless infelicities. As for Paul and Louise Ramsay, of Bamff, Perthshire, I hardly dare imagine how I would have coped without your generosity and kindness. Laurie Penny, too, for the use of her flat at a crucial time. More recently, the wit and hospitality of Ben Marshall have been life- and sanity-saving. I have almost certainly forgotten many others; all I can do is apologise and blame a (gradually, I hope) decaying brain.

This book has been typeset by
SALT PUBLISHING LIMITED
using Neacademia, a font designed by Sergei Egorov for the
Rosetta Type Foundry in Czechia. It has been manufactured
using Holmen Book Cream 65gsm paper, and printed and
bound by Clays Limited in Bungay, Suffolk, Great Britain.

CROMER
GREAT BRITAIN
MMXXV